The
History and Haunting
of the

Myrtles Plantation
2nd Edition

Rebecca F. Pittman

DEDICATION

For those who came before;
Whose footfalls still sound in empty hallways;
Whose memories of living and dying echo yet,
and are played out in the hearts of those who pause
for a time within their cherished walls.
It is a privilege to write about your history,
and find understanding in your hauntings.

John, Teeta, JG & Morgan Moss—
Owners of the Myrtles Plantation—
For this rare opportunity.

Arlin Dease—
For his expertise and hospitality.

Hester Eby—
The Myrtles Plantation's Guardian.

The Myrtles Plantation—
For yielding up a few of your secrets.

Table of Contents

The author has inserted narrative into the chapters of this book in an effort to portray atmosphere. These blocks of type are shown in italics. It is meant to be a fictional representation based on history. Some factual information is also shown in italics, such as correspondence, newspaper listings, etc.

ACKNOWLEDGMENTS

Thank you to Teeta Moss, for her permission to research and write about the Myrtles Plantation. I appreciate your acquiescence in allowing me to interview you and your staff, as well as share old photos and documents, that are represented here and in the first edition of this work.

To Arlin Dease…my dear friend for his hours of time spent with me going over the massive renovations he directed and implemented at the Myrtles, along with his partner Stephen Saunders.

For the myriad libraries, historical societies, newspapers, museums, and private individuals, who took time to help me with the research for this book... thank you so much! Your expertise was invaluable! I especially want to thank the following, who went beyond their job description to look up antiquated files, buried newspaper clippings, death certificates, family history, census reports, maps and articles: Charlene Bonnette, Head of Louisiana Collections at the Louisiana State Library in Baton Rouge; Helen Williams with the West Feliciana Historical Society in St. Francisville, Louisiana; Judy Bolton, Head of Public Services, Special Collections at the LSU Library; Barry Cowan, Assistant Historian at the Special Collections at the LSU Library; Alice Luckhardt, researcher and writer for FamilyTree.com; Tom and Myrna Hart, and Traci Liberatore of the Bradford House Organization; Lauren Davis, Curator at West Baton Rouge Museum; and my dear friend, Ann Weller, author and historian of Ruffin Gray Stirling's ancestry. A special thank you to Nicole Hobson-Morris, Executive Director of the Louisiana Division of Historic Preservation and the Office of Cultural Development. You took so much of your time to help me find the material needed for this book, and to make copious copies.

And, to two wonderful photographers who added so much to this book: Jim Zaccone Photography, and Jason Phillip Reeser.

Rebecca F. Pittman

The
History

Prologue

Jennie sat on the rough wooden steps leading to the porch of her small cabin. While darkness brought relief from the ubiquitous heat, the Louisiana humidity still wrapped the air in a moist blanket that pebbled her dark skin with dew and caused her worn blouse to droop with dampness. The rank odor of her sweat rose from her clothes as she shifted her weight. She reached for a second bowl of pole beans and continued to break them into exact lengths for the master's table. Mable sat just behind her on the porch, tunelessly humming and rocking, as she stitched clothing for the black children of their small community. The candles aligning the porch railing gave out a feeling of comfort, as they cast the slave's silhouettes across the weathered planks and out onto the parched ground.

Typical slave quarters of southern plantations.

    The familiar sounds of the night set in; a rhythm that throbbed in harmony with the cicada's song. It rose and fell like waves. A blending of accents and voices with foreign tongues leant a singsong quality to the sounds emanating from the sparse scattering of cabins. African, Jamaican, Haitian—the stories and songs from their homelands anchored these people thrown together into this strange plantation setting. Georgia, an old black woman with white hair and a waddling gait, was singing her nightly song as she walked along the hemline of the cabins: "Sun gonna set, Moon gonna rise. Shelling dem peas and makin' dem pies. Massa gonna scold if da workin' ain't done.*

Down goes da moon, up comes da sun."

    Jennie snapped another length of beans and stared off across the expanse toward the big house. Richland Plantation, the owners had named it; almost as a prayer for fertile soil and an abundant crop. There were lights flickering in most of the windows. The long building, that had been the Master and Mistress's home while the big house was being built, now sat in a wreath of wood smoke as the tantalizing aroma of roast beef wafted over to her from the kitchen's chimney. She could hear the clatter of dishes as the house slaves hurriedly assembled the vegetables, bread, and meat onto platters. Jennie waited expectantly for the sound she knew would be forthcoming. Seconds passed, and then she heard it—thin whistling noises coming from the veranda leading from the kitchen building to the dining room door of the main house.

A husky laugh broke out behind her, as her husband James came from behind the cabin, where he had been tending to their small garden.

"Yessir," he laughed, "da Whistle Walk is sure 'nuff signin' t'night. Keep dem mouths whistlin' and they ain't tastin' the food!"

Jennie laughed. James sat down next to her on the steps and stole a bean from the bowl. A breeze welled up, moving the dangling moss, that hung like grey lace curtains, into a ghostly dance. With it came the fetid smell of the indigo vats.

"I knows dis here crop is gonna be da last," James said, turning his head toward the smell. "Dem plants is givin' out…bugs everywhere. Be our bad luck too. Ben says der's talk of cotton. No matta how much I hates dealin' with dem indigo plants, it ain't nothin' to pickin' cotton. Your back break, your hands look like da skin been ripped off. Sugar ain't much better. Dats where da money is thou'…dat der sugar cane. But it's growin' better down river."

Indigo plantation 1700s

Picking indigo plants.

James stood and stretched. He patted his wife affectionately on the head as he climbed wearily up the steps to the cabin. "Dat salt pork still good?" he asked.

"It's fine," Jennie said tiredly. "It's in da pot, an' potatoes in the fire ash. Daniel ate the cornbread."

As if on cue, she heard her son's laughter coming from the direction of the hog wallow. He and the Master's son, Edmund, were tossing horseshoes. The sharp clang of metal-upon-metal bit into the night. Somewhere the delighted laughter of children could be heard as they dashed about the large laurels, oaks, and myrtle trees. The older children, those who were ten and more, were still at work, stirring the indigo "steepers" or cutting the dried blue dye into cubes or balls. Jennie watched the dark fleeting shadows of the slave children as they darted across the lawn. Their short period of freedom from the grueling sun and endless chores would be over before it had barely begun, she thought.

A sudden hush came over the quarters as a rhythmic pulse sounded from beyond the small square of cabins. It infused the night with a primitive beat, accompanied by singing and repetitive chants.

"Dat's da voodoo goin' on," Mable whispered nervously from behind Jennie's back. "Bet cats an mouses gonna be missin' t'night. Gives me da jeebies."

Voodoo ceremony, 1700s.

Several slaves stepped from their cabins into the moonlight to listen quietly from their porches. Their heads were all turned toward the darkness of the trees, where they knew the swaying figures of priests and priestesses, dressed in turbans, flowing robes and dangling necklaces, were writhing beneath the moon.

"Curses an spells," Mabel hissed. "We all gonna git murdered in our beds, mark me. Already seein' strange shapes in da trees 'round here. Maybe voodoo, maybe ghosts. Started in Naw'lins, but dey been movin' upland to bayous 'round here.

Some of da house slaves sayin' weird stuff happnin' inside too. Stuff movin' 'round...noises. Won't see me out here by myself after dark...nossir!"

Just then, an oblong box of yellow light spilled out across the grass from the dining room door of the Richland's main plantation house.

Prologue

The mistress, Elizabeth Bradford, stood in the doorway, her golden hair shining as if lit from above. She glanced nervously toward the sound of drums thrumming the humid night air. The myriad flickering lights, from the candles adorning windows and railings at the slave cabins, looked like fireflies in the darkness.

"Edmund!" she called, squinting into the night in search of her son. "Come on in now. Supper is on the table. Come on..." Glancing once more toward the huddled mass of trees to the south of the plantation, she stepped back into the safety of her home, and shut the door.

Daniel emerged from the trees to Jennie's right and ambled over to his mother. He snatched up a few beans and turned to listen to the haunting rhythm permeating the night.

"Don't you be gettin' no ideas 'bout goin' near dem drum sounds," Jennie warned him. "You hear me, Daniel? That ain't nothin' to be messin' with. You stay near the quarters, hear me?"

The 7-year-old boy nodded absently. He kept his hand in his pants pocket where it had been since he exited the trees. Keeping his side turned toward his mother, he climbed the steps to the cabin's porch. Miss Mable was eye-ballin' him. He knew she could sniff out a liar, sneak, or thief from across a field's width. Keeping his eyes down, he hurried past her and into the cabin. The air was thick with bacon smoke as he hurried to his straw cot and stuffed the ragged doll he had found in the woods beneath his covers.

The Bradford Years

1794-1817

Chapter One
The Legacy Begins

David Bradford

In 1794, David Bradford walked through the bustling port of Bayou Sara, perhaps stopping in Max Mann's Saloon for a drink of whiskey, before buying a horse at Joe and Abe Stern's extensive stables. He may have booked a room at Mrs. Burton's hotel near the river front, or one owned by Joe Mayer.

Max Mann's Saloon, Bayou Sara

Burton House Hotel, Bayou Sara

With map in hand, Mr. Bradford set off up the hill to the beautiful town of St. Francisville.

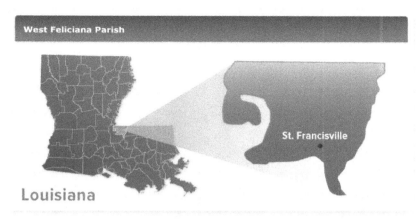

St. Francisville in West Feliciana Parish in Louisiana

The area must have looked very suitable with its general store, grocery, and other venues, that would appeal to his wife in need of fabric or staples. Bayou Sara had a post office and was a major port for merchandise sailing up, or down, the Mississippi. There were beautiful homes adorning the bluffs, churches, and it was only a short buggy ride to Baton Rouge. The bustling city of New Orleans, with its law offices and busy port, was just a few hours south. Yes, this area had everything he needed.

David turned his horse onto the Woodville Road and headed west. The air was sultry and filled with the unrelenting song of cicadas. They hung above him in the canopy of treetops, their sound drowning out that of his horse's hooves striking the packed earth. The open vastness to the north of him spread out as far as the eye could see, broken only by stands of oaks and tall grass. His nearest neighbor would be down the road several miles from here. The plantations in the south were so different from his home in Washington, Pennsylvania, where the brick houses butted up against each other, and the streets bustled with people. Plantation property could spread out for hundreds of miles..

He glanced once more at the parchment map he'd been handed in Bayou Sara. It marked his newly purchased land and where the boundaries lay. He had been on the road only a short time before he began recognizing the landmarks that would become his new home.

Louisiana wilderness

David reined the horse to the south and ducked below a low-hanging oak branch. He encouraged the mare along a small rutted path through deep foliage and unrelenting tree trunks. After several minutes of navigating the dense woods, he came upon a clearing where a large depression of damp clay held center court. He pulled up on the reins and dismounted. The thick air closed in around him as he removed his hat and ran a handkerchief over his sweating brow.

The first thing he noticed, was the overwhelming sound of birds. They seemed to inhabit every tree. There was a sweetness to the air—a perfume he did not recognize. The sound of cicadas played softly in the woods surrounding the clearing where he stood taking in the new vista. In his mind's eye, a grand plantation house rose from the ground, its front door facing east toward the road. It would have a large verandah wrapped completely around it, with rocking chairs for he and his Betsey to sit and hold their children near.

Looking off through the woods to the west and to the south, he laid out the vast fields of indigo he would plant. He would have preferred sugar, but he had been told it would not grow as well here higher up along the river. He would have his stock houses down closer to the Mississippi for exporting his goods, as well as receiving merchandise. Bayou Sara would also serve as his main avenue for business transactions.

David Bradford stooped and dug up a small clump of land. The soil was rich, and he envisioned fertile fields of indigo and gardens springing effortlessly from her mineral-laden earth.

Rubbing the soil between his fingers, he smiled. "I will call you Richland Plantation," he said aloud.

River barge on the Mississippi with St. Francisville in the background.

As David Bradford surveyed his new land, he was unaware of the destruction happening in New Orleans, a mere 153 miles to the north. The Great Fire of New Orleans was roaring through the riverport town, devouring the wooden buildings like a ravenous dog. From the area now known as the French Quarter, from Burgundy to Charles Street, and almost to the riverfront buildings, 212 structures were lost. Only six years earlier, in 1788, a fire had taken 856 buildings in New Orleans. If a wind had wafted up from the Crescent City, he may have smelled the acrid odor of burning wood.

The Great Fire of New Orleans 1794

Another historic event was happening in New Orleans, as Bradford walked his new property. Marie Laveau, a beautiful woman of Louisiana Creole descent, and born free, had just entered the world. She would become known as the "Voodoo Queen" of New Orleans, and her magic would become feared by whites, and those of African descent, alike. She, and later her daughter, became famous for their practice of Voodoo, or *Voudoun*. In 1874, as many as twelve thousand spectators, both black and white, swarmed to the shores of Lake Pontchartrain to catch a glimpse of Marie Laveau II performing her legendary rites on St. John's Eve (June 23-24).

Marie Laveau, The Voodoo Queen

David Bradford arrived in Louisiana when the state was still spinning through its metamorphosis from government rulers. 1754 had seen the Seven Year's War; 1762 had witnessed France giving Louisiana to Spain; the following year, in 1763, brought the American Revolution, followed by the French Revolution, and the upcoming year would herald the signing of Pinckney's Treaty, averting a war over Louisiana between the United States and Spain. David Bradford would not live to see the Civil War that would all but obliterate the two small towns he had just walked through. But his days at his new plantation, would see many historical moments. His chosen name of Richland Plantation would later be changed to Laurel Grove, and finally to the Myrtles Plantation. He could not have known that his architectural plans for a grand plantation home would someday be the blueprint for one of the most-haunted places in the world.

Chapter Two
The Myrtles Plantation is Born

Louisiana sign in front of the Myrtles Plantation

David Bradford and the Whiskey Rebellion

Before David Bradford began clearing the acreage on the ground that was to become home to the Myrtles Plantation, near St. Francisville, Louisiana, he had already distinguished himself in the northeast. Born in 1755, in New Jersey, David's family soon moved to Cecil County, Maryland, when David was only three. (It is often reported that David was born in Maryland, but in fact, he was born in

New Jersey.)

Later in life, David Bradford became a successful lawyer, businessman, and Deputy Attorney General of Washington County, Pennsylvania. According to the Bradford House Museum archives, the Bradford home in Pennsylvania began construction in 1786, and was completed in 1788. His home reflected his high social standing, not only by its size, but also its fittings. The magnificent mahogany staircase and the interior wood finishes show remarkable craftsmanship. The stone for the exterior was quarried near Washington, while the interior decorations came from the east and had to be transported across the mountains at great expense. It was, and is again today, an 18th century architectural showpiece. This was all the more striking at the time, because Washington County consisted of small, rustic, log buildings. During a restoration of the house, a tunnel was discovered that appears to have led to, what was then, a steep ravine nearby. It is thought that this tunnel was constructed to provide a means of escape should this obviously wealthy house come under attack.

David Bradford was admitted to the Washington County Bar in April, 1782. He later married Elizabeth Porter, from nearby Uniontown, Pennsylvania, in 1785. Together, they had five children who survived during their stay in Pennsylvania: Abelard, Edmund, Jane, Sophia, and David Jr. Two other names are listed in the Bradford ancestry—Alexander (who is mentioned as the second child born), and James (who is listed between Edmund and Jane). They are the only two children with no record of birth or death. They may have been stillborn, or, there are rumors that a child drowned during the trip from Washington, Pennsylvania, to Louisiana. The fact that neither James or Alexander were mentioned on David Bradford's land grant for the Myrtles Plantation, further proves they were not alive, or he certainly would have included them among his sons, when he divided up the acreage in St. Francisville, Louisiana. David Jr., Edmund, and Abelard are given 500 *arpents* each of the area that became the Myrtles Plantation.

The Bradford's prospered and life was good. Western Pennsylvania, however, was not content to be controlled. As early as

1775, the region petitioned the Continental Congress to be recognized as the fourteenth colony. In 1776, the people in the region, claimed by both Pennsylvania and Virginia, announced that they were the state of Westsylvania. With both states claiming the land, the tug of war began to take its toll.

There was a very serious problem with transporting goods down the Mississippi River to New Orleans, and from there to the people of the East Coast. New Orleans was, at that time, under Spanish control, and they put a very heavy tax on goods passing through New Orleans. The whiskey tariff was seven cents a gallon (the price actually varied depending on the capacity of the still, and not what was actually produced). If settlers were able to sell the whiskey in Washington County, it would bring about twenty-five cents a gallon. Selling whiskey on the eastern side of the mountains would normally bring about fifty cents a gallon. By collecting the tax at the source, instead of the point of sale, the western whiskey was taxed 28%, while the eastern whiskey had a 14% tax! Collecting the tax based on the output of the still also meant the farmers had to pay tax on the whiskey they consumed themselves.

To add further insult, stills were to be registered each June at the one tax office per county. Washington County had no tax office, due to sentiments against the East and the whiskey task. If one were to register their still, they would have to make the long and expensive trip to a neighboring county. If the locals wanted to rebel against the registration and taxation, they would have had a long trip to the Federal Court House in Philadelphia, plus pay for lawyers and witnesses. The westerners felt they were being picked on deliberately.

Whiskey Rebellion

The rebellion began to heat up. When officers were sent in to enforce the excise, they were met with resistance, and some even tarred and feathered. After a group of 500 men attacked General Neville's home on Bower Hill, on July 17, 1794, David Bradford assumed leadership of the forming band of rebels. Some say he was blackmailed and forced to take an active role.

Tax Collector Being Tarred and Feathered

By August 7, 1794, George Washington began mobilizing 12,950 troops from Eastern Pennsylvania, Virginia, Maryland, and New Jersey, under General Harry Lee, the Governor of Virginia, and father of Robert E. Lee. Washington's troops began arriving in Bedford, Pennsylvania, on October 19th. By early and mid-November, the "Watermelon Army" began rounding up suspects in western Pennsylvania. These people, suspects, and witnesses together, many of them lacking winter clothing, and barefoot, were then marched to Philadelphia to stand trial. David Bradford fled. Mr. Bradford, a warrant for his arrest at his back, left Washington, Pennsylvania, and went to Pittsburg. Contrary to popular legend, he did not jump from a window to make his escape. From there, he took a coal barge down the Ohio to what is now Portsmouth, Ohio. Charles M. Ewing, at one time, director of the historical collections at Washington and Jefferson College, who studied the Whiskey Rebellion, and is a recognized authority on the subject, felt that the Federal authorities were not too anxious to catch Bradford, as they did not want a difficult situation on their hands. The man was, after all, an Attorney General and respected lawyer. Mr. Ewing says that Bradford did not want to leave, but was persuaded to do so by some of the other leaders of the insurrection, who for their own reasons, wanted him out of the way.

All information does lead us to believe David Bradford was discovered by some of the troops while he was on a coal barge not far below Pittsburgh. The ship's captain, a Captain Keene, and his crew, apparently did see to it that Bradford was not bothered by the troops. Captain Keene was later involved in the Aaron Burr conspiracy, and lived for a while near Bradford at his new home in St. Francisville, Louisiana.

When David Bradford finally set foot on the dock of Bayou Sara, he was not in unfamiliar territory. Rumors were told of his visiting the area earlier, and even sailing as far as New Orleans, possibly in connection with whiskey sales, or for political reasons.

The Bradford family bible mentions friendships with George Washington and Thomas Jefferson. We don't know if he actually met Washington, but he may have known Jefferson, from the time David served in the Virginia Legislature. He may have also become close friends with Lafayette, as it is mentioned in Elizabeth Bradford's notes, that Lafayette stopped by Richland Plantation to pay his respects when David's daughter, Jane, died in 1826.

In 1792, David Bradford, during one of his trips down the Mississippi, stopped at St. Francisville to look into the land grants being offered by the Spanish government. During their rein, the Spanish were interested in introducing Americans to the region to settle the territory. Contrary to popular belief, that it was a "come one, come all and grab up land" mentality, on the contrary, the grants were given out to only those meeting a certain criterion. The Spanish targeted Americans from the Eastern colonies and wanted only those who were brought forth "in consideration of the favorable accounts which have been communicated to me of their excellent conduct and good principles; under the express condition, that, as soon as they shall have settled themselves with the survey, which the commandment of the post shall be furnished to each the necessary title, in form, and the settlement shall be made close to one another, and as near as possible, not admitting more American families as those named above…but in in no instance shall vagrants be admitted." E. Baron De Carondelet; given at New Orleans, the 27th June, 1797.

Baron De Carondelet

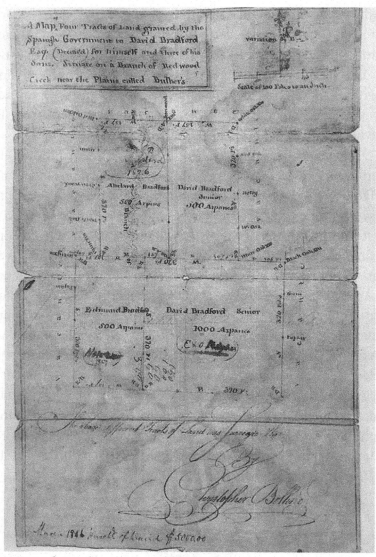

David Bradford's Land Grant w/sons' portions shown.

After surveying the verdant land surrounding St. Francisville, David Bradford purchased 650 acres at $1.40 each. Of course, the wording of the land grant Mr. Bradford was afforded was not listed in American acres, but rather in French and Spanish *arpents*. In Louisiana, during the 1700s, an *arpent* was a measurement of land that pre-dated the Public Land Survey System. It is a French, or Spanish, measurement of approximately 192-feet, and a square *arpent* is 0.84 acres. A typical French *arpent* land division is 2 to 4 *arpents* wide along the river, by 40 to 60 *arpents* deep, while the Spanish *arpent* land divisions tend to be 6 to 8 *arpents* wide and 40 *arpents* deep. This method of property division provided each owner with river frontage, as well as land suitable for cultivation and habitation.

The Myrtles Plantation today, is around 10.5 acres of land. It was an impressive acreage when David Bradford began to build his plantation in 1794, on 650 acres. The land reached down to the Mississippi River, which was common for the area plantations. The river front afforded them access to passing boats with their merchandise, to sell their own wares, and the use of the water for irrigation and other needs. It also, unfortunately, made them visible to the passing warships of the various battles that sailed along the great river. Many plantations were shelled from the water like an indiscriminate game of shooting clay decoys, as the war boats traveled by.

In 1794, David Bradford began construction on an outbuilding that would house him, and his family, while the main house was being built. The building was a little over 1,000 square feet and consisted of a small kitchen, sleeping quarters, and a main room. It is used today at the plantation as the Gift Shop. It was a simple clapboard structure, and must have looked daunting to Elizabeth Bradford, who was leaving behind in Pennsylvania, an elaborate brick home with all the amenities.

The life Elizabeth Bradford was to inherit beneath the relentless Louisiana sun would not be an easy one. The amenities that made her life pleasant in Washington would be awhile coming, as she dealt with a one-story structure with primitive offerings and as yet, untamed acreage. Husbands were often away on buying trips and other business, and childbearing was fraught with a high mortality rate.

David Bradford home in Washington, Pennsylvania.
Bradfordhouse.org

Original Bradford home at the Myrtles Plantation

While David was away in Louisiana, his wife Elizabeth tried valiantly to get his name cleared. She wrote to George Washington on more than one occasion, assuring him of David's good reputation, and his family's need of his return. Here is a segment of her first entreaty, on December 10, 1794, from Washington, Pennsylvania: (Misspellings are Mrs. Bradford's.)

Sir,

Being persuaded, that your extended Rank will prevent you from attending to the distresses even of an individual, I would willingly flatter myself that my request may obtain a favourable reception, and answer, which may relieve a heart in almost a state of ruin—Sir I am the affectionate Wife of Mr. Bradford, he is absent from me and from several tender little ones, the pledges of our cemented affections— Common fame says he is Obnoxious to the Government, that he has been unfortunately involved in a conduct which cool reflection disapproves of—it is probable, that he was precipitated into it by the Violence of some with the deliberate Machinations of others—His not acceding immediately to the Term offered by the Commissioners on the part of Government was not with a view of persisting, but knowing that the flame of the Multitude was such were he immediately to accede both his person and property would be in Danger and thereby render any influence that he might have with the people in reconciling them to a Submission inafectual & trusting rather at a proper period to explain to Government the motives actuating his Conduct, than to an inflamed Multitude thereby staining his Character with signs of guilt which Originated not with him neither cherished by him—No Sir his heart I am sure was pure; those who know him, and knows the unhappy circumstances Attending him will say of him as I say and I hope some have told you so—

After receiving no reply, Elizabeth Bradford wrote to George Washington again, on September 10, 1795, December 10, 1795, and January 22, 1796, without results.

Contrary to popular belief, Mr. Bradford did not wait for the final 1799 pardon for his role in the Whiskey Rebellion to move his family to St. Francisville. Once the simple home, that was to serve as temporary housing during the plantation's main house's construction, was completed, he returned to Washington County and gathered up his family. This is borne out by the fact that Eliza Bradford's birth record shows she was born to David and Elizabeth Bradford, on July 27, 1797, in St. Francisville, Louisiana.

The Bradford family packed up their belongings and began the trip down the Mississippi River toward their new home in the South. With them, were five small children, all under the age of 11. Abelard Bradford was the oldest of the children. His birth record was unavailable. David and Elizabeth were married in 1785, and the year of the first recorded birth of their offspring was Sophia Elizabeth Bradford, on April 1, 1791. Sophia was the 6th child born to the Bradford's, and would have been between 3-and-6, when they came to the plantation. Abelard would have been several years older, as he was five children ahead of Sophia, but again, without his birth certificate, we can only do the numbers. The best guess is that he was 11, or younger, probably closer to 9. The children traveling down the river to their new home, in order of age, were Abelard, Edmund, Jane, Sophia and David Jr. There are two other sons mentioned, Alexander and James, who would have been the second and fourth children born respectively, but as mentioned earlier, there is no birth or death certificate for them.

David Junior had just been born in Washington County, Pennsylvania, on February 2, 1796, when the Bradford's arrived at Bayou Sara. He was the last child born in Pennsylvania. On July 27, 1797, Eliza Bradford was born on the plantation that was to become the Myrtles, making her the first child delivered there. It is possible the main house had been completed, as it was finished between late 1796, and early 1797. Six boisterous children were now calling Richland home, and the heritage of the Myrtles Plantation (as it was later named) had begun. Sarah Matilda Bradford made her arrival at the plantation only a year later in 1798, and Octavia Ursula Bradford announced her debut in 1803, with a newborn's cry.

David Bradford's long-awaited pardon, in 1799, was offered, not by Washington, but John Adams, and is recorded in the following letter:

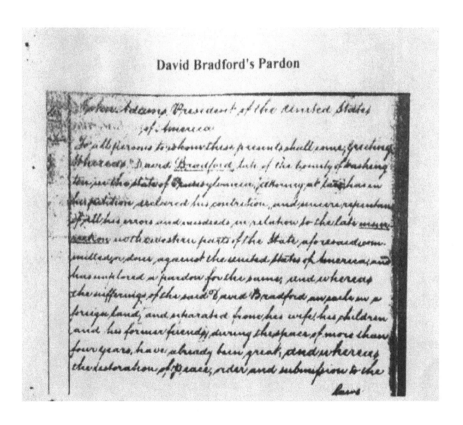

David Bradford's Pardon

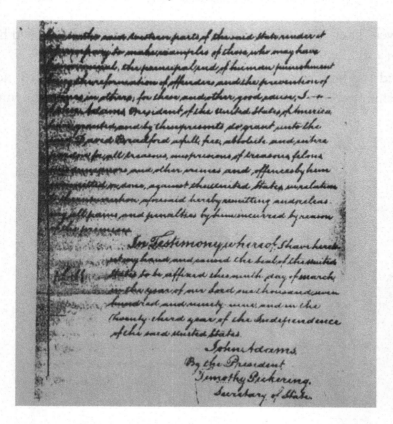

David Bradford wrote to his friend back in Pennsylvania about his new life (all capitalizations and misspellings are Mr. Bradford's):

(written on the outside of the letter is:)
Natchez March 10, 1803   David Redick, Esqr.

        Prothonotary
Washington County, Pennsylvania

Louisiana

Feb. 9ᵗʰ 1803 —   My dear Redick;

*   Your Sundry favours are at present before me— under date of 6ᵗʰ Feb. 1802 — 9ᵗʰ Mar — 1ˢᵗ April — 14ᵗʰ Aug*

and 14th Sept. all of which I have ecporused (? possibly perused. David Bradford was well known for his poor spelling and penmanship) for the purpose of refreshing my Memory on the various Subjects you mention therein. In the first place I most sincerely thank you for your punctuality and particularly in writing to me on those subjects that concern my Interest. Your anecdites (ms) respecting Electionering Business & Desk schisms & disputes afforded me a good laugh. Mrs. Bradford has charged me to assure you that she receives infinite pleasure in hearing from you, Mrs. R. and family and esnstantly (instantly) claims the privilege of reading your letters—She says you are highly improved in your handwriting which I am daily growing worse. I suppose the ground for absunation (? possibly observation) arose from yr. having wrote last letter in a very small & close hand.

Inform Madame Redick that Mrs. B has the most charming little Girl we ever had. She is named Octavian. The 12th I intend calling <u>Duadeumon</u>. My family were all inoculated last month against small pox."

The word "Duadeumon" is probably a misspelling of the word "duodenum", which has its roots in the Middle English, by way of Medieval Latin, and refers to the number 12. Octavia was child number ten, and it was probably a joke as to the number of children, if they kept coming at this rate. The reference to small pox alludes to the disease known to visit early America. Yellow fever, by far, took the greater toll in Louisiana. Also, the postmark Natchez, showed from where the letter was mailed, not where the Bradford's were living. The post was picked up at Bayou Sara and sent out from Natchez, or vice versa. In a letter to David Redick, David Bradford wrote:

"I understand there are a number of letters for me in the Post Office at Natchez. I expect them down by the next Post. I hope amongst them I will find one from you."

Life at Richland Plantation

The main house was now completed, and plantation life had begun in earnest for the wealthy owners from Pennsylvania. Records show that David and Elizabeth Bradford owned extensive properties in Pennsylvania, which they rented or sold to pay off debts while living in Louisiana. An ongoing battle with a Mr. Archibald Kerr, who purchased the Bradford home at 173 South Main in Washington County, Pennsylvania, ensued for years, with Mr. Kerr promising to pay David Bradford with flour in lieu of the asking price for the home. Bradford had returned to Pennsylvania, in 1801, to try and sell his home there. For two years, it sat empty without a buyer. He finally agreed to sell his house to a Mr. Kerr in exchange for 230 barrels of flour. New Orleans was suffering from a flour shortage and Bradford thought he could sell the flour and make back his revenue from the house trade.

Mr. Kerr mentioned at one time that the price for the home was $2200, which David Bradford vehemently denied. Correspondence back and forth between Mr. Bradford and his friend David Redick show the continuing frustration felt by David Bradford, as Mr. Kerr dodged him on many occasions. To Mr. Kerr, he wrote in the beginning of the transaction:

"You shall have it (the home in Pennsylvania) for two hundred and thirty barrels of flour delivered to me

at the mouth of Bayou Sara this Spring. The flour must be of the first quality. This will obciate (?) the scarcity of Cash complained of in your country. 230 Bls. will only be $855. Say for freight at $2 per Bbl $460 will be only $1315 an amazing sacrifice—That property cost me $4250 if it cost me one Cent. Make some repairs and you will make $1000 by the Bargain."

The fact that Mr. Kerr did indeed take over the Bradford house in Pennsylvania appears in this excerpt from a letter to Mr. Redick from David Bradford:

"I have sold all my possessions in the Town of Washington (County, Pennsylvania) to Mr. Archd Kerr. I am to receive Flour in payment deld. (? possibly short for delivered) at our landing.... Then I expected flour would have been a high price here—It has turned differently. $6 has been the common price sometimes a little more and some times under that price. Our Markets here are allways (ms) fluctuating and no calculation can be made on them."

It came to David Bradford's attention that Mr. Kerr not only didn't bring the flour, but actually sailed right past him and into New Orleans, without stopping to make the agreed upon payment. In another letter to David Redick, Bradford wrote:

"He (Mr. Kerr) need have been under no apprehensions of my suing him. Had he delivered but half the amount of Flour and showed but an honest desire to have paid the residue this Spring I should have rested satisfied. But to pass out (our) landing

thereby manifesting an Intentn. (intention) to evade complyance (ms) with any part of his contract was rather barefaced. His hope I presume was that he would get a high price for his flour & be able to make something more by it that (than) by delivering it to me. Had it been low I was bound to receive it & it would have been my loss. Whether high or law (low) he had bound himself to deliver it."

David's determination to get paid is shown in the next letter to Mr. Redick:

"Mr. Kerr did not call at the Bayou Sara as he engaged to do; but passed on I had supposed to New Orleans. On hearing that he had passed on I went on for N. Orleans. An appearance of a Storm induced us to Land the same Reason I presume occasioned Mr. Kerr to land at or near the same place. He came into our Boat. I asked him if he had any letters for (from) me—he said he had not. I asked him with some mark of surprise if had none from you—he said he had not one for (from) me but one from Mark Wilson. Waiving this subject I enquired why he did not call at the Landing agreeable to his engagement. He said he was afraid or did not like to call in the Spanish Dominions---after some further conversation he said he hoped to be able to discharge my demand against him in N. Orleans—that he had 8 or 900 $ of the money had made on Sales on his way down, and the Residue or Balance he would make on the Flour. I said I hoped he would be able to adjust all things

satisfactorily to each—as honesty was designed on my part. He assured me he would be down in N. Orleans a few days; but he had occasion to stop at Bayou Fourch with this circumstance I was acquainted. I was informed by him—he had trusted some Flour the previous year—I passed on to N. Orleans and waited for the arrival of Mr. Kerr 14 days—He did not make his appearance during my stay. I returned home much disappointed on account of Mr. Kerr's want of punctuality. Whether he returned by Sea or Land I have not been informed certainly...I was much in the dark."

David Bradford held out hope for months, giving Kerr every benefit of the doubt, until it could no longer be ignored that the man had no intention of paying him the flour, or paying him any money. He was holding the deed to Bradford's house, which for an attorney, seemed like a feckless thing to do before receiving payment, but it is gleaned from Bradford's letters to Redick, that he was not the best at handling financial matters. David owed several people money, and his debt for $38 appears on a merchant's ledger in St. Francisville, after Mr. Bradford's death.

Finally, having exhausted hope of receiving payment from Mr. Kerr, he instructed his good friend David Redick, who was also an attorney, to begin legal action:

"The Judgement is entered as you inform me— he not having complied with my propositions as stated by you. I shall insist that Mr. Archd. Kerr shall pay to me the full amount of the value of the quantity of flour which he engaged in his Covenant on the day to ascertain this you shall be furnished with every

necessary voucher—I will forward to you the prices in N. Orleans on the day the four was to have been delivered. I will also send you forward the prices which have been paid on before and at the day at the Mouth of Bayou Sara for that was the Place of Delivery & the

Criterion to Judge by." And in another letter, *"His whole language and all his promises seem to be evasions and no intention of doing any thing but to Mr. Kerrs conduct has been so unmanly and ungesous (?) that he surely now deserves rigorous treatment at my hand."*

In a letter written to Redick on July 24th, 1805 (only three years before David Bradford's death), Bradford writes of his intention to send his oldest son Abelard across country to Pennsylvania to handle the matter in person, and hopefully get the money owned them by Mr. Kerr. He mentions, in two follow-up letters, his concern over Abelard's young age to be making such a journey. At the time, Abelard would have been between 17 and 19, by my estimate:

"Dear Redick...,
I think I have mentioned in my last my intention of sending Abelard. It will therefore be extremely desireous (ms) & highly interesting to me to have the Money collected as soon as it can possibly be done. He will want it or a considerable part of it on his arrival to discharge taxes and pay surveying fees, etc. He is rather Young to send on Important Business but I much rely on your friendly assistance in giving that paternal advice that you would hope & expect from me in a similar case. I shall decree him to be

guided by your Judgement in all cases of importance."

A month later on August 20th, 1805, Bradford wrote:

"Abelard will set out for your Hemisphere in about one month from this date. I intend him to go thro by Land. I pray you to note my wishes expressed in my last letters. Leave no stone unturned to procure every legal dispatch the
money from Kerr."

Nov. 3rd, 1805, Bayou Sara, to David Redick Esquire, Attorney at Law, Washington County, Pennsylvania:

"Dear Mr. Redick,
Your last dated in the Country, I recd. I am sorry indeed to hear you have been dangerously ill; rejoice to hear from you that you are in state of recovery. I presume Abelard will soon be with you after you receive this letter, he has left us just one month past on yesterday (October, 1805). He will delay some time in Kentucky, & in the Scioto Country I hope he will arrive safe—He is a young traveler to undertake so long a journey; but I hope he will pass this safe. He will greatly stand in need of your patronage which I rest assured you will cheerfully afford to him.
I need not say more on the subject of effective measures of speedily getting the Money from Kerr. It is the object of Ableards journey. I pray you write me By every Post.
Affectionately yrs.
David Bradford"

Nov. 29th, 1805, Bayou Sara.

"Dear Friend Redick...

I hope before the period this reaches you my Son Abelard will have had the honor of introducing himself to you & to many of his former young acquaintences, who, as well as yourself, would have no knowledge of him unless he was to make himself known. I hope he will make himself agreeable & pleasing to all he formerly may recollect, as well as to those he may now make himself acquainted. He is too young to be so far abroad with a Patron and protector; but, as I before have solicited of your Goodness to council him to right & reprove him if he should happen to fall into Error. It is a friendly Office I would perform for you & shall be greatly pleased with your friendship towards Abelard..."

It is not long after this letter, that communication stops. It may be that Mr. Redick died, as in later deeds referring to David Bradford's extensive property in Pennsylvania, a "Widow Redick" is mentioned several times. At the time of Abelard's visit to Mr. Redick, his health was failing.

As a finale to this tale, that took up 90% of his communication with David Redick, David Bradford never received compensation for the sale of his home in Pennsylvania from Mr. Kerr. It is considered highly doubtful that the flour or money was ever delivered.

Often in his communications with Mr. Redick, he discussed the situation in New Orleans, and mentioned Thomas Jefferson's efforts during the Louisiana Purchase negotiations. He lamented the Spanish rule on numerous occasions, and spoke with intelligence about Napoleon Bonaparte's campaign. It must have been an amazing time to be in the midst of such evolution that would end in the creation of the United States of America.

Plantation Life

According to the Louisiana Studies in Historic Preservation, a plantation is a large agricultural business which produces a cash crop for sale on a large scale. It consists of all the things needed to grow, harvest, and sell that crop. A successful plantation region requires: 1) fertile, easily tilled land, available in large units; 2) a climate characterized by a long growing season and adequate rainfall; 3) abundant landless, and cheap rural labor; 4) bulk reduction and preliminary processing techniques; 5) abundant, cheap transportation; and 6) a network of factors, and factoring houses, to market cash crops to other regions of the world. Thus, all the elements needed for a plantation system were present in Louisiana during the antebellum period.

These six components listed above may seem efficient and succinct, and the compliance with them a guaranteed success for the plantation owner, but as many a hopeful merchant realized, it was anything but a foregone conclusion. Turbulent weather conditions and labor upheavals were only a few considerations.

Indigo plantation in Louisiana in the late 1700s.

Fact: Growing sugar cane was a riskier business than growing cotton, but sugar cane could yield a much greater profit. "It took a rich cotton planter to make a poor sugar planter," said an old Louisiana adage.

The average antebellum sugar plantation was valued at $200,000; whereas the biggest cotton plantations were valued at half that much.

Sugar Cane Field

A cat inspired Eli Whitney to invent the cotton gin! He witnessed a cat pulling bird feathers through a cage and quickly associated the action with the possibility of mechanically removing seeds from cotton by a combing mechanism. The cotton gin made the growing of cotton profitable for Louisiana planters.

THE COTTON GIN

Cotton bolls with seeds

Seeds

Brushes

Clean cotton

Cylinder

Container for cotton bolls

Container for clean cotton

David Bradford began his life as a plantation owner by planting indigo, a crop with which many of his neighbors had done well. Unfortunately, for Mr. Bradford, his timing was wrong. Two years before he landed in Sara Bayou, a bug infestation had destroyed a large quantity of indigo plants, forcing plantation owners to turn to the next cash crop—cotton. Sugar was huge in Louisiana, but the farming region to the south of St. Francisville was more conducive to sugar cane. Bradford's area was user-friendly to the cotton crop.

Tom and Myrna Hart, who run the Bradford House Museum in Washington County, Pennsylvania, and maintain a wonderful website with the history of David Bradford confirmed David originally named his land in St. Francisville, Louisiana, Richland. (www.bradfordhouse.org.) It does appear on the National Historic Register as such. It was later changed to Laurel Grove, which may have coincided with David switching from indigo to cotton, as plantations were often linked to their crop. We do know that when the Stirling's took over the plantation in later years, it was called Laurel Grove.

In a letter to his friend David Redick, on July 25, 1805, you get a sense of David Bradford's unhappiness with the political climate in Louisiana, and in particular, his area of the state. He has been on the plantation now for eleven years, beginning with his construction of the original outbuilding.

"You inform me of Jonathans Intention of coming to this Country to make his residence here. You wish my opinion the subject. I presume his intention is to practice Law. I assure you it gives me sincere pleasure to receive this information for two reasons. 1st. Because I should be only happy in seeing him in this Country and 2nd. Because I think a great field is now opening for the Practice of Law. I am almost tempted to remove from this place, which is still held by the Spanish Government, to the City of New Orleans to engage in the bustle of the Bar. My hopes that this part of the country will soon fall into the hands of

the American Government has induced me to wait the Event which I hope will soon take place. If it continues to be Spain, I shall instantly make up my mind to remove to Natchez or N. Orleans."

He wrote in a follow-up letter:

"Does your son Johnathan mean to come down to this Country? You asked my advice. I gave it if the letter was read. The Yellow Fever has raged in N. Orleans this Season."

On August 20^{th,} we get a sense of the other climate Louisiana planters concerned themselves with…the weather:

"We have had a very wet season of late—in the first part of the season it was amazingly dry. I fear out Cotton crops will be much injured by it. We have scarce had two dry days together for than two months past. The Corn Crops are excellent with us."

Notice that he does not mention indigo. It was also at this time, he was at war with Mr. Kerr, over the flour that had not arrived, and was getting Abelard ready to depart soon for Pennsylvania on his behalf. We are also told in many of his letters, that he was often ill or otherwise handicapped.

The letter was head marked: West Florida, Bayou Sara, opposite Point Couper, Octr. 10th, 1803.

"My dear Friend Redick,
Your esteemed favrs. Of June 11th and Augt. 11th both came to hand. On the receipt of the 1st I was extremely ill in the Plmucy (or Plmincy or Plcuiucy?) and did not break the Seal for many days. In short I

have been sick almost all this Summer. It has been a very sick season with (faded out) in general.... I have written you a long letter the scarcely able to sit up. It seemed to be necessary to give you some Idea of my concerns & more so as you are the only friend that will write to me."

David mentions in an earlier letter, his lament that none of his friends from Pennsylvania will write to him. Whether this was a fall-out from the Whiskey Rebellion, is unclear. The typical cost to send a letter then was 25 cents, so it is doubtful due to the expense. Most letters took an average of one week to reach Pennsylvania from Natchez.

November 12, 1803 to David Redick:

"I have been almost all this summer unwell—I am now perfectedly restored to health & I threaten you with more letters by every post—The Postage is really so trifling that I would willingly pay four times the sum for every letter you send me."

On November 7th, 1804 David wrote to Mr. Redick of his horse accident:

"About one month ago my horse fell by stumbling and so profound was his blunder that I feared he would have turned over—to extricate myself from the danger of his falling on me I threw myself off on one side & preserving myself from the fall stretched out my left hand—by the velocity of falling & my own weight my wrist was more violently sprained & perhaps some of the splintered or separated. It has been excruciating painful but now getting pretty well."

In March of 1805, David left Elizabeth in charge of the plantation and children, and went to New Orleans for four months to practice law. Whether he felt the need for additional income over that his plantation was providing, or it was merely his need to continue in the legal profession, for which he was trained, is unclear. His letters to David Redick now bore a New Orleans postmark. May 30th, 1805:

"My dear friend,
I have been in this place about 2 months. I have been admitted to Practice in the Supreme Court of this Terty. (territory). The Business has been as successful as I had expected; but I have been laid up with Disentary for some time & have not yet got released from it. I am on the Recovery."

The postmark on July 1st, 1805 saw him once more in Bayou Sara after being away for four months:

"I have been in New Orleans for some months past. I went down with the express intention of practicing the old trade of Basketweaving Viz. the Law. I was admitted without hesitation or difficulty in the Superior Court of the Tery. Of Orleans & prospects opened flattering enough; but I took unwell with a lax which terminated in a confirmed Disentary & was laid up for a long time. I had it not in contemplation to remove my family to New Orleans—The Yellow Fever which annually has visited that place forbade an Idea of that kind. I only meant to spend a few months to become familiar with the modes of practice under their new Laws & mode of Government."

There are many references in David Bradford's letters to Mr. Redick that show his affection and admiration for his wife Elizabeth. His nickname for her was "Betsey" and there are hints of a fun feistiness in their marriage and a congenial partnership. Here are a few snippets from his letters to Redick:

"...Only I must add that Betsey & all my household wish that you & Mrs. Redick may remember them & accept their affectionate Respects." "Betsey says that you are a nidling (or middling) Source that did not say more about Mrs. Redick—She said it with a Degree of airinony (alacrity?) & ill nature. I checked & made the best apology for you that I could—Haste and press of Business often prevents saying all we would wish or intent. Gratify her in the next that she may not fall out with you. She has charged me to present her most respectful & affectionate wishes for Mrs. Redicks Happiness & Prosperity." (Author's note: This may have been intended as a fun slight that she only wished Mrs. Redick well.)

There was a time when Bradford returned to Pennsylvania, after his pardon, to oversee the sale of his home and other business matters. It is believed to be around 1801. In a letter to Redick, you can see not only Bradford's pride in his wife's handling of the plantation, but also the role the plantation mistress played. It was not the image we have of Scarlet O'Hara fanning herself leisurely on the veranda with a mint julep in one hand and a lace fan in the other, adoring males at her feet, as strains of Dixie are heard in the distance.

"I have the pleasure of informing you that I had a most agreeable and speedy passage down the waters. I did not touch Land after I entered the Mississippi but

3 times—at the Chicasaw Bluffs where I found Capt. Sparks in command—Lansla Grass, & Natchez. On my arrival I found my family well & my Plantation affairs better conducted than if I had been at home. Mrs. B has acquired high reputation as a Cotton Planter. She bot. an excellent negro wench in my absence— Sent money Rowland & had four more which arrived here after my arrival. I bought two as I passed Wheeling— 1 of Col. Chaplain a young wench—a 2ⁿᵈ of Mr. South a lad of 16 years of age. Our cotton here is a (obliterated by the letter's seal) price. Industry here works with both her hands. The produce of our Soil— the high price & ready Market sets every wheel in motion."

When speaking of a business deal he is transacting, he writes,

"Mrs. Bradford hints to me while I am now writing she is sure Mr. Cunningham will not forget the female prerogative."

From David Bradford's letters, it is clear he and Elizabeth formed a team. All of their land deeds in Pennsylvania are in both their names and several were handled by Elizabeth in her husband's absence. Remember, that this was a turbulent time in Louisiana, with wars going on over the ownership of New Orleans, and epidemics claiming lives on a horrendous scale.

David Bradford died, in 1808. He was spared the onslaught of the Civil War that tore apart the towns of St. Francisville and Bayou Sara, and saw Union soldiers within the private walls of his plantation.

Elizabeth remained on at the plantation. It is a testament to the mettle and courage of the women who donned the title of "Land Barron" and "Plantation Owner" upon their husbands' death. Wills, estate titles, business negotiations, and a transfer of authority, all fell upon the plantation mistress, as their husbands were interred.

Suddenly, the slave overseers were looking to her for their instructions, while the business of running a plantation continued on. It was a role more than one wife would play at the home that would become known as the Myrtles Plantation.

Chapter Three
Elizabeth Bradford's View

A rare portrait of Elizabeth Porter Bradford.

Wind whipped the towering trees that hemmed in the plantation into a frenzy. Debris struck the side of the clapboard house with such force windows could be heard shattering in the downstairs rooms. Frightened voices called up the narrow staircase to Elizabeth Bradford, who was hurriedly making the shutters secure on the second landing.

"Missus! 'Da's glass all over da dinin' room down here!" Trudy called. "It's blowin' up real bad!" she added unnecessarily, as another gust struck the house so violently the roof threatened to cave in.

Elizabeth gathered her long skirts and hurried down the stairs. The main rooms looked like a war zone. Rain was pouring in through the damaged windows, while broken tree limbs protruded into the parlor like skeletal forearms.

"Mother, there's a man here," David Jr. cried above the howl of the storm. "He's from Fort St. Phillip. He wants to speak with you," the 16-year-old said, as he motioned to a tall shadow waiting near the door.

A man entered the room and stood in the glow of the kerosene lantern that Trudy, the house maid, was holding up with shaking hands. The rain from his soggy clothes puddled onto the cyprus planks, as he stood before the mistress of the house.

"Mrs. Bradford," he began, "I was sent from New Orleans to offer support. Friends of your late husband were concerned for your safety. I'm afraid the hurricane is a bad one. It began out of the northeast of New Orleans. Nearly all the buildings have suffered. Fifteen feet of water is covering the city. One hundred souls have been lost so far, and Fort St. Phillip is under water. Reports say the British fleet was approaching the fort when the storm hit...call it Providence, or call it the work of the Devil...it's hard to say. But I want to warn you that there may be British troops seeking refuge throughout the Gulf and inland. I would gather all your man power, M'am, and secure the house as best you can. Have you guns?"

"Yes, of course," Elizabeth said, placing an arm around her daughter Eliza, who had just run into the room. "We'll manage," she said, as she had said so many times, since her husband's death four years before.

By 2:30 the next afternoon, the winds had dropped to a pitiful wail. Laurel Grove was still standing, but the damage could be seen everywhere. As the plantation slaves rallied to repair windows, roofing, and their own damaged cabins, Elizabeth withdrew to her bedroom, and did something she had not allowed herself to do for two years now...she buried her head in her hands and wept.

Elizabeth Bradford had sailed down the Mississippi in 1796, into what must have felt like a land from another dimension. While she had been mistress to four house slaves in Pennsylvania, and indeed may have brought them along, it was nothing compared to what awaited her in a southern plantation paradigm. That so much of the mechanics of running such an institution would be left to her, may have also been absent in the "fine print."

From several accounts in David Bradford's letters to Mr. Redick, it is clear that men were often away from home on business, or for political reasons. Lawyers were especially given to long trips to handle client's matters and continue their practice in cities where the legal system was flourishing. They were often gone for months, as is noted in Bradford's four-month-long stay in New Orleans. For the mistress of the plantation, this could be a very harrowing time.

The dynamics of the southern plantation household were complex in the antebellum period. Women were in a subservient role to their husbands, who represented lord and master, not only to the slaves, but to the mistress of the house. Women's opinions were generally limited to the realm of domesticity assigned them from an early age. To quote one southern plantation owner, "My wife is not competent to advise the statesman or the politician— her knowledge, her advice, her ministry, is in a kindlier sphere."

From childhood, women of the 17th and 18th centuries, were taught primarily the graces—how to sew, and social etiquette. Many were raised by a black woman while their mothers attended to other things. It was not uncommon for babies to be suckled by a black house servant. But during this time, the young women were never once taught how to run a household or oversee workers. They tended to marry young. and many were suddenly taken from the protection of their childhood homes and role models, and thrust into the position of mistress of a plantation, with all it entailed.

It was an extremely complicated relationship: with society, with the husband, with the slaves—that now fell under her dominion when the master was away—with her own childbearing years, and with the loneliness that often-accompanied plantation life. Perhaps nowhere else, was the relationship dynamic more confusing, than that with the slaves with which she shared her life.

For Elizabeth Bradford, arriving in St. Francisville with five small children, and no knowledge of this new frontier called Louisiana, it must have been daunting, and not a little frightening. She had left behind a beautiful brick mansion, friends, a social status befitting the wife of a prominent attorney, and was now staring at a clapboard house in the middle of nowhere. Moss dangling from trees was not a sight she was used to, and she must have felt very much out of place, and homesick. Gone were the mahogany staircase, fine décor and social gatherings. At least the bustling river port of Bayou Sara, and the refined homes of St. Francisville were nearby. She would just have to start over.

Sign before the David Bradford House in Washington, Penn. "Spanish West Florida" is today's Louisiana.

David Bradford House in Pennsylvania.

Rear of Bradford's house with gardens.
Photo courtesy of Jim Zaccone Photography.

Replica of Bradford's outdoor kitchen cabin.
Photo courtesy of Jim Zaccone Photography.

The mornings in Elizabeth's new plantation home would have been filled with establishing a household, and getting used to a new routine. David had undoubtedly already hired slaves to begin clearing the land and planting indigo. There may have been a house slave or two to help Elizabeth with the children, cooking, and cleaning. Outside, were the noises of construction, as the framing went up for what would become her new home. Bricks were being made from the clay in the wallow only a few feet away from the small house she now inhabited. Many trips to nearby Bayou Sara for fabric, supplies, and groceries were probably a common occurrence. It would have been now that the confusing relationship, and often bond, between plantation mistress and black slave began.

As mentioned before, house slaves were given all of the odious chores, from cooking and cleaning, to childcare. It was black fingers that helped the little ones put on their shoes, or that wiped their tiny noses. It was unfamiliar songs from another land that rocked babies to sleep at night, and the caring heart of a "darkie" that soothed them when they were ill. It is not to say that the mother was not a prevalent presence in their young lives, but a plantation mistress was caught in a confusing mindset. On the one hand, she was "a lady," and with that title came all the social status she had hoped for. She was mistress of a plantation and wife to an important man. She was more than happy to have the chores done by others, as it may have been a household commonality she grew up with. This was familiar, in that one aspect, and expected. On the other hand, she was now an overseer of human beings.

In the southern states, during the antebellum period, slavery was accepted, as not only necessary, but an expected way of life. Without it, a plantation simply could not run. Most of the early plantations, hired anywhere from 10-30 field hands and a few house slaves. The larger plantations, hired as many as 100- to upward of 500, and sometimes more, depending on the crop and the size of the operation. Some households boasted as many as 50 slaves who managed the kitchen, cleaning, children, etc. For slaves, it was much preferred to be inside the home than out in the field, and it was a coveted position.

Louisiana Cotton Plantation.

But, therein lies the rub for the plantation mistress. The slaves knew her position was subservient to the master of the house, similar to their own status, with obvious differences. The "massa's" word was law and his opinion overruled all others. Often, slaves would stand up to the mistress of the house, knowing she was second in command. While she oversaw the daily household duties of the staff, it was the male role that counted in all other things. It was an ominous position to be in. She was dependent on these people, and they are on her. It could be an oftentimes turbulent association—especially when the husband was away.

To say that plantation owners were often in fear of their lives, is not a dramatic statement to make. The slaves far out-numbered the white people living in the big house, and revolts were not unheard of. Masters often dealt out strict punishments, sometimes maiming a servant, and the threat of retaliation was a constant stress. One can't imagine what it must have been like for the plantation mistresses to go to bed at night in the quiet house, their husbands miles away, knowing they were surrounded by people who were held against their will, in cabins just across the lawn. They were human beings, who had been taken from their homes, bought and sold, sometimes by the pound, or age, or sex. It was a degradation that formed Abraham Lincoln's most passionate campaign.

In Elizabeth Fox-Genovese's wonderful book, *Within the Plantation Household: Black & White Women of the Old South,* she talks about the burden assumed by a plantation mistress:

"Depending in some measure upon the maturity, stability, and extent of the households to which the southern women belonged, their everyday lives followed the routine of the farm day and the rhythms of the seasons, with some allowance for their own ages and stations in the plantation family. The mistress of the household—normally the wife of the master, but sometimes his daughter, widow, mother, or sister—assumed the mantle of ruling lady, whether she wore it gracefully or awkwardly. All other women of the household were subordinate to her. As symbol of her station, she carried the keys to the innumerable storerooms and outbuildings. Should the master be permanently or temporarily absent, all members of the household would answer to her, but few such women enjoyed or successfully exercised that ultimate authority, and the vast majority of those who tried recognized themselves for what they were—delegates of the master, of male authority. Women's training for their household responsibilities rarely included training in the internal running or external representation of the plantation—the disciplining of field hands, especially male, or the marketing of crops, or any of the other responsibilities that linked the household to the market and the polity. Catherine Edmonston (a plantation wife from Ms. Fox-Genovese's book) regretted her husband's absence, for "Master's eye and voice are much more potent than mistress."

In Elizabeth Bradford's world, as it would be in Sarah Mathilda Woodruff's, Mary Stirling's, and Sarah Winter's, the plantation was a community and business all rolled into one. An overseer generally handled the field hands and made sure the plantation's crop was managed. He reported directly to the master of the house, and in his absence, the mistress. Most of the slaves lived in separate outbuildings scattered about the plantation, their proximity to the house dependent on their service. House slaves lived in quarters closest to the house, while field hands were farther away on the property. Slaves often had a small garden of their own to tend and use for their own purposes on their off-time. A white child's black nurse usually lived within the main house, sleeping on the same floor as her mistress. The main house was the hub of the activity and radiated out into all other buildings.

Restaurant 1796, at today's Myrtles Plantation, sits on the site of the original carriage house, and is approximately 1,950 square feet. The original stables housed horses and cattle (when they were not in pasture); carriages and other conveyances; farm wagons and ox carts; the harness and gear for all these vehicles; plows and farm implements. A blacksmith was usually on the premises as well, and often had his own quarters, usually in or near the stables.

Typical plantation carriage house.

Former carriage house as a restaurant.
The main plantation house is on the left. Restaurant 1796 is
now in this location after the Carriage House restaurant
(pictured) burned in 2017.

The plantation grew and processed basic foodstuffs, including corn and wheat, vegetables, pork for the slaves, and beef, lamb, mutton, ham, bacon, chickens, turkey, and geese for the big house. The sewing and mending of clothes were an ongoing task that could keep a few women busy practically the entire day. Oddly enough, the plantation mistress would often undertake the chore of sewing clothes for the slaves in her dominion. Again, it was an odd co-dependency between the mistress and the slaves that peopled the plantation and called it home.

Elizabeth Bradford's day would consist in overseeing the household staff, ordering meals, peeking into the kitchen to make sure all was well, ordering the repairs or cleaning of the buildings, checking ledgers for food, linen, and other purchases that pertained primarily to the household and its upkeep. Her children's education would be attended to, either by herself or a teacher. It will fall to her to teach them social graces and etiquette that would determine their acceptance in the world. If David Bradford was away, her chores doubled. While not soiling her hands with dishes, cooking or cleaning, her mind was constantly in a whirl over the myriad instructions it took to run a plantation.

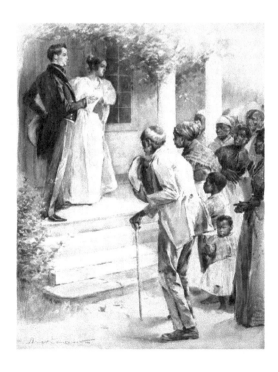

Plantation Mistress

As witnessed in David Bradford's letter to his friend Redick, Elizabeth bought slaves when needed. On December 2, 1816, eight years after David's death, Elizabeth signed Estate Record #26-A-040-032-1816 as the purchaser of 10 slaves: Henny, Comfort, Sally, Kitty, Leah, Mary, Minty, Julia and Rhoda—all black females. All but Henny were part of a group that sold for $9,800 total. Henny sold for $800 alone. A married couple, Nancy and George, went for $2,000.

It is interesting to note, that all but George are female. Women were actually the more-sought after gender for plantation work. They not only worked side-by-side with the males in the fields, they also had to cook breakfast and dinner, make clothes, spin cotton, and other myriad duties.

According to Louisiana slave records, in 1820, there were 24 slaves listed at Laurel Grove; 20 "engaged in agriculture," which may be a politically correct phrase for "working in the fields." This seems a small number, and it would be hard to fathom it entailed all the labor needed to run a plantation.

It should be pointed out, that everything depended on the crop being cultivated on these huge estates. If the crop failed, so did the livelihood of owner and slave alike. Ever dependent on the fickle weather conditions, perfection of the soil and expertise of the slaves that nurtured it, the crops were carefully tended to. This was long before irrigation systems were in place, or mechanical wonders that could do most of the work. Everything was done by hand, with a prayer to Mother Nature in constant demand. Overused soil from too many crop rotations could literally give out; its nutrients sapped. There was an exact science and timing to this precious commodity.

Once the crop was ready for harvest, an entirely new set of demands became center focus. The cotton, in the Bradford's instance, had to be cleaned, weighed, packaged and readied for market. The current asking price was strictly monitored and more than one sleepless night occurred when the market was in flux. Slaves waited as their day's baskets of cotton were weighed. If they fell behind previous pound amounts, or were not as productive as others, they were sometimes punished.

All of these components went into the everyday life of the plantation owner's wife. It is no wonder that the arrival of guests was so welcome. Here, she could finally confide in other women in her station and feel a sense of common ground. Letters were a frequent way of staying in touch with a world that sometimes felt a lifetime away. There was often an extreme sense of isolation and abandonment. The mistress's world was seen primarily from within the walls of the home, while the master's was a view from without, as he went about his departures in business and politics. Frustration, danger, and conflict exacerbated a sense of separation. There must have been, at times, a deep longing to return to the safety and surety of the home she had left behind, where as a young girl she was coddled and protected.

In all fairness to the Bradford's, their relationship seemed, from the outside, to be one of common respect. David relied on Elizabeth in his frequent absences and praised her efficiency. She seems to have been consulted in matters of property, and offered her advice on matters typically considered the master's domain. One gets a feeling of camaraderie and feisty playfulness from David's letters.

Elizabeth Buys Laurel Grove

After David Bradford's death in 1808, at the age of 53, his will, whose deposition lasted several years, and was finally metered out in 1816, provided for his heirs and their families. Listed in the settlement of the estate are Harrison, James M., Elizabeth, Eliza, Octavia, Edmund, David Jr., James B., Leonard, Isham, Samuel, and Charles M. Bradford, and Nancy Reams. Documents on file at the

LSU Library include a personal letter by David Bradford, detailing the disbursements of his property in Pennsylvania. Papers include Spanish Land Grants, surveys, plats, conveyances, appraisals, and mortgages for land owned by Bradford and his family; chiefly in West Feliciana and East Baton Rouge Parishes.

On December 3, 1816, Elizabeth buys Laurel Grove for $8,000, putting it legally in her name. It could be the plantation was left to several of the heirs and she bought them out, leaving them with other properties or money. We know that the land surrounding Laurel Grove had been partitioned out to Abelard, James, and Edmund at 500 *arpents* each. In any case, Elizabeth was now the owner and overseer of a large plantation and all it entailed.

In 1816, several of the Bradford children were still living at home. Jane Bradford had married Henry Q. Spear at Pointe Coupee Parish, Louisiana (just across the river from Laurel Grove) in 1807, one year before David Bradford died, and was possibly living elsewhere with her new husband. Sophia Elizabeth Bradford married James M. Bradford from Pennsylvania, and David Bradford, Jr. married Amanda Davis, on Nov. 6, 1820. Eliza Bradford married M. James Challen, May 9, 1827, in the West Feliciana Parish. Their wedding was no doubt celebrated at the plantation, as was Jane's, and probably David, Jr.'s. Octavia Ursula Bradford, the youngest of the children, married Issac A. Smith, and after his death, was married again to B.G. Martin. There are no marriage records for Edmund and Abelard. We do know Abelard died, in 1826, and Edmund, in 1825.

Sarah Matilda Bradford, the 9th child of David and Elizabeth Bradford, married Clark Woodruff, on November 19, 1817, at Laurel Grove Plantation, in St. Francisville, Louisiana.

Chapter Four

The Layout of the Myrtles Plantation

Myrtles Plantation, also known as Richland, and Laurel Grove.

Most Southern plantations had very similar layouts. Buildings made an arc around a yard, or courtyard, with the owner's mansion at the top, domestic buildings on one side of the arc, and farming buildings on the other side. There were usually domestic buildings, that included a kitchen (closest to the main house), a smokehouse, chicken coop, washhouse, coach house and stable. There was also usually a yard for doing laundry, a kitchen garden, and paddock in this area. Some plantations also featured rooms for tutors and gardeners.

On the other side of the mansion, there were usually buildings more associated with farm work, such as a storehouse, barns, rain shed, cotton gin, mills and blacksmith shop. Some also featured an office for the planter or owner, and a pottery shop.

Field slaves were housed in quarters to the side of the work buildings. Most slaves shared cabins, while overseers and drivers usually had separate dwellings. Domestic slaves lived in cabins closer to the mansion near the other domestic buildings.

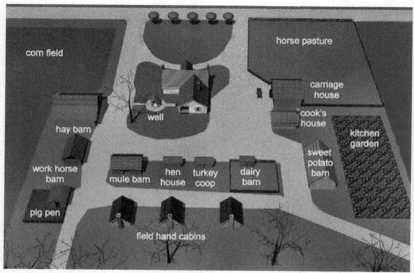

Typical southern plantation layout.

The majority of land on a plantation was used to grow a crop, such as cotton, corn, rice, tobacco or sugar. These fields were portioned off around, or sometimes in front of, the main living areas, with woodlands or forest surrounding the entire plantation, and usually a river running through it, or nearby. Rivers were used as a means to transport crops to the marketplace, and goods and supplies to the plantation owner. Typically, one field was used as a pasture for cattle or horses, and one or two other fields were left idle for yearly crop rotation.

Some very large plantations had churches, schools, hospitals and stores, called commissaries on their land. *Garconnieres* and *Pigeonniers* were also found on plantation grounds. A *Garconniere* was a separate quarter for older boys, allowing them their freedom to come and go at their own convenience. This is the beautiful building you see at the entrance to the Myrtles Plantation, on your right of the entrance.

Myrtles Plantation garconnierre

Pigeonniers, or Dovecotes, were used where pigeons were raised for food, and their droppings collected for fertilizer. Usually, owning a pigeonnier was a sign that the plantation owners were very wealthy indeed.

A pigeonnier.

The antebellum (Latin for "before the war") period was known for the plantation era. At the start of the Civil War, cotton had overtaken both tobacco and sugar, as the largest crop traded in the world. Food crops included peas, pumpkins, corn, potatoes, and other vegetables, used by the plantation's habitats.   When David Bradford received his pardon for his part in the Whiskey Rebellion in 1799, Laurel Grove was two years old and cotton was doing very well. He had built a beautiful plantation home with the original 1000-square-foot structure now acting as the kitchen, pantry, storage, and domestic food prep area for the main house.

Stephen Saunders researched the Myrtles Plantation in 1975, when he acted as the plantation curator during Arlin Dease's ownership, along with Mr. and Mrs. Robert F. Ward. Stephen's exhaustive research on every square inch of the plantation is impressive. He also worked on its renovation with Mr. Dease, (who was the contractor on the refurbishing job, as well as part owner), painting shutters and doors, and many other tasks to restore the mansion to its former glory. The two also did the impressive restoration of the faux painting on the fireplaces and mantels. Thanks to this research, which was done in part to nominate the Myrtles Plantation to the National Register of Historic Places, we have the following information about the early plantation's architectural elements, in Mr. Saunder's words:

Stated in David Bradford's will, dated Jan. 4, 1808, at the West Feliciana Court House, the site of the present Myrtles Plantation is on a portion of the original tract, which was a Spanish Land Grant applied for in 1792, by General David Bradford. This was dated in Madrid, January 20, 1792, but granted under authority of Baron de Carondelet, Governor of Louisiana and West Florida, and dated July, 1797. (It would appear Mr. Bradford had already built the original outbuilding before the final grant was filed. It may have been a timing thing with the document's official posting. Author's note.)

The same boundaries are set forth in a survey by Cosby dated

1813, resurveying Bradford's property, after his death in 1808. This survey showed David Bradford's property on the S.E. Longitudinal boundary fronting the Old Woodville Road.

A pond of approximately 1 ½ acres is located on the top of the bluff in W.N.W. quadrant. This area is assumed to have been formed first by buffalo, using it as a wallow, thus exposing the clay. The fact that the pond is atop this bluff, having no water entering by feeder streams or drainage, it is presumed that it was formed by buffalo, as there are many such ponds in the vicinity. Since there are no other excavations nearby, combined with the fact the clay had already been exposed, and finding wedge-shaped brick in the edge of the pond, we are led to believe this excavation was enlarged with the production of brick.

The Myrtles pond. Photo courtesy of Jason Phillip Reeser.

As clay was needed later for the production of brick being used to construct the foundation for the home, underground cisterns, well and fireplaces, this wallow was deepened and enlarged. Located on the southern shore of this pond are three red cypress trees approximately 125-years-old. These trees also help in dating the pond, as they could not have survived without having had water at their base. (The dating of the trees may be a little off, as it would put them in 1850, based on Mr. Saunder's estimation, and if it was indeed a buffalo wallow, it would have been there at the time Bradford began construction in 1794, as it is doubtful buffalo were still roaming through the plantation once it was being planted and excavated. The dating of most trees allows for a discrepancy of time. Author's note.) An orchard of considerable age and still bearing fruit is located in the northern section of the property and includes peach, pear, cherry and pecan trees.

The architectural style can best be described as an elaborate Louisiana 2-story raised cottage. The materials from which the home was constructed consisted of cypress for framework, flooring, exterior siding, lathe work for wall, ceilings and original shake roof, brick being used for columns making up foundation of the home, fireplaces, underground cisterns and also for the well. Plaster mixed with cattle and deer hair adhered to the cypress lathe work provided the interior walls, ceilings and elaborate plasterwork. Hand blown glass was affixed to the windows, decorative cast iron grillwork and standards helping to support the roof and hand hammered iron nails were used for securing.

David Bradford's plantation home was designed much like his home in Pennsylvania. The style is called a "saddlebag house," meaning it has four rooms upstairs and four rooms downstairs, with an exterior staircase on the center of the backside. The original house forms the western six bays of the main façade. As you look at the main house, the original portion (before it was expanded in the mid-1800s to the south), almost doubling its size, begins with the first set of stairs to the north which lead up to the veranda. The second set of stairs to the front of the house, the stairs closest to the parking lot, represent the newer portion created by the Stirling's, in 1835.

The original main house consisted of two parlors on the main floor, separated by a hallway leading from the front door. The Ladies' Parlor was to the left as you entered the hall and the Gentlemen's Parlor was to the right, again emulating the "saddlebag" architecture. The Ladies' Parlor was for the mistress of the house to use in writing letters, overseeing the plantation help, entertaining female guests, or for other female members of the family to engage in sewing or crafts.

The Gentleman's Parlor was used for the men to sit, share a cigar and discuss business, politics, or news of the day. The windows in these two parlors could be raised up into the ceiling to allow a welcome breeze to permeate the home. The jalousie shutters could be closed, still allowing air flow through their slats. Both rooms featured fireplaces and cypress floors. The original fireplace mantels were made of cypress. These were later changed out when the Stirling's took over the plantation, and did an extensive remodel and expansion, that resulted in the two parlors being combined, separated only by a pocket door.

A door to the east of the Ladies' Parlor leads to the formal dining room with its own large fireplace. The Dining Room has two doors. This is important as doors were taxed, so having two doors in one room said to the world, "We have money." The large windows overlook the back property and the original outbuilding, which contained the kitchen. The kitchens were always located in a separate building from the main house in case of fire. A kitchen might feed 200 people a day, depending on the size of the plantation.

From the Gentlemen's Parlor, one could enter the Game Room, which was originally the children's dining room. The adage "children should be seen and not heard" may have originated in this era, especially when company was present. Children were taught table manners and other etiquette, and when old enough, were then allowed to join the adults at the main dining table. Often several families lived under the same roof, as was the case with the Myrtles, so often a separate dining room for the children was more pragmatic, as there was not enough room at the main table.

The back staircase can be accessed from the Game Room (Children's Dining Room) and the Dining Room, and it literally split the home in half. It is very steep and leads to the second floor. A large gallery at the top of the landing separates two wings of rooms. This gallery served as both the schoolroom and the chapel. Platforms were found at either end of the expanse, one for the teacher and her desk— the other for the minister or priest, or sometimes the father.

Flanking this gallery were the bedrooms. These rooms have seen changes over the years in their size. The Fannie Williams Room may have been one long wing that accommodated traveling guests. Today, that wing is separated by a wall culminating in two rooms. The platform at the south end of the gallery is now home to guest bathrooms. The entire second floor has been reported to have a good deal of paranormal activity, each area touting its own experiences.

Original back staircase from the Bradford era.

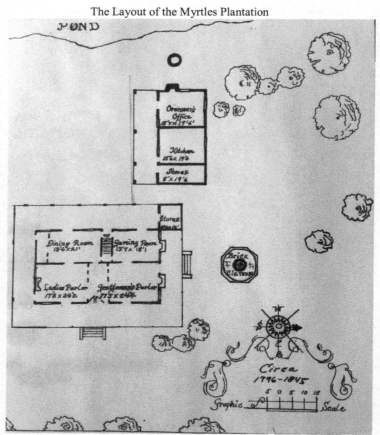

Floor plan drawing depicting home during Bradford's time
(Remodel of Stephen Saunders drawing)

To the left of the gallery, was a long bedroom, used as the master suite, and lady's dorm, where females of that era were expected to rest during the afternoon before the party in the evening. Visiting ladies would lie down on beds and mats. You might remember a similar scene from *Gone with the Wind*. To the right of the gallery were two large bedrooms, each with a fireplace. One was usually designated as a nursery where the small children slept; the other room was for the nanny, or other adult.

Lady's dorm in a scene from Gone with the Wind.

Outside of the main house, was the original building Bradford constructed to house his family in 1794, as work on the plantation house was underway. It was not originally in the location you see it today. When it was given to the overseer, it was moved closer to the fields and slave quarters. When the original kitchen, which was built on the backside of the pond, burned down, sometime between 1840 and 1850, the Stirling's brought the original Bradford outbuilding to the location it is now.

That building later became the main kitchen, pantry and storage, and the overseer's quarters. Meals were brought from the kitchen outbuilding to the main house. The prepared food was carried in large kettles into the butler's pantry near the dining room. In a floor plan of the Myrtles, during the Stirling's ownership, the small room outside the current Game Room was called a Warming Room, and may be where the food was kept warm during serving. It was then arranged on serving dishes and delivered to the dining room by way of the outside verandah. (This wooden porch is often called a gallery, and the name gallery and verandah are often interchangeable. In my research, I found that a gallery is usually a balcony on the second story of a building, while a verandah is the porch that wraps a house on the main floor. Galleries were very popular in New Orleans' townhouses and indeed are the images one gets of beautiful ladies leaning over the balconies beckoning to strangers for beads during Mardi Gras. The Author.)

Food was brought to the house along these verandahs which were nicknamed "Whistle Walks." They were so called due to the fact that the slaves were often told to whistle while bearing in the food from the kitchen to the dining room. If they were whistling, they couldn't be sneaking bites of the food. As the meals was placed on serving boards, or offered directly to the table, a house slave would stand discreetly to the rear of the main dining table, pulling on a long satin cord that moved a large "shoo-fly", or "punka," above the heads of the diners. This wooden, loom-like device would sway back and forth keeping flies from the food. An original shoo-fly can be seen in the Myrtles' dining room today. There were also small glass vases at different locations around the table that were slightly raised. Inside these glass receptacles was a small cup. Syrup, sugar, or something sweet was put into the cup, and the flies would crawl under the raised edge and become trapped inside the glass.

Fly Catcher

A photo of a shoo-fly or "punka."

Due to the plantation's cotton production, there would have been a building on the property set apart especially for cultivating the cotton and removing its seeds, packaging it, and getting it ready for market. Boats may have stopped at the Myrtles' dock, or in nearby Bayou Sara, to take the precious commodity to market in New Orleans where a broker typically handled the transaction. Often brokers made more than the plantation owner himself in the sale of goods.

During this era, a privy, or small outhouse, or shed, containing a crude toilet would have been situated close to the house. They may have used chamber pots that were located in each room, generally stored under the bed, and then the contents tossed out. During the 1800s, people realized that poor sanitary conditions caused diseases and began looking for better accommodations. Having toilets and sewer systems that could control human waste became a priority. In 1829, The Tremont Hotel of Boston became the first hotel to have indoor plumbing, and had eight water closets built. In 1840, indoor plumbing could be found only in the homes of the rich, and better hotels.

Old cistern at the Myrtles Plantation.
The Caretaker's Quarters can be seen in the background.

Two cisterns are still in evidence today at the Myrtles' Plantation, located outside to the south and northeast of the main house. A cistern is a waterproof receptacle for holding liquids, usually water. In the case of the Myrtles Plantation they were created to capture rainwater and store it. The water ran from the large 4-foot-wide gutters along the top floor roofline and down a pipe into the brick-lined cisterns. During the Civil War, it is believed that the cisterns were also used as a hiding place for the family silver and other valuables, by placing the objects in burlap sacks and sinking them into the depths. Other plantation owners had gone to great lengths to hide their heirlooms from the advancing armies. One story told of the plantation mistress placing their silver in a bag and burying it in the mud of the property pond.

Cisterns differ from wells, in that a cistern is designed to store water, while a well taps into a supply of groundwater, such as a spring or underground stream. Wells are built by digging into the earth and inserting reinforcements so that the sides of the well do not collapse. One such well is located near the Myrtles' pond and it is said several slaves lost their lives while digging its 100-foot depth.

Somewhere on the property, would have been a family burial ground. One rumor is that it may have been located where the parking lot is today. Once Grace Church in St. Francisville was constructed, a year before the Civil War broke out, future owners of the plantation tended to have their burial sites there.

The other current buildings, brick patio, gazebo, and other amenities you see on the Myrtles Plantation property, will be discussed as we get into the impact each new owner made on this fascinating home and grounds. Each of the plantation rooms will be gone over in detail, including descriptions of their furnishings, frieze work and décor. The evolution of the Myrtles was truly brought about as an act of love for this historic site and continues on today under the watchful and caring eyes of the current owners, Teeta, John, and Morgan Moss.

The Woodruff Years

1817-1834

Chapter Five

Clark Woodruff Comes to Laurel Grove

Clark Woodruff

Clark Woodruff was born in Litchfield, Connecticut, in August, 1791. Having no desire to follow in his father's footsteps as a farmer, he left Connecticut at the age of 19, and sought his fortune on the Mississippi River; ending up in Bayou Sara. He arrived in 1810, two years after David Bradford's death, and the same year the citizens of the Feliciana Parish rose up in revolt against the Spanish garrison at Baton Rouge. They overthrew the Spanish and set up a territory, with its capital being St. Francisville. The territory extended from the Mississippi River to as far east as the Perdido River, near Mobile. We do know Clark Woodruff was listed in Captain Jedediah Smith's

Feliciana "Troop of Horse" from September 28, 1814, through March 24, 1815.

Still seeking to make his fortune, Woodruff (spelled Woodroof at that time) placed an advertisement in the new St. Francisville newspaper, *The Time Piece*, in the summer of 1811. He informed the public that an "academy would be opening on the first Monday in September for the reception of students." He planned to offer English, grammar, astronomy, geography, elocution, composition, penmanship, and Greek and Latin languages. The academy was apparently short-lived, for in 1814, he joined Colonel Hide's cavalry regiment, from the Feliciana Parish, to fight alongside Andrew Jackson at the Battle of New Orleans. When the smoke cleared and the War of 1812 had ended, Woodruff returned to St. Francisville with the intention of studying law. In 1816, he was the incorporator of the St. Francisville Library, Baptist Church (1823) and Presbyterian Church (1828). He was a state representative for West Feliciana Parish (1826-36), and the first auditor of public accounts for New Orleans. His brother, Morris Woodruff, was a merchant in South Farms (now Morris) and Litchfield, Connecticut, associate justice of Litchfield County Court, a representative for Litchfield County in the General Assembly, and a major general in the Connecticut militia.

Woodruff, after returning from the War of 1812, and setting up his law practice, met Sarah Matilda Bradford. Although it has often been told that Clark Woodruff met Sarah while studying law under her father, the dates don't match up, as David Bradford had been dead since 1808, and Woodruff landed in Bayou Sara for the first time in 1810. With Woodruff working only minutes away in St. Francisville, it would have been an easy matter to meet the lovely Sarah when she was in town, possibly using the library he resided over, or they may have been introduced.

Courting, during the 1800s in the south was a very chaperoned event. While couples in the northern states could get away with sitting alone in a parlor or on the front porch, the south strictly forbade a young woman and gentleman to be left unsupervised, even after they became engaged. For Clark Woodruff, who was between 21 and 25, when he came to the plantation with the intention of courting young Sarah Matilda, (who was 19 when she married Woodruff in 1817), it was probably a little daunting to face the remaining family housed within the beautiful home. David Jr. was still at home, along with a few of the other children, and Mrs. Bradford was still mistress of the plantation.

Beneath the canopy of myrtle trees and moss-draped oaks, Clark Woodruff wooed Sarah. With a chaperone always near, the couple tried to get to know one another. In Southern parlors, they were never left alone, and if the mother, or some other member of the family, was not in the room, a female slave would sit on a rug near the door to keep an eye on them. One story of a young southern suitor, tells of a time he was so desperate to steal a kiss from his fiancée, that he gave the attending servant a drugged peach to put her to sleep.

Girls began to think about courting when they were quite young. There was a tradition of putting a slice of wedding cake beneath their pillows with hopes of dreaming of their "young gentleman" who would someday come calling. It was called the "Dreaming Cake."

Young women were told to "behave honorably and sensibly." They were also warned that the ways in which they conducted themselves during courtship would have a lasting impression on their husbands. Many girls were quite young when they began courting. Marriage in the late teens to early twenties was the norm, and girls were sometimes considered "old maids" if they had not married by their mid-twenties. In rural areas, girls sometimes married as young as thirteen or fourteen. However, the average age for most antebellum brides was between nineteen and twenty-three.

Clark and Sarah's conversation would have probably followed the correct etiquette for the day. Relationships between men and women played an important role in the new code of good manners. When women were involved in conversations with gentlemen, they were never supposed to ask them about their health. Gentlemen were advised against asking a lady a personal question, period! If they wanted to give a gift to a particular lady, a bouquet of flowers or a book were the only suitable gifts. The slightest contact, however, was to be avoided between ladies and gentlemen in public.

Dancing was probably the one issue that caused the most problems. The sexes were simply kept apart as much as possible. The only body part that was allowed to be touched during a dance was the elbows. The men never put their hand around the woman's waist. That was not acceptable. Her waist was forbidden. Other etiquette, strictly enforced among women included: never allowing anyone to help her with her coat, shawl, etc. Certain words were forbidden. For example, a woman called her chest her neck, and she was to call her stomach, her chest. Never was it acceptable for women to show their legs in public. There were strict social prohibitions against antebellum women sunning themselves. Refined southern ladies did not want to overexpose themselves to the sun; some did not want any exposure at all. Southerners viewed beauty measured by several standards—one of the most important was that of facial pallor. Freckles were seen as natural blemishes; whereas tanned skin became viewed as an unnatural and an unforgivable departure for the refined southern woman. Unfavorable racial connotations were associated with darker skin, as well as the stigma of a non-pampered lifestyle, and resulted in a lack of status in the social structure. Thomas Jefferson, in a 1786 letter to his daughter

Maria said, "Remember too as a constant charge not to go out without your bonnet because it will make you very ugly and then we should not love you so much." (Clinton, Catherine, *The Plantation Mistress: Women's World in the Old South,* p. 63.)

Mealtime, also, had its own set of manners. It was not appropriate to blow your nose with your napkin, nor was it acceptable to pick up your soup bowl and drink from it. Women were expected to always remove their gloves as soon as they sat down at the table, spread their napkin in their lap, or sometimes pin it to their dresses. They were also encouraged not to stare at anyone if that person were eating loudly or happened to spill something on themselves. It was never appropriate for men or women to make any noise chewing. Such noises would be classified as inconsiderate.

Clark married Sarah Matilda Bradford on November 19, 1817, at Laurel Grove. In antebellum America, the covenant of marriage was an important rite of passage, particularly for women. The accepted role of women was that of wife and mother, making marriage a crucial apex in a young woman's life. In a society where women played secondary roles in politics, economics, education, and everyday life, the wedding was one occasion where females commanded the spotlight. Regardless of their socio-economic level, weddings spotlighted the bride.

Though the institution of marriage was not always glamorous, many nineteenth century Americans began their marriages with beautiful wedding ceremonies. Weddings were frequently elaborate social affairs, especially for well-to-do brides. At no other time in her life, would any young woman be as important as she was in the weeks leading up to her wedding. In addition to a religious ceremony, the wedding was an important social occasion in the community, particularly in the South. Weddings provided an opportunity for distant relatives and friends to join together in a joyous celebration. Antebellum southern weddings were social events that marked a coming-of-age for many young women. (*Wedding Customs in Antebellum America*, Megan Cooper)

Laurel Grove Plantation was alive with activity. Slaves worked around the clock preparing the wedding feast and gathering fresh flowers for centerpieces and garlands that covered the cypress mantles in the four downstairs' rooms. Music filled the house as the fais-do-do (dance in Louisianan lingo) dominated the parlors. Succulent aromas permeated the air as a cochon de lait (pig roast) took place; the golden-brown pork was finally brought into the dining room table and grandly displayed. Sounds of laughter and animated conversation, gaiety and the enthusiasm that heralds a life event were everywhere. Long gowns swept along the verandah and softly against the polished cypress flooring. The distinctive smell of cigar smoke wafted on the evening breeze as gentlemen strolled the grounds beneath the twinkling starlight, their long black coats and stovepipe hats lending an air of formality to the occasion. Small slave children sat perched in trees, peering out from between the branches, as they watched the twinkling candlelight through the rippled glass windows, and listened to the laughter and music that was everywhere.

For Elizabeth Bradford, her emotions must have been mixed. The thrill of seeing her daughter married to a prominent lawyer, who would one day become a judge, was a mother's dream come true. But there must have been moments when she looked across the rooms, alive with candlelight, and thought of her departed David, who was not here to witness his daughter's wedding in the plantation he created for his family. In the absence of the patriarch, the matriarch, or other head of the family, would have to sign a document giving their consent to the marriage. These were official certifications requiring witnesses.

The wedding certificate, giving Elizabeth Bradford's consent to her daughter Sarah to marry Clark Woodruff, is written in a lovely hand. It says:

I Elizabeth Bradford of the Parish of Feliciana and State of Louisiana herby consent to the Celebration of the bonds of matrimony between Clark Woodroof of the Parish and State aforesaid and my minor daughter Matilda Bradford; in witness wherof I have signed duplicates this 19ᵗʰ day of November 1817.

Several witnesses affixed their names, as well as Clark Woodruff (Woodroof).

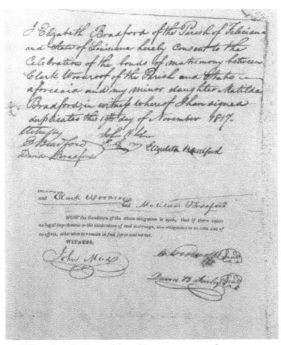

Elizabeth Bradford's consent document

Clark Woodruff also signed a document, made out to John H. Johnson, Parish Judge of the Parish of Feliciana, procuring a promise of two thousand dollars. It was signed, sealed, and witnessed, on the wedding day, November 17, 1817. It is a

"License to celebrate a marriage between Clark Woodroof and

Matilda Bradford."

What purpose the payment of two thousand dollars was intended, is not clear. It may have been used for what is called a "bride price," or "progeny price." This is an amount of money, or property or wealth, paid by the groom, or his family, to the parents of a woman upon the marriage of their daughter to the groom. The agreed bride price is generally intended to reflect the perceived value of the girl or young woman. It was also a way of helping the bride's family, since they were losing their daughter's help in the household. In Sarah Matilda's case, her father was gone, and she may have been one of the few children remaining to help Elizabeth with the plantation. Clark Woodroof may have paid this sum in an effort to help. (You will notice he is spelling his name Woodroof at the time, changing it later to Woodruff, after he became a Judge in New Orleans.) Sarah's first name is left off the document; simply calling her Matilda Bradford.

1800s-style wedding ring

Clark Woodruff (Woodroof) marriage agreement

That the Myrtles Plantation saw so much happiness within its walls is evident. Young lives, just beginning their joyous entrance into the accepted world of matrimony, celebrated beneath the myrtle trees and clinked their glasses in tribute in the dining room. But there would be heartache, as well. David Bradford would not be the only one to die here.

The Woodruffs Take Over Laurel Grove

When the wedding guests departed, and the exhausted newlyweds returned from their honeymoon at Hermitage—the Tennessee home of Clark Woodruff's new friend, Andrew Jackson—it was time to make a decision about their future home. Elizabeth Bradford was now 54, and needed help with the plantation. Most of the children were married, or off beginning lives of their own. Clark and Sarah decided to take over the plantation and manage it for Elizabeth. Laurel Grove would now be their home as husband and wife.

Clark wasted no time in improving the operation. He planted about 650 acres of indigo and cotton, expanding the original holdings. Together, he and Sarah had three beautiful children, and Elizabeth was once again surrounded with the laughter and hectic movements of little ones. Twins were born to the Woodruffs, a boy they named James (possibly for the brother Sarah lost so early in life) and a daughter, Cornelia Gale. There are references that mention the nursery in the upstairs of the house was nicknamed the "Twin Room." Today, is it called the Ruffin Stirling Room. Mary Octavia (named for Sarah's youngest sister) made her entrance on October 3, 1818. Sarah and Clark's family was complete.

The plantation flourished and the twins played happily amongst its flowering shrubs and secret hiding places created by the trees and outbuildings. Clark and Sarah purchased Laurel Grove from Elizabeth Bradford for $2.50 an acre. For the first time since its creation, the plantation is listed under a name other than Bradford, although Sarah's name appears on the document in the National Register of Historic Places.

For many years after the twin's birth, life at Laurel Grove was filled with happiness and promise. Mary Octavia was only six- years-old and undoubtedly followed her older siblings about the property. The house slaves were involved in their upbringing and watching out for them as they grew. They would help with the dressing of the children. Very young infants wore what are referred to as 'long clothes.' This was a dress that was longer than the baby, usually white in color. The extra length could be folded up for extra warmth or to protect the legs. When the baby got more active, the clothing got shorter to allow for more freedom of movement. These were then referred to as 'short clothes.'

Toddlers of both sexes wore dresses. The fancier the dress, the more money and social position the family had. These dresses included wearing petticoats to fill out the skirt. Cotton was the most common fabric from which clothing was made, although wealthy families would dress their children in silk. Fabric colors were bright, and patterns were cheerful. Often, small white caps were worn with the dresses to complete the look. It is not until after the toddler years that children dressed in accordance with their gender.

Boy wearing a skirt in the 1800s

'Breeching' is known as a time when a boy transitioned from wearing dresses to wearing trousers. Even though this usually happened when the boy was about 4 years old, it was considered a rite of passage into manhood. The first suits boys wore were called 'skeleton suits.' These suits were tight to the body, and the pants attached to the jacket with buttons. They were worn with a white blouse.

Typical children's attire in the 1800s:
skeleton suits and dresses.

Girls continued to wear dresses, with age dictating the length of the skirt. Until a girl was approximately 12 years of age, her skirt came to her knees. From that age until 17, her skirt reached her ankles. After that, women wore floor-length dresses. The dresses for all ages were usually heavily decorated and made of cotton, silk, sateen, fine wool, and poplin. Hats were a must and also were very ornate.

The mention of the dress style of the early 1800s is to clear up some confusion as to the sex of the twins born to Sarah and Clark Woodruff. Many stories have referred to them as two girls. With both sexes wearing dresses at an early age, it would have been easy to confuse James as a girl. Boys' hair was sometimes long and often curly.

With his bustling family around him, Clark Woodruff conducted affairs pertaining to his law practice, political affiliations, and things regarding running a plantation, from the Gentlemen's Parlor. The door would be shut to allow for privacy. Slaves had been cautioned against interrupting such meetings and it was strictly enforced. In the 1820 Census, Clark Woodruff is listed as owning 5 house slaves. In a following census, it shows a young black female, age 14, residing in the Woodruff household. Many believe her name was Chloe, and it is her story that took on a life of its own.

Chloe

Chloe was in a coveted position at Laurel Grove. She was a house slave, spared the hours of endless toil in the cotton fields beneath the blistering sun and humid Louisiana heat. She was entrusted with the children's care and it is said she deeply loved the Woodruff children. She wore simple clothes—a blouse, long skirt, apron, and a turban wrapped around her hair.

Portrait of a young black girl.

Wearing turbans began as a means to play down a house slave's attractiveness in the southern household. Their long, luxurious hair was seen as a means of asserting their allure and competing with white women for a white man's attention. Later, the turban became a symbol of status and respectability. Only the trusted chief house servant was allowed to wear the starched white "tignon." This was the "mammy" and her word was law among the house slaves. Second to the turban, as a symbol of respectability in the hierarchy of female slaves' head coverings, was the often-colorful bandana. Like the turban, the bandana was tied at the forehead with the ends tucked in and was a snugger fit than the higher, thicker, and more authoritative-appearing turban that was created from larger swaths of cloth.

Legends of a ghost wearing a green turban have swirled around the Myrtles Plantation for centuries. Some thought she was a governess at the plantation a long time ago that returns to watch over the children of the great house, often tucking guests in at night. But the most persistent rumor is that the ghost is that of the young black slave girl, known as Chloe.

Chloe had found a way to make herself useful to her fellow slaves by listening at the closed door of the Gentleman's Parlor in the hopes of hearing news regarding the buying and selling of slaves. If she overheard news that might affect one of her fellow laborers, she would pass it along. It also served to establish her own sense of well-being, as to her continued status in the household, if her own name was not overhead in a derogatory manner.

The Louisiana humidity wrapped itself around the young slave girl like a shawl. Chloe wiped her brow as she stepped inside the plantation dining room. She placed the bouquet of flowers she had cut from the garden into a cut-crystal vase and centered it on the dining room table.

Chloe walked through the Ladies' Parlor on her way to the front door. The children were out front playing and it was time for their studies. A murmur of voices could be heard from the other side of a closed door. It was coming from the Gentlemen's Parlor. Chloe looked about her. She was alone. Tiptoeing stealthily, she crossed through the hallway to the closed door. Gently she pressed her left ear to the warm wood and listened. It was the Master's voice, along with several other men. They were discussing the price of cotton and some embargoes going on at the port in New Orleans. This did not interest her.

As Chloe grew bolder, she would often open the door a small degree, in order to hear well. There she would crouch, ever alert to anyone coming along the hallway, as the combined parlors were not yet created. On a few occasions, she was caught by Mr. Woodruff and reprimanded. No doubt, she made an excuse, such as polishing the door frame or dusting, as a reason for being there. Nevertheless, she was warned that if she was caught there again, her punishment would be severe.

Punishment for slaves was a common occurrence. Plantation owners and even the black overseers (not wanting to lose their own elevated rank), would punish the wayward worker with physical pain. They were careful not to hurt the slave in a way that would hinder his work or make him less valuable on the auction block. Hence, the wounds were often carefully placed. Teeta Moss, owner of the plantation, told this author that if a slave stole something, "a digit on one finger was cut off. If all digits on the finger are cut off, it signified he had stolen something of great value. This way the buyer of slaves, when brought to auction, could tell their history by looking at their wounds."

Chloe went about the household, caring for the children and helping Sarah. She may have behaved herself for a time, frightened off by the severe warning from being caught eavesdropping the last time. But soon, the temptation grew too great. It may be she had committed an error in the house and was concerned about being sent to the fields. Carefully, she crept to the door, and cracking it ever so slightly, pressed her ear to the opening to overhear Clark Woodruff's discussion with a visiting gentleman.

Suddenly, the door was thrown open and the imposing form of the master loomed over her. Without preamble, he grabbed her by the arm, and dragging her behind him, angrily told her she had been given the last of her pardons. It is doubtful that Woodruff metered out her punishment. He may have had a slave driver do it, or it has been rumored Woodruff's nephew, Ichabod, who was living at the plantation as overseer at the time, may have been instructed to inflict the punishment. In any case, Chloe's earlobe was cut off, as a symbol of her eavesdropping. The green turban she affected now had a dual purpose…it covered the disfigurement. She was cast out of the main house and sent to work in the hot, grueling kitchen. Here, she fumed and worried.

There must be a way back into the Woodruff's graces. After all, wasn't she the beloved children's nanny? Hadn't she been there for the mistress?

Mary Octavia's 9th birthday was coming up on October 3rd, and Chloe thought of a plan. She had watched the other slaves in the kitchen concocting the meals for the family's consumption. Chloe asked to be allowed to be in charge of making the child's birthday cake.

On the morning of October 3rd, Chloe assembled her bowls and ingredients for the cake she was making for the little girl's birthday party. The oleander springs were hidden in a box on a shelf beneath the pump-handle sink, where she had placed them the day before. Her hands shook as she blended together the flour, milk and eggs for the batter. When the kitchen was empty of other slaves for a few minutes, she hurriedly heated a pot of water, and dumped in the red flowers and leaves from the poisonous oleander plant. Hurriedly, she stirred the boiling mixture, constantly looking over her shoulder for prying eyes. It gave off a sweet, earthy odor she had not accounted for.

Oleander plant

"What in God's green world are you puttin' in dat cake?"
Chloe jumped, and turned to see the kitchen mammy staring at her,
with her plump hands planted firmly on each hip.

"I thought you tol' me you wuz makin' chocolate. Don't you be
messin' 'round with some fancy smancy new recipe on da mos'
'portant day of dat child's life!"

Chloe looked into the boiling pot and thought fast.

"It' jes' vanilla root," she lied. "I got it special."

Mammy stared   at   her   through   slitted   eyes.

"Uh huh," Mammy said skeptically. "It be yer head if da
Missus ain't happy with dat cake!"

Clark Woodruff was off on business as the table in the children's
dining room was prepared for the little party. Chloe brought in the
beautiful cake and set it before the gleeful eyes of the children and
their smiling mother, Sarah Matilda. The cake was lovingly sliced
and served. Chloe stood back nervously watching, as bite after bite
of the heavenly confection was devoured.

It didn't take long for the results to begin. Hours later, the twins, Mary Octavia, and Sarah began having severe stomach pains. Chloe, knowing the cause of the illness, now went into her plan. She had hoped the oleander would make the four just sick enough that she could rush in and administer herbs that she felt would counteract the poison. Then, when she had nursed the family back to health, they would be so grateful, she would be reinstated as the beloved house servant. They might even think she was a Voodoo Priestess with magical powers! It was a plan hatched by a fourteen-year-old brain.

The family's illness worsened, so much so, that Chloe became fearful she had added too much of the poison. The children's vomiting increased. In a wild panic, the young slave ran into the kitchen house and grabbed one of the young black cooks.

"Ya gots to help me!" Chloe begged in a strained whisper. "I think I made the Missus and the chillin' sick!"

The young female cook laid down her towel and stared hard at the shaking girl.

"What did you do?"

Several of the other people in the kitchen were taking notice of Chloe's panicked state. Mammy walked over and grabbed the girl by her shoulders.

"Did you go and make dat family sick? I tol' you not to be 'sperimentin' with no 'gredients!"

"I jes wanted dem to need me!" Chloe cried. "Now dey gonna die and dey's gonna hang me!"

Mammy began shaking and slapping the girl.

"What did you put in dat cake?" she screamed.

"Oleander," Chloe whimpered. "I didn't know it was too much...I swears I didn't. Please don't let dem kills me! Tell me hows I fix it!"

She dropped to the floor and grabbed Mammy's stained apron. A black youth ran from the kitchen toward the house to see if the story was true.

The children and mother did recover, but Chloe's relief was short-lived. The kitchen slaves, fearful for the safety of the slave community, if it was found out one of their own had poisoned the owner's family, told the other field hands. Chloe was attacked by a mixed mob of black and white laborers and dragged to a tree on the far end of the property.

Beneath a watchful moon, the men tied the rope around a large oak branch. The other end was looped around the neck of the screaming girl and pulled taut. They hoisted her into the air. After several minutes, she was cut down and carried along the slope to the shore of the Mississippi. They watched as her small form disappeared downstream.

Portrait of Clark Woodruff near a vase of oleander in the foyer of the Myrtles Plantation.

The various legends of Chloe have grown. One such story tells of her being Clark Woodruff's mistress, and when he had tired of her, she feared he would send her to the field. She had begun listening at the door for incriminating words of her demise. Another legend tells of the cake finding its poisonous target and killing the twins and their mother. But, we know all three lived several years after that fateful birthday, and died later from yellow fever.

Photo taken by Teeta Moss showing what appears to be a female figure in slave clothes and a turban on Myrtles' back property.

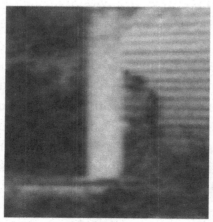

You can see the clapboard siding through the figure.

The story of Chloe has been called a legend. But legends tend to evolve from a kernel of truth. Somewhere, the story began and it changed over the years, added to in bits and pieces, like cloth to a growing quilt. Too many people have seen Chloe's ghost, complete with turban, including the current owner who unwittingly captured her in a photograph on the back property. The photograph, on the previous page, has been gone over by an expert, who went into painstaking detail to not only verify its authenticity, but show through a graph the anatomical make-up of the ghost; complete with the clapboard slats showing through her body. As an amazing caveat, the shapes of two children sitting on the roof near the "ghost in the turban" (when no children were at the plantation) were captured in the same photograph.

Many guests visiting the plantation tend to end up with one missing earring. This occurrence is so frequent, that some females on the tour have placed their jewelry in their purses for protection. It is always just one earring that goes missing on the unsuspecting visitors. This is assumed to be the direct result of Chloe only needing one earring, as the lobe of the other ear was cut off. Young girls on the tours have found their hair clips or bows missing as well.

Many feel an affinity for the hapless slave and have left her ghost an earring as a gift. These varied pieces of jewelry can be seen in a lovely display case in the main entry hall of the plantation. Above this case, hang two photographs of the original plantation.

Legends are not new. In today's world we have on-going instant reporting of worldwide news and events but still seem to get contradicting accounts. Therefore, it is not surprising that accounts of what happened 200+ years ago are often reported incorrectly. Births, deaths, number of children, and events all have been argued about for centuries.

Earring display case in foyer of the Myrtles Plantation.

Did Chloe exist? This author believes she did. I believe the story happened as told here. Somewhere, it evolved into the deaths of the mother and two small children. The interesting aside here is that I came across several references to a fire that reportedly broke out in the upstairs of the original plantation house, and that "a mother and two children" possibly perished in that fire. We know several families were living under the same roof, and in those days, visitors would often stay for extended periods of time, after traveling a long distance. Was there a fire? Did three people perish? Are the children's ghosts the two small girls that have been witnessed over and over again playing on the grounds of the plantation, long after they should have departed this earth? It is quite possible, that over the years the two stories—that of Chloe and the birthday cake, and that of the deaths of a mother and two small children in a house fire—were combined by mistake to create a common misconception.

The other legend touting Chloe as Clark Woodruff's mistress is one with no basis, other than the common practice of that time for

plantation owners to dally with the female slaves. It was, unfortunately, something that happened all too often. In her book, *Within the Plantation Household: Black and White Women of the Old South,* Elizabeth Fox-Genovese writes of the Southern
Plantation mistress, "They would have been happy to have their husbands, brothers, and fathers cease trifling with slave women."

Sarah Bradford Woodruff's Death

In 1823, only a few years after Chloe's fateful birthday surprise, another yellow fever epidemic raged through the state of Louisiana. Hardly a family was left untouched. Sarah Matilda contracted the disease, and lay languishing in the upstairs' bedroom, her body ravaged by fever. Her mother, Elizabeth stayed by her side, applying wet cloths to her beautiful daughter's forehead. Elizabeth Bradford was now 60-years-old, in a time when the mortality rate was much less. Clark Woodruff must have paced the cypress boards of the upstairs' hallway over and over, knowing the death toll the epidemic had accrued. Despite the efforts of her family, Sarah Matilda Bradford Woodruff died on July 21, 1823, at only 25-years-of-age.

St. Louis Cemetery in New Orleans late 1800s.

The blow to the plantation household had to be a large one. Gone was the vibrant bride and mother of three small children. Elizabeth had now lost three children in her lifetime: James, Alexander, and now her precious Sarah. Clark Woodruff was devastated. For the sake of his small children and his aging mother-in-law, he went on, running the plantation and continuing his law practice. And then, only one year later, his only son James, at the young age of 12, succumbed to the same deadly fever raging over the housetops of Louisiana like a Grim Reaper. Before he had barely laid his son in his grave, two short months later, his small daughter Cornelia Gale, also died from the deadly plague. It was the beginning of a landslide of deaths in the family. A year later, in 1825, Edmund Bradford, Sarah's brother died, followed by their sisters Jane in 1826, and Sophia in 1827, both married women. Sophia had one daughter, Sophia Elizabeth. Abelard Bradford, the oldest son, and the one entrusted by his father David to ride to Pennsylvania to conduct family business, also died in 1826.

For Laurel Grove, the walls that had once echoed with the celebration of joined hearts and the cries of newborn babies entering the world, were now stained with the inconsolable sounds of weeping and pain. It would not be the last time the plantation witnessed both celebration and death.

Clark Woodruff's Last Days

In the Census for 1820 and 1830, Clark Woodruff's occupations are listed as teacher, lawyer, judge and friend of Andrew Jackson. He had an estimated 5,000 acres with 450 field hands and thirty house servants in 1830. Gone were his wife and two of his children. Mary Octavia, his only surviving child was now 12. Elizabeth Bradford was now 63. She had buried her husband, daughters Sarah Matilda, Jane, and Sophia Elizabeth (who was named after her), and two grandchildren (James and Cornelia Gale) on the plantation grounds. She had outlived six of her children! Even with the common occurrence of deaths in the 1800s, from frequent outbreaks of yellow fever and other rampant illnesses, it is a formidable and heartbreaking task to place one's husband and so many children into graves. Five years after Elizabeth's death, her youngest daughter, Octavia (not to be confused with Mary Octavia, Elizabeth's granddaughter), whom had been married twice— to Issac A. Smith, and upon his death to B.G. Martin—died in Herculaneum, Missouri. Eliza Bradford died in 1882, and David Bradford, Jr. passed away, on March 13, 1844.

It was in the year, 1830, that Elizabeth Porter Bradford died. Perhaps, feeling a release from his duties as her helpmate at the plantation, the heartbroken Woodruff gathered up his small daughter Mary Octavia and turned his back to Laurel Grove. Leaving the plantation to the management of a caretaker, he and young Mary Octavia moved to Covington, Louisiana, where he was appointed Judge in District D of that county. He served in that capacity until 1835. Finally, on January 1, 1834, Woodruff (who had recently changed the spelling from Woodroof), sold Laurel Grove to Ruffin Grey Stirling, and his wife Mary Catherine Cobb, for $46,853.00.

By this time, Woodruff was living on Rampart Street in New Orleans. Mary Octavia was sent to a finishing school in New Haven, Connecticut, but she returned home to live with her father in 1836. Two years later, on May 10, 1838, in New Orleans, she married Colonel Lorenzo Augustus Besancon, and moved to his plantation, Oaklawn, five miles north of New Orleans. Together, they had four children: Leoline Francesca Besancon (1839- 1919); Julia Besancon (1841-1878); Octave Besancon (18431905), and Clark Woodruff Besancon, born February 22, 1848 in New Orleans, and who died January 5, 1901. He was a lawyer, like his grandfather.

In the 1860 census, it states Mary Octavia Woodruff Besancon was a widow at 42, caring for her four children. She had $21,000 in land value and $5000 in personal property. She had two slaves. She died November 30, 1889, in New Orleans.

In 1840, the Louisiana governor, Issac Johnson, appointed Woodruff to the newly created office of Auditor of Public Works and he served for one term. At 60 years of age, he retired and moved to Oaklawn, to live with Octavia and her husband. He devoted the remainder of his life to the study of chemistry and physics. He died on November 25, 1851. He was buried in the Girod Street Cemetery, in New Orleans.

There is a sad ending to Clark Woodruff's story. The graveyard where he was buried, fell into disrepair and was eventually abandoned. In the 1960s, the city hoped to renovate this part of New Orleans and sent out a notice to families that the cemetery was going to be moved to a new location on Canal Street. The bodies that were not claimed were gathered and placed in large drums, and then buried in a mass grave under the Hope Mausoleum. Clark Woodruff was one of those unclaimed bodies. Today the New Orleans Superdome stands where the Girod Street Cemetery once lay.

Girod Street Cemetery before it was destroyed.

Ruffin Gray Stirling

The Stirling
Years

1834-1854

Chapter Six

Ruffin Gray Stirling

Ruffin Gray Stirling's Family Coat of Arms.

As mentioned, Clark Woodruff sold Laurel Grove to Ruffin Gray Stirling and his wife, Mary Catherine Cobb, in 1834, for the sum of $46,853. The slaves and all the plantation holdings were included in the price. The plantation had been in the hands of an overseer for four years, after Woodruff departed with young Mary Octavia for New Orleans. It was about to undergo a major transformation.

Ruffin Gray Stirling was the son of Alexander Stirling and Ann Alston. Alexander Stirling was born in 1753, in Lethan, near Forfar, Angusshire, Scotland. He served in the military in 1773, in Manchac and Baton Rouge, West Florida. At the time of his death on June 6, 1808, he was living on Egypt Plantation in West Feliciana, Louisiana. He was "an Alcade, and Planter of Cotton and Sugar Cane, in 1784, in West Feliciana Parish, Louisiana." Alexander was in the First

Regiment of Grenadiers under Spanish General Don Bernardo de Dalvez, against the British, at Manchac and Baton Rouge, gallantly siding in the defeat of the British and regaining control of the area for Spain.

Egypt (now Rosale) Plantation, West Feliciana, Louisiana.

It was a strange quirk of fate which led Alexander to find a wife whose father was a loyal Tory, not in sympathy with the revolution against England. John Alson, Ann's father, traced his ancestry back to Alfred the Great of England. John had moved his family to the area from North Carolina, obtaining a large land grant from the British near Natchez. After the Spanish ousted the British, John Alson was jailed in Natchez; the circumstances for the arrest were not made clear. He sent his wife and children (of which Ann Alston was one) to Pointe Coupee Parish. He was sent to prison in Moro Castle in Havana. His daughter Ann met Alexander in Point Coupee and they were married, in 1784.

Alexander Stirling came to this continent as a young man, eventually making his way to the Spanish settlement just west of the Mississippi River in West Florida. The area is now part of Louisiana; thus, this branch of the family is known as the Louisiana Stirlings.

Alexander and Ann had the following children:

Lewis Stirling (born after 1784); Henry Sterling (born June 5, 1785); Alexander Stirling (born on June 23, 1791); William M. Stirling (born on August 17, 1792); Ruffin Gray Stirling (born on April 5, 1795); Ann Stirling (born on November 27, 1797); and John Sterling (born on September 19, 1799).

The Stirling's genealogy can be a little confusing. Names are often repeated through the generations, making it hard sometimes to understand to which Lewis or which Ruffin you are referring. Ruffin Gray Stirling was a wealthy gentleman, owing largely to the inheritance left him after his father, Alexander's, death, and through land holdings of his own. The Scottish people are known for their frugality and Ruffin obviously was good at obtaining and keeping money. Mary Catherine Cobb's mother, Sarah Matilda Bingaman (not to be confused with Ruffin and Mary's daughter Sarah Matilda, who was named after her grandmother) died at age 70, in West Feliciana Parish. Her plantation, known as the "Sleepy Hollow Place," was purchased by Ruffin Gray Stirling, along with its 1300 acres, and all improvements thereon. He also obtained 1600 barrels of corn and 7 stocks of fodder. Mary had tried to obtain a division of the property upon her mother's death, but a division was impossible, so it went up for sale and Ruffin bought it. It is noted that when Mary Cobb married Ruffin Gray Stirling, she was a minor and required her mother's permission.

According to court house records, Ruffin and Mary owned several pieces of land, to the extent that the listing of the properties took several pages. Their holdings are listed in both Feliciana's, West Baton Rouge, and Pointe Coupee Parishes.

According to the title, when the Stirling's purchased Laurel Grove in 1834, the property was listed as being about six hundred *arpents* located on the Woodville Road. "They brought up large timbers from the Cobb plantation on Bayou Maringouin to the Greenwood landing…"

Though Laurel Grove was purchased by the Stirlings in 1834, they did not live on the plantation for some time. Renovations to the property took several years, while the family continued to live in Chowan, North Carolina. Their time in that area is marked with the sorrow of losing several of their nine children: Lewis Stirling (1831-1854, died at the age of 23, no wife); Sarah Mulford Stirling (1833-1878); Clarence Stirling (18361849, died at the age of 13); Ruffin Gray Stirling, Jr. (Feb. 9, 1840-July 24, 1840, died at 5- months of age); Ruffin Stirling III (1842-1844, died at the age of 1); Mary Stirling (1845-1863, was the only child born at the Myrtles and died of typhoid fever at 18); Stephen Stirling (1847-1926, died in Locust Grove, West Feliciana at the age of 79); William Stirling (1850-1886, born in Chowan, NC and died at 36); Henry Stirling (1853-around 1900, born in Chowan, NC).

It is interesting to note that Mary Stirling was born at the Myrtles, but the two subsequent children were born back in Chowan, where the family came from. Perhaps the typhoid fever was still prevalent in the area surrounding Laurel Grove and Mary preferred to give birth elsewhere. At any rate, Mary Stirling is the only child noted as having been born at the plantation. Tragically, only four of the nine children grew to adulthood and were married. At the time of Ruffin Gray's death in July, 1854, Mary became a widow at the age of 41, with four young children living at home on the Laurel Grove Plantation: Mary Ann, Stephen, William and Henry. Sarah Mulford had married William Winter in 1852, two years before her father's death. Lewis Stirling died the same year as his father, in 1854, at the age of 23.

The 1850 Census shows Ruffin (55), Mary Cobb (38), Lewis (19), Sarah M. (17), Mary Ann (5), Stephen (2), William (0; she had just given birth to William).

Judging by Mary Ann Stirling's birth date, at Laurel Grove in 1845, we know the family was living at the plantation by that time. We do know that the 1850's are filled with details of the extensive renovations to the home. It was at this time, the plantation received a new name—one which would live in infamy. The newly-remodeled home and its acreage was now christened the Myrtles Plantation. One can only assume, that between the time Ruffin bought the home in 1834, and Mary Ann's birth at the Myrtles in 1845, the construction of the new half of the house was being undertaken. The interior elements and finishing details seem to have fallen around 1850, but it is noted that the Stirlings spent years traveling to France and around Europe, purchasing lavish chandeliers, furnishings, and other amenities for the home. They hired European artisans to come to Louisiana and decorate their new plantation dwelling.

Art Gallery in the Gilded Age.

The Stirlings owned several plantations on both sides of the Mississippi River, as well as a townhouse in Natchez. Since they were so well thought of in the community, they needed a house that reflected their social status. Up until now, Laurel Grove had served primarily as a functional, pragmatic home for the Bradford's and Woodruffs. Ruffin Sterling expanded the planation land to 5000 acres, taking its boundaries all the way to Bayou Sara. He employed 500 slaves in the fields and 50 slaves to run the household. It was now the largest working plantation in the area.

The Stirlings were building up their wealth at a period in history that would become known as the Gilded Age. While this era shows its bookend dates as 1870-1900, the 1850s were beginning to feel the pull of "showcasing your affluence." Culture, art, and furnishings, mirroring the mansions and castles of Europe, were all the rage for those who could afford it—and the Stirlings could afford it.

According to the West Baton Rouge Museum, the following detailed description is given of the newly renovated plantation home:

The house itself is a broad, low, rambling frame mansion with a clapboard exterior. The main (east) frontal gallery is 107 feet long and the main façade is composed of ten irregular bays. The present house was built in two halves. The first half, which was built in 1796, forms the western six bays of the main façade. This part consists of four large rooms, two at the front (the ladies' and the gentlemen's parlors) and two at the rear (the dining room and the gaming room). The present sizes and generous proportions of these rooms are largely the result of a mid-19th century renovation. At that time, walls were moved, the Adam's Cypress mantles were moved upstairs, and the present elaborate detailing was installed. Also, at that time, the house received a southward extension which almost doubled its size.

The extension included a 16-feet wide entrance and stair hall, which ran from the front to the rear of the house, three chambers, and the present cast iron supported galleries. The old pitched roofline was extended to encompass the new addition, and the old dormer pattern (a wide, two window, pediment dormer flanked by single dormers) was continued over the addition. This created the present dormer pattern of two large pediment dormers with three interspersed smaller ones.

The Stirling expansion began to the left of the 2nd dormer shown. The new front entrance was now where the stairs are to the left.

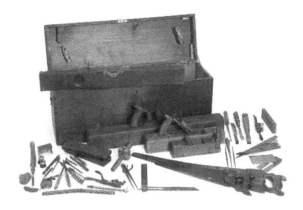

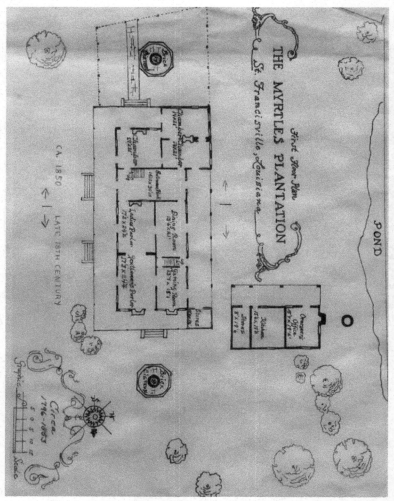

Stephen Saunders drawing of Stirling expansion.

The addition has a ceiling height of 13'6", which is one foot higher than the original house. However, a common roofline was maintained in the two halves by raising the floor in the second story of the addition by one foot.

Exterior showing expansion, with original Bradford entrance steps on the right, and Stirling's new entrance on the left.

Myrtles Plantation cast iron railings.

The exterior detailing is worthy of note. The entire house is encompassed by a heavy entablature which dates from the 1850's renovation. It presents open galleries on all facades with cast iron supports in the front and sides, and wooden posts in the rear of the house. The cast iron supports are rich and elaborate with scrolled vine and grape patterns. (This railing and supports were originally painted purple and green, and the clapboard siding was whitewashed white...quite a dramatic sight. Courtesy of *Tour Guide Notes at the Myrtles.*) Most of the windows reach to the floor and have ear molded frames with louvered shutters. The front door has a similar design with transom and side lights. The roof is particularly handsome with the large dormers articulated in full temple fronts with four Tuscan pilasters. The small dormers are decorated with framing and corner blocks.

Myrtles Plantation's front door.

Elaborate ceiling medallions of wealthy antebellum homes.

Perhaps, the most important feature of the house, is its interior detailing. Most of the ground room floors have fine marble, arched mantles in the Rococo revival style, with central console keystones or cartouches. Most of the rooms have plaster ceiling medallions, no two of which are the same. Several are based upon the acanthus motif, but the most unusual one occurs in the gentlemen's parlor. This medallion, which is formed of fruits, cusps, crockets, and stylized foils, may best be described as Rococo-Gothic. The medallion in the large frontal chamber has an elaborate interlacing of fruits, carved heads, and acanthus leaves. All of the ceiling medallions in the house are of characteristic fineness and delicacy, and depict an extraordinary naturalism in the fruit, leaf and foliage motifs.

The entrance and stair hall, the ladies' and gentlemen's parlors, and the dining room have elaborately pierced and carved plaster cornices, with the delicacy of lace work. Most of these are executed in flower, or vine and grape designs.

Ornamental ceiling frieze work with vines, fruit and figures.

Antebellum parlor during the William Morris period. Note the plant beneath the glass container; a popular feature during this period emphasizing botany and nature.

All of the flooring, and most of the windows, in the house are original. The rear frame kitchen dates from the late 18th century. Most of the glass, clapboarding, shutters and doors are original. The house and kitchen dependency are set on the ground, which was terraced in 1850. To the rear of the house, is a pond. There are several alleys of live oaks in the front, and a cistern on either side of the house. The garden also contains five carved stone statues of cherubs, symbolizing the five senses.

(I would like to thank Alice Leblanc and the West Baton Rouge Museum for their research, wonderful detailed description and kindness, in sharing their notes with me. The Author.)

Original statues of the 5 Muses that once lined the front garden of the Myrtles Plantation.

In 1954, the cypress shake roof was replaced with slate asbestos shingles, and the cypress lathe strips, with tongue and groove decking. Electrical wiring and plumbing, at this, time were carefully installed.

Myrtles Plantation front entry after the Stirling's expansion. The window to the left marks the exterior wall of the original Bradford house.

Mary and Ruffin Stirling's New Home

Mary Cobb Stirling hired the finest craftsmen in France to create the beautiful detailing you see today in the Myrtles Plantation. The front doors are especially lovely and filled with meaning. The French doors contain exquisite hand-painted glass in ochre and white etching. The design in the elaborate rendering is of the French Gothic Cross, also called a Maltese Cross. This insignia graced the swords of the Crusaders and Knights Templar, and holds a special place in history. It represented all that was good, and was a symbol that evil would be abolished. Mrs. Sterling may have chosen it for that reason—a talisman of sorts against evil, and to keep her beloved new home safe. It is apparent that her need to keep evil spirits at bay permeated many of the designs she incorporated into the Myrtles' motif. One of the more interesting ideas Mrs. Stirling had, was to place many of the doors' keyholes upside down. This superstition believed that spirits lived in the trees outside and could enter the home or rooms through the keyholes. By placing them upside down, the spirits would become confused and go away. Obviously, none of the departed souls were locksmiths in a former life.

Myrtles Plantation upside-down keyhole.

The French Room was used by Mrs. Stirling as her Day Room, or Morning Room, where she spent most of her time running her household, writing letters, and taking care of domestic accounts. There may have been things happening at the plantation at this time that were making her uneasy. The Myrtles Plantation's history of unexplained noises, shadows and atmosphere, may have begun with the home's renovation. At any rate, Mrs. Stirling made sure she was protected by installing talismans in every facet of the house.

In the 1800s, people thought the evil spirits would hover in the corners of the room during the day and come out in the evenings. They believed that religious icons in every room would protect the family. Mrs. Sterling used the beautiful chandelier in her Day Room to carry out just such a purpose. At the base of the chandelier are cherubs whose faces watch the corners. They guard the lower portion of the room. The medallion piece anchoring the chandelier to the ceiling is engraved with the images of four nuns, who guard the top half of the room.

Another belief at the time, was that salt could ward off evil spirits. At one time, salt was a rare commodity and thought to have magical powers. It has long been used as a preservative, in medicine, and is also used in magic, ritual, and superstition, to purify, bless things, and drive away evil. Packets of salt were placed in the Myrtles below the windows in the house, hoping to keep spirits from coming in through the glass. These small bags were usually secreted behind the long, puddled curtains.

As long as we are on the subject of superstition, you will find several black cats making their home at the Myrtles. They are strays who frequent the patio area. Ironically, if a black cat is walking toward you, it is considered lucky, while one walking away is said to be stealing your luck. Just make sure you keep the cute kitties facing you while walking the grounds.

Black cat on the porch of the Myrtles Plantation.

Mrs. Stirling's French craftsmen created all the open-pierced frieze work found throughout the house: Entry, Ladies' Parlor, Gentlemen's Parlor, and Dining Room. They are created from a mixture of plaster, clay, Spanish Moss, and hair from cattle and deer. Francis Kermeen, in her book about the Myrtles plantation, said it very well when she likened the feeling of the pastel walls, topped with the white, lacy design of the frieze work, as a feeling akin to being inside a wedding cake. It is truly lovely.

Faux painted fireplace to look like marble.

These artisans also painted the doors, moldings, and fireplace mantels in what is called *faux bois*, meaning "fake wood." It was more distinctive to have the cypress wood painted to look like heart of pine or mahogany. Other faux finishes included the facades of marble or malachite.

In the entry, Mrs. Stirling had the walls papered in 1848, in a truly elaborate design. To glance at it, it looks like any wallpaper depicting a floral and bird motif. But upon closer inspection, it is something quite amazing. This paper is called eggshell paper. It is French. There are actually 12 layers of paper on this wall, each layer depicting one simple element of the design. Then the additional layers are lined up and carefully added, each building upon the last to create a finished look. The paper was very fragile and transparent, and expensive. Other homes in the area have this technique, with some requiring as many as 35 layers of paper! It is much like the more elaborate stencil designs today where each stencil builds upon the pattern, adding new elements and depth of color.

Myrtles Plantation foyer frieze work above the haunted mirror, and the elaborate eggshell wallpaper.

This wall is worth mention for other reasons. It was the exterior wall of the original main house when Bradford built it, in 1796. The door in the wall to the left of the banjo clock, once looked outside, whereas now it separates the new entry hall from the older Ladies' Parlor.

Upon this wall, also hangs the notorious mirror, where handprints from unknown sources refuse to be cleaned away. It sits above a beautiful antique Bombay chest where a bust of a woman's head looks out serenely toward the main doors. Only a few feet away, stands an antique grandfather clock, its banjo shape dating it back to the early 1800s. The banjo clock was developed by renowned clock maker Simon Williard in Roxbury, Massachusetts, at the beginning of the 19th Century. These elegant antiques are prized by collectors and keep remarkably good time.

The gigantic chandelier in the main entry is truly extraordinary. It originally hung in a castle in France. It is made of 'tole' and Baccarat crystal. It is one of the first uses of color in crystal. The largest of these crystals weigh 3 ½ pounds. The smaller ones are 2 ½, 1 ½, and ½ pounds. The entire chandelier weighs more than 300 pounds.

Myrtles Plantation foyer chandelier.

The entry hall showcases another testament to the wealth that crossed over the threshold of the Myrtles Plantation when the Stirlings acquired her. At the base of the beautiful main staircase, you will see a newel post. Look closely and you will notice an ivory button set into the top of the post. This was called a "brag button," or a "contract button." If the property was mortgaged, the newel post was nothing more than a solid piece of wood without adornment. But once the property was paid off, and the deed and title in hand, a hole was drilled into the newel post and the deed was inserted into it. The hole was then covered with a brag button made of carved ivory, like the one at the Myrtles, or sometimes a large jewel. It was a "subtle" way of letting your friends and neighbors know, upon entering your hallway, that your mortgage was paid off and you were 'stylin'!

Myrtles' newel post brag button

Newel post at base of Myrtles' main staircase with ivory "brag button" atop it.

The main entry also houses a beautiful antique baby grand piano, which at the time of this writing, sits beneath the main staircase. A family portrait hangs on the wall above the staircase, and is that of an unknown man with wandering eyes. The portrait has some famous hauntings associated with it, as does the piano, which we cover in *The Haunting* section of this book. Clark Woodruff's likeness is found in an ornate gold, easel-style frame near the front door. Above that picture hangs an antique mirror in gold gilt, reminiscent of the Civil War era.

An unknown man in the portrait above the stairs
keeps a watchful eye over the main staircase.

French doors with the hand-painted French Gothic Cross on the side panels and transom lead from the large entryway and out onto the back verandah which overlooks the patio. Here you can rest in the comfort of swaying high-backed rocking chairs while sipping a mint julep, and watch the moss sway softly in the breeze. To your right is the original house Bradford built for his family while the main house was being constructed, and is today home to the Gift Shop. This where tour tickets are sold and overnight accommodations are confirmed. It is also at the juncture between the two houses that Teeta Moss, owner of the Myrtles Plantation, captured the now famous image of Chloe's ghost standing near the clapboard siding of the original outbuilding.

Myrtles Plantation Gift Shop area.

For the Stirlings, maintaining a presence in the community was all important. The Myrtles must become a place of social gatherings befitting their wealth and station. We have already mentioned that the rooms were enlarged and the ceiling raised, but in order to accommodate the impressive galas and parties they wanted to throw, the Stirlings came up with an ingenious idea. Why not take the Ladies' Parlor and the Gentlemen's Parlor, which were identical in size, with matching fireplaces on each end, and combine them? They removed the original hallway that separated the two rooms. Now they installed a pocket door between the two parlors that could simply disappear into the wall, creating one large ballroom! The servants could remove the other doors and the furnishings, raise the floor-to-ceiling windows up into the ceiling, and now you had the equivalent of a pavilion with the partiers dancing out onto the verandah. The band could be set up inside or outside, and the night filled with music; or for simpler parties, the harmonium provided the lilting notes that floated into the night like fireflies. Guests would travel for days by horse and buggy in order to attend these lavish parties that went on for days. A special wing on the top floor of the 21-room mansion accommodated the lady guests, while the men stayed in the *garconniere* outside, which was customary. The Ball Season was spring and fall, doubtless due to the grueling heat of summer. Invitations to the Stirling's galas were coveted. The Myrtles Plantation was now one of the Grand Party Houses of Louisiana!

Back verandah overlooking the patio at the Myrtles Plantation.

Party guests could dance out onto the verandah through the raised windows in the twin parlors.

Today, guests to the Myrtles Plantation can see the amazing detail the Stirlings lavished on their plantation home.

Myrtles Plantation from the driveway. Photo courtesy of Jason Phillip Reeser.

The William Winter Years

1854-1871

Chapter Seven

William Drew Winter

Reconstruction Period in Louisiana

The Civil War ravaged the South. The once affluent plantations, that had made their fortunes in cotton and sugar, were looking around at the devastation and wondering what to do next. The labor they depended upon had been liberated, as a direct result of the North conquering the South, and enforcing
Abraham Lincoln's slavery edicts. Without the labor force, a plantation could not operate. After emancipation, once the initial euphoria of freedom died down, former slaves—with nowhere else to go—often drifted back to the plantations, where at least they had a roof over their heads and regular meals. They worked as tenants, sharecroppers, or paid laborers, under contracts negotiated through the newly-organized Freedmen's Bureau. Although the conquered

Louisianans were deeply divided about reconciliation with the United States once the Civil War ended in 1864—as Abraham Lincoln was reaching the height of his political power—delegates drafted a new state constitution that embodied Lincoln's conciliatory approach. Emancipation was already in effect in the Confederate parishes, but the new document abolished slavery throughout the state, without compensation to the slave owners.

During Reconstruction, however, Louisiana was caught up in the same racial bitterness as the rest of the South, and in 1865, the Louisiana legislature passed a Black Code similar to those in other states in the defeated South. Although it did permit blacks to own property, marry, make contracts, and testify in court, it did not extend them voting rights. Furthermore, it restricted their movements and opportunities, in an effort to restore the plantation economy. The Civil Rights movement had gained momentum, however, and in 1868, Congress approved the Fourteenth Amendment, instituting universal male suffrage, and other rights for black people.

These Reconstruction laws, while extending the rights of blacks, also caused resentment among whites throughout the South. Conflicts erupted, including a major riot in New Orleans, in 1874. Even after Reconstruction ended, lingering bitterness, and the deeply established social order of the South, kept the color barrier firmly in place for another century. White supremacy organizations, such as the Knights of the White Camellia and the White League, used terror tactics to maintain the status quo. The Ku Klux Klan, in Louisiana, did not debut until the twentieth century.

Mary Cobb Stirling had suffered staggering blows in the 1850s and '60s. Her husband Ruffin was gone, fallen by consumption in 1854, followed only a few months later by the death of her son Lewis. The Civil War literally rode up to her doorstep and pillaged her home, leaving much of their holdings in worthless Confederate money. Other nearby plantations were also looted, with no regard for tearful families begging that their heirlooms remain intact. The "spoils of the war" was a common occurrence. Into this climate, came the racial unrest that would ultimately be the swan song for plantations hoping to make a living off the land.

To add to Mary's despair, she had invested heavily in sugar planting, when Ruffin left several plantations to her upon his death. The War had ruined both cotton and sugar operations, and she was now looking at not only the Myrtles, but Ingleside, Crescent Park, and Botany Bay plantations. In desperation, she turned to her son-in-law, William Drew Winter, to help her manage the plantations.

William Drew Winter

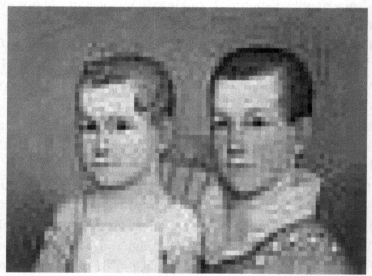

William Winter with his sister Marcia as children

William Drew Winter was born to Captain Samuel Winter and Sarah Bowman, on October 28, 1820, in Bath, Maine. In 1839, he graduated from Harvard, and in 1844, married his first wife, Lucretin Bass, who died during childbirth. Not much is known about William, until his marriage to Ruffin and Mary's daughter, Sarah Mulford Stirling, in 1852, at the Myrtles Plantation. The event was heralded the "Wedding of the Decade." Ruffin lived to see his oldest daughter married to the prominent attorney.

The Wedding of the Decade

On June 3, 1852, Sarah Matilda adjusted her wedding gown with fluttering hands, as her mother Mary Cobb and sister Mary, who was only seven, hurried about the upstairs suite Sarah had lived in during her days at the Myrtles. The smell of flowers permeated the air, as the happy bride looked into the mirror and made her final touches. Downstairs, the strains of music from the violins and band the Stirlings had hired for the occasion, could be heard in the upper story of the plantation. Laughter, animated conversation, and the excitement of the guests, resonated throughout the antebellum home.

William Drew Winter paced in the Day Room, as his family and soon-to-be father-in-law, tried to soothe his nerves. The wedding license had been filled out and witnessed earlier in the day. Lewis G. Sterling had stood in as William's security.

The deed read:

We William D. Winter as principal, and Lewis G. Stirling as his security, do acknowledge ourselves to be indebted to Charles B. Collins, Clerk of said Court, in and for the Parish of West Feliciana, and his successors in office, in the sum of five hundred dollars, for the payment of which we bind ourselves, jointly and severally, by these presents.

Whereas the above bound William D. Winter has thus obtained from the Clerk aforesaid a license to marry Sarah M. Sterling and should there exist no legal impediment to the marriage of the said party, this obligation is to be null and void, otherwise it remains in full force and virtue. Made and dated this Third day of June, A.D., 1852.

It is signed by William D. Winter and Lewis G. Stirling.

William, no doubt, received last minute instruction about the ceremony that would begin in mere moments, as he fussed with his top hat and tails. The house pulsated with energy and happiness.

Suddenly the music stopped, and an expectant hush fell over the attending party; dressed in their finest ball gowns and top coats. After a few seconds, the recognized tune of a popular wedding song began. It was time.

1800s French Wedding Tiara.

1800s Wedding Gown

William took a deep breath, and along with his family and father-in-law, opened the door to the Day Room, and stepped out to the sea of beaming faces; all the attention turned to him. He and Ruffin Gray Stirling took their places at the foot of the grand staircase, as other members took up their stations in the Ladies' Parlor, where the ceremony would take place. As the music swelled, they pressed toward the door to get a clear view of the staircase.

An appreciative gasp filled the room as Sarah Mulford Stirling exited the doorway from her suite, and stood at the top of the stairs in white perfection. Her mother Mary stood by her side, quickly adjusting the gown's train behind her daughter. Grasping her small bouquet of flowers, Sarah began her slow descent down the stairs, her eyes fixed on the man who waited anxiously below—her future husband, William Drew Winter. Hearts filled with happiness, as the plantation, that had seen so much tragedy, was tonight effused with love, romance and gaiety.

William claimed his bride at the bottom of the stairs, only to turn her over to her father to escort her to the Ladies' Parlor, where Ruffin would give her away to the beaming young man the Stirlings had come to love. Wedding guests filled the Gentlemen's Parlor and the large entryway, witnessing what would be dubbed by local papers as the "Wedding of the Decade." Garlands of flowers were everywhere, the smells of a roasted pig and other savory dishes wafted on the wind from the outdoor kitchen, as slaves carried in preparations for the enormous feast that would follow the formal ceremony. Mary and Ruffin Sterling stood, arm and arm, and beamed upon the happy couple as they exchanged rings and vows. The Myrtles Plantation

was witness to one of its happiest moments. In an ironic duplication of a marriage that took place in those very rooms 35 years earlier, it was the second time a bride named Sarah exchanged vows with her attorney husband. Only this time, the bride would outlive the husband.

Sarah and William Winter

The next nineteen years were a mixture of blessings and sadness for the Winters. After the wedding flowers faded and the last of the feast had been consumed, William took his new bride to his plantation near Clinton, Louisiana. The home was called Gantmore Plantation. Their first child, Mary Stirling Winter, was born at Gantmore, on November 14, 1853. Shortly after, William moved his new family to a plantation he purchased in West Baton Rouge Parish, called Arbroath Plantation, on the west side of the Mississippi River. Here, two other daughters are born to the happy couple: Sarah "Sadie" Bowman Winter in 1855, and Kate Lyle Winter, on September 28, 1858. A boy, Ruffin Stirling Winter, entered the family on May 18, 1862, and was the last child born to the couple at Arbroath.

Sadly, it is on record that Kate Lyle Winter died at the Myrtles on January 29, 1861, of typhoid fever at the age of 3. Since her younger brother, Ruffin Stirling Winter, was born a year later in 1862 at Arbroath, it indicates the Williams were still living at that residence. It could be assumed that Kate was taken to the Myrtles during her illness to keep her contagious fever from the other children, or for Sarah to have help from her mother Mary Cobb in treating the deadly disease.

Little Kate Winter became consumed by fever in 1861. Sarah and William Winter were desperate. They had witnessed children dying all over Louisiana from the dreaded disease; a raging plague that would claim Sarah's own sister Mary two years later, in 1863. The twin fevers of yellow and typhoid were visitors that, once crossing the threshold of a home, seldom left without a fallen companion. Doctors had been summoned, night-long rituals of "bleeding" and applying rags to the feverous brow, had done nothing to cure their little girl.

Mosquito Bier used during the Yellow Fever epidemic to keep the disease-carrying insects out.

Stories of miracles wrought by Voodoo medicine, so prevalent in New Orleans, reached the Winter's ears; possibly carried into the little girl's sick room by a house slave helping with her care. It was their last hope, and one not unaccustomed to finding its way into the white household. Taking a slave aside, they admonished her in hushed tones to bring a Voodoo Priestess to the house. This must be a secret not to be shared with others. It was still a practice not openly condoned in "good society."

Beneath the cloak of night, a woman dressed in strange clothes and an elaborate turban, is secreted up the back staircase and into the room closest to the top of the stairs on the left. Rumors have reported her name as Cleo. She approaches the little girl lying in sweat-soaked bed clothes and holds a candle over her pale face to study the disease's effects. The child's parents stare on, wide-eyed, half-pleading, half-fearful that they may have done the wrong thing in bringing this strange person into their home. The Priestess sets the candle down on the small table near the bed and raises a hand for all to be silent. Slaves huddle outside the doorway, afraid of the powerful magic about to begin.

Drawing a strange brown sack from a burlap bag she has brought with her into the room, Cleo raises it above the prone child, and begins to chant, her body swaying to unheard rhythms. Slowly she shakes the gris-gris bag over little Kate. A white powder filters through the sack's cloth and dusts the child's bedclothes. Swaying and chanting, the Voodoo Priestess tilts her head and stares sightlessly at the ceiling. She closes her lids as her lips murmur words from strange, faraway places. Her intonations become louder, her body spasms, and the gris-gris shakes violently over the bed, as Kate's parents look on in horror. With a final shuddering jerk of her body, the Priestess collapses in on herself, and all is quiet. No one dares move or utter a sound. All eyes are now on the stricken child, praying for a sign of recovery.

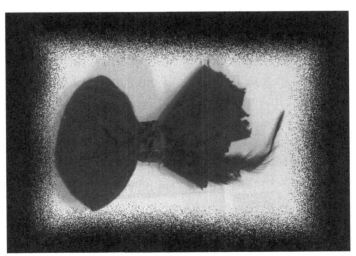

Bag of voodoo gris-gris.

The Priestess replaces the gris-gris in her bag, noticeably shaken by the ceremony, and turns to leave the room, assuring all around her that the child is now cured and will be better by morning. She leaves by the back stairway and disappears into the trees.

Throughout the night, the Winter's keep vigil by Kate's bedside, watching for the fever to break or her eyelids to open. Her small frame seems to diminish before them. The long hours are broken by the light of morning filtering through the lace curtains. It is January 29th, and young Kate Lyle Winter is dead, at the age of three.

Agonizing cries are heard throughout the upper story of the Myrtles Plantation. Sarah cradles her dead daughter in her arms, despite warnings from others that the fever is contagious. The failed protective powder from the gris-gris falls away, along with the family's hopes.

Several legends followed the death of Kate Winter, who is today buried in the cemetery at Grace Church in St. Francisville, Louisiana. It was said that the Voodoo Priestess was found and hung, much like Chloe, by her fellow tribesmen, out of fear of retribution from the plantation owners.

Other stories, have her fading away into the protective cover of other Voodoo practitioners in nearby New Orleans. This author tends to lean toward the latter theory, as most of the slaves of the 1800s lived in fear of Voodoo magic, and would doubtless not take it upon themselves to slay one holding the title of Priestess. Voodoo eventually began to lose its hold on Louisiana, and by the 1930s, the true religion went underground, when New Orleans became a tourist attraction.

Sadly, Sarah Mulford's sister Mary died a year later, at the age of 18, of typhoid fever at the Myrtles Plantation. It must have been heart-wrenching to see so many children under one roof pass away from such an insidious disease.

Yellow Fever

Typhoid's sister, yellow fever, ravaged Louisiana. The disease occurs in three stages. In the first stage, headaches, muscle soreness, fever, loss of appetite, vomiting, dizziness, and jaundice are common symptoms. During the next stage, multi-organ failure, such as liver and kidneys, internal hemorrhaging, delirium, and seizures, are generally followed by death. Victims may die as soon as four-to-eight-days, after being infected.

Yellow fever was also called the "black vomit." It was called "yellow jack," as areas under quarantine traditionally displayed a yellow flag. "Jack" was sailor's slang for "flag."

The plethora of bayous and Louisiana swampland, undoubtedly, fostered the breeding grounds for mosquitoes. Thousands of the winged creatures found their way in through open windows and doors. The loss of life due to these tiny insects was astounding.

Major epidemics began occurring in 1811, and again in 1817. The latter epidemic, spread from New Orleans to Baton Rouge, Saint Francisville, and then to Natchez. In the summer of 1853, generally considered the worst year of the epidemic, 29,120 people contracted the disease, and 8,647 died from it. On a single day in August, 230 deaths were reported. Newspapers touted it as the "Black Day." In August of that same year, 1853, an average of 1,300 died each week! By the end of that epidemic, approximately one out of every twelve people had died from yellow fever. Sadly, most did not know how to treat the malady. The archaic methods of bleeding the patient, purging, inducing vomiting, and even administering mercury, were used.

Yellow Fever attacks in Louisiana began to decline after the Civil War, but the death toll was astronomical, often felling the smallest members of the family not strong enough to fight it off. Meanwhile, Mary Cobb Sterling, who had just buried yet another child, when she placed her beloved Mary in the ground at Grace Church, in St. Francisville, was barely hanging on at the Myrtles Plantation. With Ruffin gone, it had become too much to run four plantations. The crops were failing due to the after effects of the War and the scattered fall-out from the Reconstruction Period. She turned to her son-in-law William Winter and asked if he, Sarah, and the children, would leave Abroath, and live at the Myrtles with her.

The Winters moved into the Myrtles, and on May 30, 1865, William Winter, Jr. is born there. Once again, the plantation was filled with the laughter of young children. But the Myrtles was hanging on by a thread financially. On December 5, 1865, Mary Cobb offered to hire William Winter to oversee her properties, which included four plantations. In her gratitude, she gave the Myrtles to William and Sarah. In the estate partitions, the property was listed as "2300 acres more or less, comprising all the land between Bayou Sara on the West, and the Woodville Road on the East, and between lands of Mrs. Harriet

Mathews on the North, and lands of D.S. Lewis and others on the South."

Francis Anderson Winter, a healthy son, was born to Sarah and William, on June 30, 1867 at the Myrtles Plantation, but the happiness was short-lived. William had been doing his best to recoup Mary's wealth, but the properties were too much in debt. The prosperous years of the Cotton and Sugar Kings were over.

On December 23, 1867, William had to declare bankruptcy.

April 15, 1868, the Myrtles Plantation was sold by the U.S. Marshall to the New York Warehouse & Security Company.

Only eight days later, it reverted back to Sarah Mulford Stirling Winter, as her father's heir. The Winters continued to try and farm the land, and bring the Myrtles back to its former glory. Unlike the other children, who had not lived long at the plantation, the Winters, with the exception of young Kate, seemed to have broken the curse that cut short so many young lives. Their other five children lived to maturity. Mary Stirling Winter was attending school at the age of 16, in 1870, while living at the Myrtles. All of the children grew up and married. Other than their financial worries, life at the Myrtles was good, and everyone was thriving. Mary Cobb, Sarah's mother, was still living with them, and was, no doubt, a great asset in coaching Sarah in the ways of motherhood and running a plantation household. But the worst tragedy to befall the home was about to come calling— not by plaque or bankruptcy, but on horseback.

The Murder of William Drew Winter

Perhaps more stories have been told about the fateful last day of William Winter than were told about the hapless slave Chloe. Yet this murder was documented by the local paper at the time, the *Pointe Coupee Democrat* newspaper, as well as others.

William Drew Winter

On January 26, 1871, William Winter was in the downstairs section of the original portion of the house. Reports vary that he was either in the Game Room or the Gentlemen's Parlor, giving lessons to his children. The date falls on a Thursday, so it is assumed they were school lessons, although reports that he was teaching Sunday School lessons, also surfaced.

It was evening, shortly before 7 p.m. Young Francis, who was only 4 at the time, may have been put to bed. The other two boys, Ruffin Sterling Winter, who was 9, and William Winter Jr., who was 13, on that fateful night, may have been the only two members of the family in attendance at the lessons. Mary Winter was 18, and Sarah "Sadie" was 16, on that January evening, and may have been upstairs with their mother, or not at home.

Suddenly, the sound of a horse approaching the front of the house at great speed was heard. The pounding hooves were accompanied by a deep voice calling out, "Gentleman to see the lawyer!" The horseman circled around to the north side of the house, where the candlelight could be seen through the tall windows, and repeated his request, "Gentleman to see the lawyer!"

William Winter left his children and walked to the French doors next to the fireplace in the Gentlemen's Parlor and opened them wide. He stepped out onto the verandah to see a man on horseback. Obviously, Mr. Winter did not recognize him in the darkness, as all he said was, "I'm a lawyer." Reportedly, the rider said, "Are you William Winter?" to which William replied in the affirmative. At that, the mysterious rider pulled a gun, and aiming it point blank at the attorney's chest, fired. Reports vary as to how many shots were fired, but according to the newspaper article, Mr. Winter was hit "in the breast."

It is from this point, that stories concerning Mr. Winter's next actions take on various forms. The one most-associated with the hauntings at the Myrtles Plantation find him making it to the main staircase in search of his wife.

The north verandah at the Myrtles Plantation where William Winter was shot by a man on horseback.

Panicked family members came running as the sound of gunfire filled the night. The horseman reined in the horse, spun it around, and bolted away into the darkness, leaving Winter mortally wounded on the north verandah.

A newspaper reported the following story at a later date, as it was printing a social announcement concerning William's son Francis:

Francis Anderson Winter, Lieutenant Colonel, Medical Corps, U. S. Army, has been the distinguished guest of his relatives, Mr. and Mrs. S. C. Stirling of Locust Grove. Col. Winter is a native of West Feliciana, the son of Judge Wm. D. Winter, whose murder aroused the people even amid the injustices and horrors of reconstruction days. This able jurist was called to his door, one night, at his home, Myrtles plantation, and shot down. For awhile the assassin was not known, but it gradually transpired that a mulatto named Swayze, an agitationist of the worst type, had done the shooting. He left for unknown parts, and was warned never to return to West Feliciana. In 1891 or '92 he ventured back, but was hanged by a mob as soon as he set foot on parish soil. Mr. Winter has been held in revered remembrance as a martyr of those troublous days. His son receives the welcome due such a father.

The True Democrat. (Bayou Sara [La.]) 1892-1928, October 10, 1914

William Drew Winter died from the gunshot wounds, and was buried at Grace Church the following day.

—Mr. W. D. Winter, was murdered at his residence about one mile
from St. Francisville, on the night of
the 26th inst., at about 7 o'clock P.
M. The following is a version of
the affair as we heard it from Deputy
Sheriff, James Smith : It appears
that the deceased, was sitting in his
room teaching his son his lessons for
the morrow when a person called to
him from outside of the house to
come out quick. He at once went
to the door and on opening it he was
shot at with a double-barrel shotgun, several buck-shot taking effect
in his breast.

Mr. Winter was a lawyer of considerable practice at the West Feliciana Bar, and much esteemed in this
community. He leaves a wife and
three children to mourn his loss.

Official report in The Feliciana Republican newspaper.

A recounting of the tragedy, also blames an unnamed assailant, perhaps harboring a grudge due to the troubles of the turbulent Reconstruction era, when nighttime violence was commonplace. Newspaper dispatches mention angry mobs of former slaves armed with torches and guns marching on St. Francisville. But actual newspaper accounts of Winter's demise, refer to an upcoming trial of one E.S. Webber for his murder. Whether it was Swayze or Webber, no one went to trial for the murder. Though a $1,000 reward was offered for the capture and indictment of the murderer, the case was never solved and no arrest was ever made.

Those who have stayed at the Myrtles, and heard the sounds of footsteps made by an unseen person climbing the main staircase, have attributed those steps to the late William Winter as he attempted to reach his wife Sarah who was upstairs. The legend says the footfalls against the creaking stairs always stop on the 17th step where William supposedly expired in his wife's arms. This author has heard the steps on the stairs when no one was there, although the sounds this author heard, only made it to the fourth step before stopping.

Myrtles main staircase.

William Winter was shot in "the breast" according to the newspaper report. It also stated "several buckshot took effect." The author spoke with two police detectives, including Tom McLellan, a retired detective of the Fort Collins Police Department in Colorado, about the shooting, and they both agree the injury would not be immediately fatal. Scattered buckshot is not a concentrated load, and depending on his wounds, he could have lived a day or more. Without knowing the load used, they could not say with certainty the duration of his likelihood to live.

William may have leaned on one of his sons, who had raced to his side, and asked to be taken inside the house, perhaps fearful the horseman would return. As it was, after all, January, and it would have been cold out in the evening hours, he may have been pulled inside the doors for that reason. Another son may have run ahead, calling for his mother, who had been upstairs at the opposite end of the house. It is possible, William made it to the stairs and tried to meet her half-way up, only to collapse when he reached her arms. A gunshot wound can take time to bleed out, as can other bullet wounds. As with many of the stories reported in an era when newspapers relied on word of mouth, and are not delivered with today's rapid-fire technology, things could be distorted and told a hundred different ways.

An account of William's death is told in the Family History Book of Alexander Stirling and Ann Alston as follows:

> *"The death of William, as told by Amanda Smith,*
> *Wife of Stephen Sterling"*

> *"Amanda had the floor in the game room shaved to remove the bloodstains. Lucile Lawrason, and other family members, dispute the tale of William dying on the 17ᵗʰ step in his wife's arms. They say that he was teaching Sunday school, when a man rode up on horseback and shot Winter. They also state that he died right there in the game room/study."*

It is said, that following William's death, Sarah retired to her room and would not come out until her own death. Friends would travel form Natchez and New Orleans bringing gifts, some of her known favorites, but she refused to greet them.

Whether the sounds of footsteps climbing the main staircase, only to stop on step 17, are those of William Winter, or some other plantation occupant from the past, they have been heard by too many people, myself included, to be discounted. It may be the grief-laden steps of Sarah Mulford Winter climbing to the room that became her reclusive retreat after her husband's body was carried away.

Sarah was devastated by the murder and never remarried. She remained at the Myrtles with her mother, Mary Cobb, her children, and a few other family members, until her death, in April, of 1878. It is her sobbing that many report hearing when they stay in her old room, which is today called the Woodruff Suite.

Mary Cobb Stirling, the mistress of the plantation, who did so much to renovate it, bringing in French craftsmen and overseeing the property as it doubled in size, died only two years after her daughter Sarah passed away. She had outlived so many of her precious children, and for over 30 years called the Myrtles Plantation home. She was buried next to her husband Ruffin Gray Stirling, in the Grace Episcopal Church graveyard, in St. Francisville, Louisiana. Today, you can visit their impressive monument there.

The Myrtles Through the Ages

1880-

Chapter Eight
A New Legacy Begins

Two families created the Myrtles Plantation home's structure that you see today: David and Elizabeth Bradford, and Ruffin Gray and Mary Cobb Stirling. It is not to say that subsequent owners did not put their mark on the property; to the contrary. As for the Stirling home, however, it was never expanded upon again, though many owners that followed put in copious hours to renovate it and maintain its historical integrity. The grounds surrounding the Myrtles Plantation house did evolve and we will go into those improvements, along with the owners who created them, as we proceed with the plantation's history. Other guest rooms were added to the grounds, along with changes to the Carriage House, Bradford's outbuilding (that had served as his original home while the main house was being built), and so many other upgrades which continue today.

Stephen and Amanda Stirling

In 1881, shortly after Mary Cobb Stirling passed away, Stephen Stirling bought out his two surviving brothers, William and Henry, of their shares in the plantation for the purchase price of $3,000. The property was heavily in debt and it would be a huge undertaking for Stephen and his young family to bring it back from the ashes.

According to the 1880 census, Stephen Stirling was 33 when he bought the Myrtles. His wife Amanda was 26. They had two small daughters, Nannie who was 3-years-old, and Maud who was 1 ½-years-old. The two little girls filled the large nursery with their squeals of delight as they played and ran about the rooms, as so many children had done before them. Sightings of two young girls in ringlets and pinafores have been reported by hundreds of people visiting the Myrtles. Perhaps it was these two young daughters of Stephen Stirling. So many young girls lived at the Myrtles, many of them dying there, that it is hard to say. Stephen and Amanda tried for five years to turn the war-ravaged plantation around. As with many of their neighbors, they found it a daunting task. Finally, in 1886, Stephen could no longer handle the debt that hung over the roof of the Myrtles; debt as tenacious as the Spanish moss from nearby oaks. With a heavy heart, he let the family home pass out of his lineage and into the hands of a stranger.

Oran D. Brooks

Oran D. Brooks was born in 1845, in Louisiana. The 1880 census shows him living in St. Francisville, Louisiana, as an apothecary. He probably owned a small shop in the town of St.

Francisville, where he lived with his wife, Ewdolie, and their two small children, Ewdolie and Cerile.

In 1886, Oran bought the Myrtles Plantation from Stephen Stirling for $10,000. When Oran took over the plantation, he was 41, his wife Ewdolie was 31, and the two children, Ewdolie and Cerile, were 11 and 9. The Nursery was home yet again to young people exploring the small closet near the dorm window, running up and down the back staircase, and petting the horses in the carriage house outside.

But the dream lasted only three years, when the property was split between Harrison Milton Willams and Aaron Schlessinger, in 1889. It is unclear why it took two more years for Harrison to buy it outright, unless there were legal procedures going on between himself and Schlessinger, as to the ownership. It is also unclear if the property was empty at that time, or if the Brooks remained in residence until 1891, when Williams finally bought it.

Harrison Milton Williams & Fannie Lintot Haralson Williams

Harrison Milton Williams was born February of 1845, in Wilkinson, Mississippi. Records show he was married to a woman who died in 1880, leaving Harrison a widower with a young son, Hunter, who was born in 1872. Harrison remained a single father, raising his son on his own, until he met and fell in love with Fannie Lintot Haralson. After the customary courtship, they married on December 18, 1890. Fannie was 25-years-old and Harrison was twenty years her senior. It was at this time that Harrison began proceedings to acquire the Myrtles for his new bride, and his son from a former marriage. Hunter was now 18, and according to subsequent census records, did not live long at the Myrtles. Follow-up records could not be found, showing whether he married and moved on, or not, but by the 1900 census, he is not listed as living at the plantation.

The Williams moved into the Myrtles Plantation, in 1891. It would not be long before the home was once again filled with the sounds of small children. On November, 1892, Harry entered the world, filling the antebellum home with the cries of a healthy newborn male. Only two years later, Lucille was born in January, of 1894. A short 11 months later, Samuel joined her on December 1894. Young Fannie had her hands full! There was a two-year respite before Fannie (named after her mother) bounced into the world in January, 1896. Zuleika became daughter number three in August, 1898. Two years after that, the last son was born. Fannie gave birth to Surget Minor Williams in March, 1900. There was an unusually long pause between Surget and the birth of his sister, Jeanne Hereford Percy Williams, in 1909. At any rate, the Williams now filled the Myrtles with seven healthy children.

The 1900 census (9 years after their move into the Myrtles), shows the following family members living there, and their ages: Harrison (56), Fannie (35), Harry (7), Lucile (6), Samuel (5), Fannie (4), Zuliecka (1), Surget (2 1/2 months). Jeanne was born later, in 1909. The census also shows a new face added to the family, that of Fannie's sister, Kate Haralson, who was born November, 1874, and is listed as 25-years old.

Kate, or "Aunt Katie," as the children called her, was a five-foot, 90-pound ball of fire. She wore long skirts, black stockings and high-top shoes, and her voice thundered throughout the plantation house as she barked out directives to the staff, and undoubtedly, the seven children she helped to raise. Her outspoken nature earned her the nickname "the Colonel" and many a household member bowed beneath her glare. Her nickname for his sister Fannie was "Tansy." Kate never married and was considered a spinster. She was still in residence at the plantation in 1910, at the age of 40, according to the census of that year.

Harrison Milton Williams planted cotton at the Myrtles, once again striving to revive the plantation's opulent era. He gained a reputation as a hard-working and industrious man. He and Fannie, along with their growing sons, kept the plantation going during the hard times of the post-war South. To bring in extra income, Harrison spent 15 years as a Confederate Calvary Courier in the post-war era.

It must have been daunting to hear the news that the Spanish American War was about to break out. The South was still picking up the pieces when the war hit in 1898. For the families of the Louisiana Plantation Country, it was akin to sounding the death knoll. The last thing they needed was for their men to go marching off to another war. Luckily, the Spanish-American War lasted briefly, from April to August of 1898, and was fought over Cuba. America won the war and gained Guam, Puerto Rico, and the Philippine Islands. Louisiana did help in the fight with several infantries headquartered in Baton Rouge, "mustered out" at New Orleans, Jacksonville, Florida and other areas.

Harrison Williams died in 1909 at the Myrtles. Sadly, it was the same year his daughter Jeanne was born. He was 65-years- old, a respectable age in those days. A 1910 census does show Fanny "Tansy" Williams as head of household at the age of 43. Her oldest son Harry, is 17, in that year, Lucile is 16, Samuel, 14, Fannie "Lintot", 13, Zuleika is 9, and Jeanne is 1. Aunt Katie is still onboard, at the age of 40.

Sometime after 1920, Harry, who is listed in the 1920 census as 26-years-old and still living at the Myrtles, drowns in the Mississippi River. From a copy of the February issue of *Louisiana Life*, the headline ran "Son Harry drowned in the Mississippi River trying to round up cattle scattered by a storm." Fannie had now lost her husband and oldest son. In that same census, Surget is now 19.

Death of H. M. Williams.

There are other men in the parish whose death might have caused more demonstration than that of H. M. Williams, but none where the record of esteem and regret was more general and harmonious. Though a man of strong convictions, sturdy thought and intelligence, he had no enemies. He pursued the even tenor of his way, honest in his dealings with all, and while holding his own opinions invincibly, antagonized no one thereby. A planter of indomitable energy and preseverance, he did not despise laboring with his own hands, as so many Southern farmers do. His life is an example of unflagging industry and endeavor. His ideas on agriculture were progressive and embraced every portion of the farmer's domain: field, pasture, garden, stock- and poultry yard. Myrtles, his plantation two and a half miles from town, was an object lesson of what can be done by one man with means due to his exertions. There are few plantations in West Feliciana, which show such all-roundness of effort as Myrtles, where too, a kindly Southern hospitality was always unostentatiously dispensed.

ry. In post-bellum days his natural reticence and modesty prevented his mention of his military record, but there was no better soldier than young "Harry Williams" as his comrades testify.

For a number of years he taught school in St. Francisville, and many of the older set of young men remember him as a just and able preceptor. Later, he went to planting, and after the purchase of Myrtles plantation devoted his entire attention to that avocation.

He first married Miss Lida S. Austin, a young lady, who came South to teach. His son, Hunter, by this marriage, survives him and resides in California. In 1890, after being a widower for a number of years, he married Miss Fannie Harrison, who, with their six children, Harry, Lucille, Linton, Sam, Surget, Zulelka, mourns the loss of as kind and good a husband and father as ever lived. He has one sister, Mrs. Rodney of Wilson, La., who grieves over him, as do his wife's sisters, who found in him a true brother.

Of such as he the Psalmist spoke: "Mark the perfect man, and behold the upright: for the end of that man is peace."

Obituary in The True Democrat, Feb. 20,1909 praising Harrison Williams' integrity and hard work at the Myrtles Plantation.

Shattered with grief, Fannie turned the plantation over to M & E Wolf, on June 16, 1909. She bought it back the same day, for $7,313. This was probably a necessary deed transaction putting the property in her name, so that she could bequeath it to whomever she chose.

> ## Succession Sale.
>
> State of Louisiana, Parish of West
> Feliciana, 24th Judicial
> District Court.
>
> Succession of H. M. Williams
> No.
>
> BY virtue of a commission to me
> directed by the Honorable Court afore-
> said, in the above entitled succession,
> I will sell at public auction on the
> premises of the late H. M. Williams
> in Ward 3 of said parish, at the hour
> of 11 o'clock a. m.
> SATURDAY, JUNE 12, 1909,
> the following property to-wit:
> A certain piece or parcel of land
> known as the "Myrtles" plantation,
> containing six hundred and thirteen
> (613) acres, bounded on the North by
> Mrs. Sallie M. Ventress and A.
> Schlesinger; on the East by the Wood-
> ville and Bayou Sara road; on the
> South by A. Schlesinger and John W.
> Leake; and on the West by lands now
> or formerly of Freyhan, situated in
> the parish of West Feliciana, La.,
> with all buildings and improvements
> thereon.

Ad placed in newspaper announcing the sale.

The Louisiana plantation economy had pretty much ground to a halt. With the end of slavery, the plantation economy gave way to extraction industries. Logging was the first, developing in the late nineteenth century. The discovery of oil near Jennings, in 1901, led to a boom that lasted eight decades. At first, oil was shipped out of state for refinement, but in 1909, Standard Oil built a refinery near Baton Rouge, and soon refineries and petrochemical plants sprang up along the Mississippi River and around Lake Charles. Next up, was sulfur, and the invention of the Frasch method, which could recover sulfur from deep deposits. These innovations soon put sulfur as the third major industry to the state.

For the Myrtles Plantation, the cotton and indigo days were all but gone.

A Wedding Celebration at the Myrtles

During the hard days of war, death and economical change, the Myrtles regained a sense of days gone by. On December 30, 1913, Miss Maud Haralson stood beneath the Christmas decorations at Grace Church in St. Francisville, and exchanged wedding vows with W. H. Richardson. Mrs. H. M. Williams, being a cousin to the happy couple, offered the Myrtles Plantation as a place to hold the wedding reception and celebration. According to the newspaper clipping (opposite page), the "spacious parlor was decorated with vines and white flowers, and the dining room in Christmas greens. An immense bell of white flowers was suspended from the center of the parlor, and beneath it, the young couple received the family greetings with natural grace and charm."

The article stated "a sumptuous menu was enjoyed," and "later there was dancing, one of the features being the dancing of an old-fashioned quadrille by the older members of the family."

BARROW-HARALSON.

Following the custom of several years past, that of there being always a bride to stand beneath the Christmas decorations in Grace Church, a popular young couple, Mr. Robert Ellason Barrow and Miss Maud Haralson, plighted their marriage vows, Tuesday, Dec. 30, at four o'clock in the afternoon. Only the immediate relatives and the W. H. Richardson family were present, as the aim was to keep it as simple as possible.

As Mrs. O. Leonard struck the first notes of the wedding march, the bride entered the church with her father, Mr. Bertrand Haralson, and was met by her bridegroom and the rector at the chancel steps. During the ceremony and signing, low, sweet music was played by Mrs. Leonard. The bride was chic and charming in a midnight blue suit with hat to match, and never looked better than when in the light of happiness she stood at the marriage altar with the handsome young man to whom she was committing her love and her future. She carried snowdrops and asparagus fern, arranged in a graceful bouquet.

After the ceremony the bridal party repaired to Myrtles plantation, the home of Mrs. H. M. Williams, a cousin, where an informal pleasant time, was had, the relatives only being present. The spacious parlor was decorated with vines and white flowers, and the dining-room in Christmas greens. An immense bell of white flowers was suspended from the center of the parlor, and beneath it the young couple received the family greetings with their natural grace and charm.

Supper was served, thirty covers being laid, and a sumptuous menu was enjoyed. Later there was dancing, one of the features being the dancing of an old-fashioned quadrille by the older members of the family. The bride, whose unfailingly cordial manners is one of her greatest charms, was, with the bridegroom, the life of this family circle, enlarged by their marriage.

The young couple are guests of his parents, Mr. and Mrs. Robert H. Barrow, at Rosale, until he begins farming at the Phillips place. Some pretty and useful presents were received. Relatives from a distance for the occasion were Mr. and Mrs. Wilson Rumble and Miss Katie Haralson of Natchez, Miss May Haralson, Mrs. Bryson Stirling and children and Reeve Barrow from Baton Rouge.

The Myrtles Plantation was once again in the headlines with the following article on Mrs. Fannie Haralson Williams, on Feb. 24, 1917. It touts the property as a haven "with a placid pond in the middle distance and woodland against the western horizon...Nearly everything on a Southern farm can be found thriving at 'Myrtles.'"

"Myrtles," the home of Mrs. Fannie Haralson Williams, three miles from St. Francisville, is a typical Southern house of the better sort. It was built by Mrs. Mary Stirling, mother of Mr. S. C. Stirling, who sold it. After passing through several owners, it reached Mrs. Williams and her children, Mr. Williams having bought it nearly thirty years ago. The house has a wide veranda almost entirely around it, and late Fergus Haralson and cousin of Parish Assessor Bertrand Haralson: a good old parish name, and highly connected. Her husband, the late Harry M. Williams, was a fine scholar and conducted a school in St. Francisville for years after the war, before taking up planting. Their children are Harry M., Samuel, Surget, Misses Lucille, Lintot, Zuleika, and Jeanne.

Mrs. Williams, assisted by her eldest son, manages the place, and is success-

the back view is as lovely as the front, with a placid pond in the middle distance and woodland against the western horizon.

Mrs. Williams is the daughter of the ful in so doing. Mr. Williams set a good precedent at "Myrtles," and it has been maintained. Nearly every thing on a Southern farm can be found thriving at "Myrtles."

The walls of the Myrtles Plantation absorbed the sounds of myriad families living within her shelter—the echo of newborn babies, the laughter of children, music that played throughout the night as revelers swept through the parlor doors and out into the moonlight, the home-sick song of the slaves, and the soul wrenching cries of sorrow. Yet, not all who haunt the plantation today, lived within.

Another Murder at the Myrtles

In 1927, an elderly caretaker, staying in a cabin on the property, was said to have been robbed and killed. No one was ever arrested for the murder. Perhaps for that reason, or because he has nowhere else to go, the caretaker's ghost has been seen by too many people to be dismissed.

Baton Rouge About.com, July, 2001, reported: "In 1927, an overseer of the property was killed and robbed and the crime was never solved. Many who visit complain of a rude man at the front gate, dressed in a straw hat and overalls, who has tried to turn them away from venturing on to the main house. The Myrtles management claim to have no such man employed but do admit to the knowledge that the murdered overseer was dressed in overalls and a straw hat often while working on the grounds."

Hester Eby, long-time docent at the Myrtles Plantation, has related "some folks report a white man in overalls and a straw hat has met them at the front gate." She has been told that the man is rude and "testy" and will not let them in.

The odd thing, according to Eby, is that "no one reported seeing him until the 1960's, after workers tore down his cottage. A new cottage went up in its place. It's an overnight guest room now, and some people say they see the shape of a man looking out the windows in their photographs. Some people react strongly to the cottage, and ask for other accommodations."

And Yet Another Murder on the Property

Fannie William's brother, Edward, moved onto the Myrtles Plantation after Harrison's death, no doubt to help his sister after the staggering loss of her husband and oldest son. He stayed in a different building somewhere on the property.

Edward B. Haralson was born in 1876, and died June 3, 1942, at the age of 66. Records indicate he too was involved in a robbery and killed. The Louisiana Statewide Death Indices do indicate that he was living in the West Feliciana Parish, in the Ward attributed to the Myrtles Plantation, when he died on June 3, 1942.

A man, 66-years of age, living in the 1900s, would look "elderly" by today's definition. Perhaps his ghost has been confused with that of the caretaker. It was not general knowledge that Edward wore overalls however. He was not the hired help; he was a member of the family. Nonetheless, that makes three documented murders at the plantation. As mentioned earlier, the 1900s were a turbulent time of unrest and shootings; murder and robberies were common. The murder of Edward Haralson was documented and the killer caught. The man would later be the first to die in Louisiana's electric chair for the crime.

While we are on the topic of murders at the Myrtles, it was reported that while Fannie owned the plantation, she had tried several times to remove the blood stain left by William Winter's murder. A relative of the family, "Puddin" Bankston, reported spending nights at the plantation and witnessed Fannie "shaving" the wood floor in the Game

Room, trying to eradicate the dark brown stain from where they had led Winter into the house after being shot. Puddin also remembers still seeing the blood stain on the front verandah where Winter was gunned down, and said the owners finally replaced the board when several efforts to remove the stain met with futility.

The Myrtles Plantation 1930s

Surget Minor Williams and Jessie Davis "Teet" Folkes

Surget Minor Williams was born on March 1, 1900, at the Myrtles. He had been a first-hand witness to the turmoil swirling about the plantations in the early 1900s-mid-1900s. His mother Fannie finally turned the plantation over to Surget in 1948, and asked him to manage it. Surget would have been 48-years-old at this time, and married to a woman named Jessie Davis "Teet" Folkes.

Jessie was born April 22, 1891, and according to the census report, lived to the golden age of 95, when she died on April 18, 1986. The couple had no children, which allowed room for dear maiden Aunt Katie to remain on at the plantation, along with Surget's mother,

Fannie. He managed the property for two or more years, until it was divided up among the William's heirs and put up for sale in the 1950s.

Ghost Stories Are Told

Whether or not other owners at the plantation had seen or heard strange things leading up to this time, we are not sure. We do know that bags of salt were placed beneath windows, keyholes were inserted upside down, a plethora of angels, nuns, and cherubs found their images adorning chandeliers and mantels. Neighboring plantation owners had reported seeing strange lights on the property, but it was not documented until Clarence John Laughlin came calling, while Surget and Jessie ran the Myrtles. Clarence Laughlin was going throughout the South taking pictures of plantations to document their glory days and show those that were already left in ruins. His wonderful picture book, *Ghosts Along the Mississippi*, published in 1948, was the result of that journey. While at the Myrtles, taking photographs, he took notes of several conversations he had with Surget and Jessie. He mentions that there was not much information about the Woodruffs, but the ghost stories about the house came pouring out.

"A number of ghost stories have been associated with the Myrtles. One of these concerns an infant, who, throughout the night, cries in its former death chamber. Another is that of an old French lady who wanders, sometimes at night, from room to room, lifting mosquito *biers*, and searching, evidently, for some unknown person she never finds."

The mention of mosquito *biers* is very interesting. These were nets, or drapes, made of gauze or cotton, that hung over the beds like a tent to keep mosquitoes out while people slept. They were done away with by the early 1900s, when the yellow fever epidemic came to an end in Louisiana. Someone witnessing the ghost of a woman peering beneath mosquito *biers* was seeing something that happened before 1905, when the last epidemic was reported.

So, the stories had begun before 1950, when Marjorie Munson of Oklahoma, buys the notorious plantation, and the tales of unexplained phenomenon begin to find their way into print.

Chapter Nine
The Myrtles and the Twentieth Century

1950s LA Tourism Brochure

Marjorie Munson

In 1950, a wealthy widow, who had made her money in chicken farming, came to the Myrtles, by way of Oklahoma. Her name was Marjorie Sawyer Munson. In December, in 1953, Ms. Munson purchased the Myrtles Plantation for $40,000. She immediately began to notice that her new home came as a package deal—it included

175

unexplainable sounds, smells, objects moving, and a few apparitions that were, quite frankly, unnerving. She also reported hearing her name called on several occasions by different voices; both male and female. It was with Ms. Munson, that the story of a turbaned black woman roaming the property first began to be spread with aplomb. Worried that her beautiful plantation was haunted, she began to ask neighbors if they had heard of any stories of the unsavory variety concerning the Myrtles.

Neighboring plantation owners, and some people from St. Francisville, related to her the story of a young slave girl who supposedly poisoned the birthday cake she had made for the Woodruff children back in early 1820s. The girl was named Chloe and she wore a green turban on her head. This is now 130-years later, but neighboring plantations had heard about the legend. It is hard to believe that at least some portion of the story of Chloe was not based in fact, if it was still being repeated over a hundred years later.

Mrs. Munson began to wonder if the turbaned ghost she had been seeing at her plantation home might be this "Chloe." The problem was, the stories of the ghost she was hearing about were those of a young girl. Ms. Munson was being haunted by a much older-looking woman, somewhat homely, with a square jaw and thick frame. She had already seen the ghost on countless occasions, walking the hallways of her home as if it owned the place. How many other owners at the Myrtles had seen it?

Lucile Lawrason, the granddaughter of Harrison and Fannie Williams, remembered her aunts used to talk about the ghost of an older woman, who haunted the Myrtles, and who wore a green bonnet. It became a family tale, told with nervous laughter, and handed off as a joke, possibly to deflect criticism from outsiders, or from being labeled "crazy." Ms. Lawrason also confirmed that Fannie's brother Eddie Haralson, who lived in a small house on the place, was killed while being robbed.

With this information, Ms. Munson set out to search the archives of any historical society or library she could get her hands on; trying to find the answer to the mystery of the woman who was haunting her property. She spent 16 years of her life looking into the history of her home. One sincerely doubts that someone would put in that kind of time, unless they had witnessed things happening around them and were determined to find out the cause—and to give it a name. Her research also gave her invaluable historic information about the house and grounds she now called home.

Marjorie Munson was an artist and owned an antique shop. She also had a gift for music, and her obsession with the ghost in the green turban led her to pen a song about her. She went in search of someone to set the lyrics to music, and met Delor Michaud.

Delor Michaud was a violinist and composer from Hollywood, California. Ms. Munson approached him with her "haunting" lyrics and asked him to compose the music for them. During this collaboration, love bloomed, and Marjorie Munson became Mrs. Delor Michaud. Delor moved to the Myrtles and together the couple began to restore the mansion. The room that had been called the Gentleman's Parlor for over a hundred years, was now christened the Music Room. A Steinway piano was set up, along with a collection of 12 violins dating back to the 17th century. A cello and several small harps were also placed about the room.

In 1955, the Michaud's opened their doors to tourists and to those responding to invitations to opulent music recitals held at the Myrtles Plantation. For the first time, the home was offered to the public, instead of solely acting as a private residence. It was also the end of the planter and slave; an era that literally built the Louisiana southland before oil, lumber, and petrochemicals took over.

The Gentleman's Parlor was not the only room to be showcased in a cultural way. Mrs. Michaud filled the Ladies' Parlor with her collection of Carnival Glass and china, which was part of her antique shop offerings. The two parlors and the dining room windows were encased in lively floral curtains with oblong valances.

Carnival glass that comes in over 2,000 patterns with vivid colors.

The Ladies' Parlor featured a long table in the center of the room, draped in a lace cloth and filled with items that Ms. Michaud collected. The mantel top, side tables, and small serving tables were crowded with knick-knacks from another era. A large, high-backed couch dominated the wall between the east-facing windows, flanked by matching tables with Ming Vase lamps, dating back to 1644. An Italian Bombay chest, from the mid-1700s, was also on display, along with a portrait by John Hooper, who was the court artist for George III.

It may have been at this time that the carriage house was turned into an antique store and gift shop. The subsequent owner, John Lambert Pearce, was using it as such while living at the plantation.

The décor was repeated in the Gentlemen's Parlor with a highbacked couch anchored on both sides by matching end tables and Ming Vase lamps. Mrs. Michaud's own artwork was seen hanging throughout the home. It was truly a cultural time during the 1950s and '60s, when the plantation was host to both music and art. The couple lovingly cared for the home well into their nineties before retiring in California, where they died.

During her stay at the Myrtles Plantation, Mrs. Michaud repeatedly told people of seeing a beautiful lady in a black gown, wearing a headpiece with a veil. She called her the "French Lady" and said she would go from room to room as though looking for something. Perhaps, this was the same ghost that Surget and Jessie Williams reported seeing searching the rooms and peeking beneath mosquito *biers*. The ghost was also seen repeatedly on the main staircase where she would stand and look longingly at the French doors in the main entry, as though awaiting someone's arrival.

There were several widows at the Myrtles Plantation over the years, and each would have worn black and a veil for a period of time. Why Mrs. Michaud nicknamed the woman the "French Lady," could not be ascertained. Perhaps, the period of dress was of a French influence. Unless the ghost spoke to her in an affected accent, there would be nothing to give away a person's nationality, especially that of an apparition. Sarah Winters was a widow in the house, as well as Elizabeth Bradford, Mary Cobb Sterling, and most recently, Fannie Williams. Could the lady in black, a sheer veil flowing from her headpiece, be the ghost of one of these women? Of them, only Sarah lost her husband to murder.

Until her death, Marjorie Munson Michaud stuck by her story that a large, African-American woman, wearing a long dress with a white apron, and sporting a green turban, or "bonnet," frequented her home. She never felt threatened by the ghosts, or the noises of doors banging shut, or that of a horse's hooves thundering up the driveway, when no horse was in sight. She became used to hearing her name called, and would simply smile and say "Hello" back to the unseen guest. Without rancor, she would rearrange her carefully displayed antiques that unseen hands had set askew in the night, while she and Delor slumbered. Nothing was ever broken and she appreciated that. The black cats that began appearing on the property were welcome, as long as they stayed outside. All-in-all, it became a home where a mutual respect was established between the living and the departed, and there was room for all to share the Myrtles Plantation.

Chapter Ten
The Restoration of the Myrtles Plantation

Arlin Dease, and Mr. and Mrs. Robert F. Ward

Mrs. Hilda Bird Toups Williams bought the Myrtles from the Michaud's, and owned it for a brief period in the 1970s, before selling it to Mr. and Mrs. Robert F. Ward, and Arlin Dease, for a reported $146,845.69. A massive restoration of the plantation began, culminating in a nod from the National Register of Historic Places.

The Author was very fortunate to have the opportunity to interview Arlin Dease, who, along with his partner, Stephen Saunders, did so much to restore the plantation home to its former glory. Here are Mr. Dease's words concerning his time at the Myrtles Plantation:

Arlin Dease

"My name is Arlin Dease, and I am a resident of Baton Rouge, Louisiana, and a native of Mississippi, but I have lived in Louisiana since the age of 10. The Myrtles Plantation in St. Francisville was the first renovation I did. I had started a small construction company building residential homes and I was told that the Myrtles Plantation was going up for a Sheriff's sale. I approached the lady that was occupying the house and about to lose it, and with her permission, I checked with the bank and stopped the Sheriff's sale. I was designing and building a house for Bob and Mary Ward in Baton Rouge, so I had the money to purchase the home, but I didn't have the money for the purchase *and* the restoration. So, between me, Bob and Mary Ward, we made a 50/50 purchase of the house and 12.5 acres. The first goal was certainly to restore the house, place it on the National Register, and get it income-producing.

"At that time, it was 1973. There were many Louisiana homes needing extensive renovations. The Myrtles was in desperate, dire need of foundation work, and the fundamental plaster work that the house is so noted for. Huge pieces of that had completely fallen and had been sitting like that for decades. The front façade of the house—the front wall—had completely slipped off the supporting beam. Actually, in the double parlors, the mirror image parlors, you could stand on one side of the parlor and actually look through an 8" gap at the bottom next to where the baseboards were and see the person on the other side through the cracks. The front wall had separated from the house completely.

"We had to do extensive work on the research in order to place the house on the National Register. In 1973, the State of Louisiana did not have a department designated for just helping an owner of an historic house, or even a museum; a department of preservation just did not exist. The first person that was hired for that position was Jonathan Fricker. Jonathan Fricker was very, very helpful in giving us the information for placing the Myrtles on the National Register. But that is a huge task!

"My great friend and partner, Stephen Mark Saunders, was the curator for the Wards and I. We hired him to research the property, the period furnishings, and everything needed to place the house on the National Register. He did an excellent job, spending days in the court house here in West Feliciana, researching, and going back as far as the Spanish Land Grants, which each owner of the plantation had. He looked up birth and death certificates of each of the occupants of the house. This was the most important aspect of the Myrtles Plantation, because the research was almost non-existent.

"Steve did an unbelievable job. He never received an award for his accomplishments and all of the wonderful things he did. He was an Art History major at New York University. He lived in the borough of Queens, New York City, and he was a foreman in the Navy. Once leaving the Navy, he became the curator for the Myrtles Plantation and the Mount Hope Plantation, and the major restoration that was started in 1980 of Nottoway Plantation, in White Castle, Louisiana.

(Note: On June 18, 2012, Stephen M. Saunders was posthumously issued a certificate of recognition from the Office of Historic Preservation for the State of Louisiana for his research and efforts that culminated in the Myrtles Plantation becoming recognized on the National Register of Historic Places. Thank you so much to Nicole Hobson-Morris, Executive Director of that office, for all her efforts to bring this to pass. The Author)

"Through the guidance and use of professional craftsmen, the house was rewired, and air-conditioning was placed in so that the walls would not sweat," Mr. Dease continued. "It had a dehumidifier in the system, very similar to those that are placed in first class museums. This was almost unheard-of restoration work in the early 1970s. This was due to a very good engineering firm I had hired, Walker Heating and Air. They did an excellent job. That pretty well stabilized the house as far as moisture is concerned.

"Stephen and I built a small kitchenette in the back room behind the French Room. This was originally the Stirling Suite and the area where we built the little kitchen was a sitting room. When we entered that room originally, it was in bad shape. The Michaud's had not used it, and large chunks of plaster had fallen from the ceiling. Those rooms are underneath the large troughs that take the water off the roof, and the water damage was extensive in the bedroom, sitting room, and in the French Room. We found a wonderful artist in his middle 70s, Carl Dean of Dean and Associates in Baton Rouge, and he worked with us on it."

Stephen Saunders, who was so instrumental in the repairs and restoration of the plantation at this time, wrote the following details:

"The primary objective was to strengthen and reinforce the foundation of the main dwelling. This was accomplished by repairing some of the original brick columns which supported the house, as well as the addition of more brick columns being constructed, utilizing a similar old brick, so as not to detract from the integrity of the original foundation.

"Plaster walls and ceilings were carefully repaired. To replace missing sections of the cove molding, wooden "mules" were patterned after the plaster and were run by hand. (A mule is the old name for a tool, which was made of wood, cut into the design with which the artisan would shape the desired type of molding.) Missing segments of the elaborate open-pierced work molding were carefully hand cast in rubber molds and inserted into place by a skilled artisan, so the plaster molding throughout the Myrtles has been restored to its original condition.

"The original cypress floors were cleaned by light sanding, the patina restored with a mixture of oil, cornstarch, and sawdust saved from the shavings."

Arlin Dease continued to elaborate on the restoration processes undertaken at this time:

"The faux finishing work is of granite and marbleized baseboards and it is one of the finest examples of faux finishing in Louisiana. The faux work on the grand staircase in the center hall is all original. The glass in the French doors is absolutely original, and it's made of stained, as well as etched glass, and it is stunningly beautiful. The chandelier that hangs in the main center hall is of extreme quality.

"I have examined the chandelier and it is made of tole, a metal alloy, that may look like iron but it isn't. It is a wonderful example of early American lighting. It was lighter and easier to work with. Fireplace screens were made of tole, as it didn't conduct the heat as much, which was preferable back then when a lady's makeup was made of wax and could melt and run. Prior to electricity being introduced into the home, all the lighting was either "chandeliers" or oil lighting. The house never had any evidence of gas. The gasolier in the Game Room was never run on gas. It dates to the 1880s.

"I put all the statues on the ground in 1972, and they are of cast stone, not concrete. My mother got on a plane and we went to Miami where there was an importer of Italian statuary. We hired a U-Haul truck and drove back to the Myrtles, and arrived back there about 4 o'clock in the morning, and found every light in the house on. I pulled up, and Steve and Charles Celestine said, "We knew you were driving all the way back, because you didn't call us and let us you know you were stopping. So, we thought we would welcome you home." So, I had a U-Haul filled with statuary that we placed around the property.

One of many statues on the Myrtles Plantation grounds.

"We put in the maze in front of the house in 1972. We also built the *garçonnéirre* out front. I designed it. The windows are leaded windows that came out of an antique shop that Steve and I owned, and there is something very unique about the *garçonnéirre*. Even though it was built in 1973, there was a lightning rod built on top with a blue milk glass ball, and it's still there. The reason you would have lightning rods on your house, and have this glass ball, was not for decorative use at all. If lightning was to strike the lightning rod, then it would break the glass ball, alerting the owner that lightning had struck and you needed to check your cables and things. You can drive up to the Myrtles and still see the blue ball.

The maze at the Myrtles Plantation

"During this time, we would serve the tour buses coming through on the back gallery, with a cold plate of stuffed tomato and chicken salad. We didn't need a commercial kitchen for that and it worked very well. The Wards were never in favor of opening a restaurant on the property, which was something I would have liked to have done.

"We sold it to John L. Pearce, whose father owned Mt. Hope Plantation," Arlin Dease told me, "so for my share of the equity of the Myrtles, I took the Mount Hope Plantation, and 4 ½ acres, and $50,000 in cash, and that was my portion of equity. Bob and Mary Ward financed their part to John L. Pearce. Then John L. sold it to Frances Kermeen-Meyers. John L. bought the house back later and sold it to Mark Sowers."

"When you have ownership of a piece of property that is historical in nature, and you are placing it on tour, and you are talking about spirits of the past, you have many, many, many Doubting Thomases," Mr. Dease told me. "So, living in the Myrtles, there were many things...feelings, that were unexplainable. To tell you right now, this happened on this day, there are many hair raising experiences, not just in the day, not just in the night, has nothing to do with the full moon, has nothing to do with Friday the 13th, or any of these things we may think of as spiritual or magical nights of Halloween. It's there all the time.

"One day there were two couples, and the two ladies, walked in to go on the tour of the Myrtles. The men were in the car and I approached them to welcome them to the Myrtles, and all. One gentleman turned to me and said, "This really is just a crock of s**t...all these haunted houses, right?" I was a little defensive because I always felt the historic value of the Myrtles far outweighs the spirits of the house. *The Ghost Hunters* and all these shows have become very popular now. So, I looked at the man and said, "Have you ever been in a large stadium, like at a football game, and you are concentrating on the game, but for some unknown reason you had a feeling that you should turn around. And you turned around, and five or six rows above you, you see someone looking down at you and waving, and saying 'Hey...Hey!' I said, 'Has that ever happened to you?' 'Well, yes," he said. I said, 'You know you couldn't see that person, you couldn't hear that person...only thing is, you could sense a presence. And that's what you sense inside the Myrtles, 24 hours a day, 7 days a week...a feeling of never, never ever quite being alone.'

Arlin paused and said to me, "That sums up the whole deal, right there, Honey."

I asked Mr. Dease about the segment I saw on *Unsolved Mysteries,* where he is depicted as a young man riding a lawn mower and comes around the corner of a tree, and stops. There before him is a "vision" of an elderly gentleman in overalls and a bent straw hat. The vision stands there looking at him for a moment and then fades from view.

"Did that happen the way they said it did on the show?" I asked Mr. Dease.

"Oh yes, it was truly something you never forget."

Arlin Dease is a multi-faceted entrepreneur, craftsman, and successful venue owner. He now owns and operates Hemingbough, a breathtakingly beautiful plantation, dedicated to the arts and wellbeing, only a few minutes down the road from the Myrtles. The acreage is absolutely stunning, and he is known for his Easter Sunrise Services and opulent weddings. If you are in the Saint Francisville area, you must ask to see the grounds, or book a room there.

The Concert Hall at Hemingbough Platation

My eternal thanks to Arlin Diese for all the time he gave me. The Myrtles Plantation would not be what it is today without the expertise, skill, and care he and Stephen Saunders proffered it. And without Mr. Saunders help, it may not have made it onto the National Register of Historic Places.

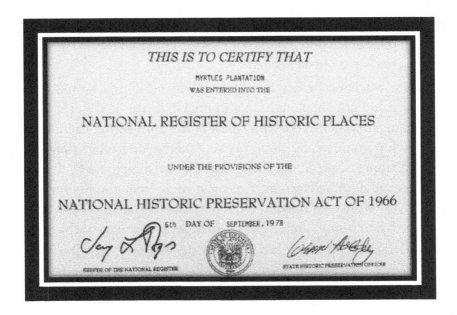

THIS IS TO CERTIFY THAT

MYRTLES PLANTATION
WAS ENTERED INTO THE

NATIONAL REGISTER OF HISTORIC PLACES

UNDER THE PROVISIONS OF THE

NATIONAL HISTORIC PRESERVATION ACT OF 1966

6th DAY OF SEPTEMBER, 1978

KEEPER OF THE NATIONAL REGISTER   STATE HISTORIC PRESERVATION OFFICER

John Lambert Pearce

John Lambert Pearce, "John L," as he is called by most who know him, purchased the Myrtles Plantation, in 1977. Arlin Dease, and Mr. and Mrs. Roberts, had put the plantation up for sale for $350,000. The price included an almost 7,000-squarefoot house, 10.25 acres of land, and a 1 ½ acre pond. Mr. Pearce was the former curator at Mount Hope Plantation, in Baton Rouge. John L.'s melodic southern accent and soft gentility reminded all who met him of the romantic era of the antebellum period, and a by-gone feeling of civility and hospitality.

Mr. Pearce owned the plantation for three years and enjoyed offering it to the public for historic tours, and even taking in overnight guests as a bed and breakfast. He took over the French Room on the main floor, and allowed the guests the use of the main suite upstairs, that is today called the Woodruff Suite. The Michaud's had put in a private bath in the sitting area of that room and it worked well as a suite for the paying public. One other room in the upstairs older wing had been remodeled and a bathroom added in the gallery. These two rooms were rented out as needed.

As Mrs. Michaud before him, John L. loved antiques, and ran a small store and gift shop out of the original carriage house. He loved entertaining, and the Myrtles was usually host to visiting friends and family, who would enjoy his proffered sherry, and other libations, along with quiet conversation. The Saturday evening tours were often done by candlelight, returning the guest to another time before the rude glare of electricity flooded the rooms and the senses. Daily tours were also offered sporadically, as curious people arrived at the door.

It was during Mr. Pearce's reign at the Myrtles, that the ghost stories were squelched, at least within his hearing. He played up the plantation's historic wealth while downplaying the reports of other-worldly phenomenon. Some have said that he would become outwardly nervous when asked about the legends surrounding the home's ancient past. At other times, such questions were waved away, as though swatting at annoying flies. Guests would arrive, eager to hear the stories, and were welcomed by Mr. Pearce himself, bowing them into the house, as his soft cadence soothed their nerves. At other times, a maid, clad in a crisp uniform with apron and cap, opened the door and smilingly admitted them into the entryway, where they waited beneath the 300-pound Baccarat crystal chandelier. Outside, statuary played among the bushes of the plantation, as the Spanish moss caught a passing breeze and rode along as far as its tether would allow. Humidity laced the ancient windows with a sticky frosting in the summer months, as fireflies darted in and out of the Myrtle trees like a fiber optic side show. Some things at the plantation have not changed at all.

John L. Pearce finally put the Myrtles up for sale, in 1980. The sound of children running through its hallways had not been heard in a long time. The past three owners had no children at the plantation, unless they were visiting…or had never left.

Frances Kermeen and Jim Meyers

Frances Kermeen was on her way back from a trip to Haiti with her boyfriend, Jim Meyers, when a couple they had met on the trip diverted their plans and asked them to join them in New Orleans, instead of returning to their home in San Jose, California. Frances and Jim agreed, and ended up touring the plantation country, after their friends returned to the west coast.

Ms. Kermeen had made a good reputation for herself back in California for her skill in renovating old homes to their original glory. She also had a love of the South, which came from her father's side of the family, who were from Hammond, Louisiana. Her love of antiquity came from her maternal grandfather who was a world-known authority on Victorian architecture. He actually designed Main Street in Disneyland and was art director for numerous movies and television shows. Glancing about at the run-down mansions of New Orleans, and antiquated plantations between the Crescent City and Natchez, whetted her appetite to follow a life-long dream…to open an Inn in the South. After spending the night at a couple of plantations, Frances and Jim arrived in St. Francisville, and on an impulse, stopped in at Audubon Reality to see what was on the market. After the agent showed them several homes in the area, Frances asked what she had that was "older and bigger." As it turned out, the listing for the Myrtles had just come on the market. Frances remembered seeing the plantation from an earlier trip she had taken with her father, when they sailed up the Mississippi River on the *Mississippi Queen*, stopping along the route from New Orleans to Vicksburg, to view the plantations. She had loved the different façade of the Myrtles. It stood out from the cookie-cutter Greek Revival mansions that dotted the hillsides of Planation Country, with its white clapboard and aqua-colored shutters and elaborate grillwork railings.

The appointment was made, and Frances and Jim approached the Myrtles with awe, as the agent's car made its way up the winding driveway. Jim commented it looked like the haunted mansion at Disneyland, mainly due to the color and grillwork. They were met at the door by John L. Pearce, who graciously showed them through the house and proffered his preferred glass of sherry. Frances fell in love with the home immediately, and her mind went into overdrive on how she could decorate the unfinished rooms upstairs and turn the mansion into a working bed and breakfast.

According to Ms. Kermeen, she talked her boyfriend Jim into buying the plantation with her, though the money for the purchase was from her bank account. There was a hitch. The belief that a couple should be married if cohabitating was alive and well in the South, especially if one was going to take over an historical place like the Myrtles Plantation. So, Frances Kermeen became Frances Kermeen-Meyers, and after the paperwork went through, she moved into the plantation properly.

Ghosts at the Myrtles Make an Appearance

Frances spent several days there alone with John L., as the slow grinding process of transferring titles took place. During that time, she reports a plethora of supernatural activity, including hearing voices, smelling perfume, having her name called, lights turning off and on, footsteps outside her bedroom door, cupboard doors banging shut in the kitchen, pots and pans being tossed about, doorknobs rattling, a phantom wheelchair in the parking lot (that came crashing up to the fence), clocks ticking (that had been silent for years), a naked Indian girl ghost at the pond, the sounds of parties (when no one was around), and being locked into her room, where the door and windows refused to let her out. Ms. Meyers also reported seeing the apparition of a slave girl with a green turban standing over her, holding a lit candle, as she slept on a couch. Jim had returned to California to settle things there, and Ms. Meyers dealt with the ghosts, and John L. Pearce's refusal to talk about them, on her own.

During her 10-year ownership of the Myrtles Plantation, Ms. Meyers did many things to improve the property. According to her accounts, she removed a plastered-over door that connected the main bedroom suite (now known as the Woodruff Suite) to the adjoining sitting room, once again making it one unit. She turned several rooms in the old wing into guest suites by putting up dividing walls and installing bathrooms so that each room had its own. With full enthusiasm, she dove into decorating each room, putting up period-style wallpaper and painting the walls to match. She and a friend searched out authentic antiques to turn each room into a themed perfection. From draperies to knickknacks, four poster beds to rugs, she worked day and night to prepare her Inn for guests.

When Jim Meyers finally joined her at the Myrtles, they launched into turning the carriage house, which had been used as an antique shop and gift store, into a Victorian tavern which they named "Spirits." They also determined, that more rooms could be added on the property that would allow handicap access to guests who could not navigate the steep staircases. Four suites, complete with private baths, were added behind the carriage house, and given the numbers 1-4. Teeta and John Moss later bought the plantation and changed the numbers of the rooms to the names of the many beautiful flowers that grace the property: Azalea, Camellia, Magnolia and Oleander. They were later nicknamed *"The Garden Rooms."

* Today, the Garden Rooms are located next to Restaurant 1796 on the grounds and offer six guest rooms with names befitting the South: The Amelia, the Octavia, the Bordeaux, the Carondolet, the LaSalle, and the Prytania Garden Rooms.

Previous entrance to the Garden Rooms at the Myrtles Plantation

At this time, the Meyers also cleaned up the pond area, and put in a blue bridge, in honor of Monet's famous painting, and installed a Gazebo on the small island in the middle of the pond. Towering cypress trees border the island while a lone statue of a cherub waits at the entrance to the Gazebo.

Cypress Knees in the Myrtles Plantation pond.
Photo courtesy of Amanda Folce DeVille.

Bridge and Gazebo at the Myrtles Plantation

Close-up of Gazebo with cherub statue

Mark Sowers

Mark Sowers bought the Myrtles Plantation in 1990, with eccentric dreams of resurrecting the plantation planter's lifestyle. He owned it for a year only, and his vision of reviving the long ago past was never realized.

Mr. Sowers finally called Arlin Dease and asked if he would be interested in purchasing the Myrtles. Mr. Dease said, "Mark, I will be there in ten minutes!"

Arlin Dease

"In 1991, I bought the Myrtles back, twelve years after selling it the first time," Mr. Dease told this Author, during an extended interview. "I bought it for less money than I sold it for the first time. We signed the papers at noon that day, and a van pulled up and loaded up Mr. Sower's things. They were loading things out the back door as tours were coming in the front door," Mr. Dease said, laughing softly. "There was a large group of construction men there on the site that I had hired, and I told them, 'Men, come back after lunch, and we are going to start knocking out walls to build a restaurant in the carriage house. So, the restaurant was put in.

"I brought the Coco House onto the property, and the Mosses later moved it to where it is now. The Mosses also put in the Caretaker's Cottage. At this time, we restored the bridge and gazebo at the pond, that needed repair. We also added the gates and picket fence up front by the *garçonniérre*.

The Coco House guest cottage at the Myrtles Plantation.
Photo courtesy of Morgan Moss.

The Caretaker's Cottage at the Myrtles.
Photo courtesy of Amanda Folce DeVille.

Garçonniérre/pigeonnaire at the Myrtles.
Photo courtesy of Amanda Folce DeVille.

During this point in the interview, I asked Mr. Dease about the floor in the upper section of the main house, where the foyer is outside the William Winter Suite.

"I noticed when I was walking along this floor, next to the back staircase, that you can feel the floor sloping down toward the Winter Suite. Have you noticed that?" I asked Mr. Dease.

"I did, and that is a puzzle," he answered. "If you walk up the back staircase the floor really looks like it has bowed and settled. That floor is directly above the double parlors downstairs and their ceilings are perfectly level. They do not slope down at all. I have no idea what happened there."

"Another interesting thing is about the plaster frieze work at the Myrtles," he continued. "It is exactly like the pierced frieze work that adorned the ballroom on the third floor at Afton Villa before it burned down. The same plasterer that did Afton Villa at that time also did the Myrtles. The medallions at the top of the chandeliers in the Myrtles' parlors are exactly like the ones shown in pictures of Afton Villa, in such books as *Ghosts Along the Mississippi*. An artisan would come into towns like Natchez, and have molds for a medallion motif, and do it over and over again.

"As for the faux finishes on the fireplaces and baseboards, Steve and I repaired the faux finishes over a weekend. We did the fireplaces in the Game Room, the marble baseboards, and the ones in what is now the Bradford Suite. Steve took denatured alcohol and cleaned them, and we painted them, and added varnish. You have to remember, those fireplaces were made of slate, and when slate gets hot, the paint runs or flakes off. Back then, they used coal in the fireplaces instead of wood because it would burn all night without burning down the house. We copied the baseboard in the Game Room to reconstruct the finish on the fireplace in that room. We went to Harrison Paint Company in Baton Rouge, and we bought little tubes of Benjamin Moore paints, and did the faux finishes on the fireplaces. I remember we did a lot with yellow ochre. No one was doing faux finishes in 1972, and all the fancy paints they have today were not available. We were told faux painting was a lost art. But we did it," he told me with pride.

The faux painting in the Game Room is especially amazing. To be able to emulate the work of French Old-World craftsmen is no small feat. Mr. Dease and Mr. Saunders sincerely did the Myrtles Plantation proud!

Main entrance sign to the Myrtles Plantation.
Photo courtesy of Amanda Folce DeVille.

Chapter Eleven

Today's Myrtles Plantation

The Myrtles Plantation.
Photo courtesy of Amanda Folce DeVille

John, Teeta, JG and Morgan Moss

On December 18, 1992, John and Teeta Moss moved into the Myrtles Plantation, only two weeks after arriving in the St. Francisville area. The plantation was a Christmas gift from John to Teeta. Both had ties to the area: John Moss' grandfather, Boyce Middleton, was the nephew of Lt. General Troy Houston Middleton, the namesake for the Middleton Library at LSU, and Teeta had relatives in the area, some of whom were directly tied to the plantation.

Teeta Moss is an amazing woman. I had the pleasure of getting to know her while researching this book. She is a devoted wife and mother, often putting her schedule on hold, as she tours the country following her son's racing career. Her affection for her staff at the Myrtles is palpable and they adore her. There is no feeling of owner/employee here. They work together as one to insure the historic integrity of the plantation, as well as its maintenance. Each guest is welcomed, as one would be invited into a private home.

Mrs. Moss' face would light up when talking to me, as she described her vocation as a teacher. Teeta spent the next ten years teaching students grades 9-12 English, Journalism, and Speech in high school. Politics was also in her resume; she took a sabbatical in 1984 to work for a year on the 1984 President Reagan/Bush campaign in Louisiana and Washington, DC.

"While I loved working on the seminars and campaigns, I began to get restless and I missed my home," Mrs. Moss told me. "A Cajun has to have a gumbo pot! I was tired of hotels."

It was at this time, the school board asked her to work with them on a new program. They were looking for teachers to go into hospitals and work with in-patient children. Teeta spent the next ten years working with hospitalized children in Baton Rouge, Louisiana.

"I learned so much about how to teach while working with these children one-on-one in a hospital setting," she told me, her eyes filling with gratitude and tenderness. "They were from four-to-eighteen-years of age. Those were amazing years for me!"

We talked about the transition to "Innkeeper" and she smiles. Her love and careful attitude about the plantation are obvious.

"We have to walk a tight line about the history—architectural history and folklore here. This is now on the National Historic Register and there are rules about what you can, and can't, put out there concerning a landmark!"

Teeta went on to say that they "meet people from all over the world! It's amazing. We lost the tour bus business after Katrina. It used to bring people from St. Louis, Memphis, Natchez and New Orleans, as Jazz touring buses would come by. The international tourism was also a boon for us. People from France loved to visit New Orleans and the area, due to the French heritage here. Business people from all over the world would fly into New Orleans, and while they attended to corporate matters, their wives and children would go sight-seeing. We called them 'Spouse Tours.' Then 911 hit, and international travel took a nose dive. No one wanted to be flying. We saw a steady decline in the touring business. When Katrina hit, it was pretty much the final nail in the coffin. Today, it is a different kind of traveler. The FITs (Family of Individual Travelers, not those with a group) make up a large demographic of people we see here. The buses are slowly returning, not so much internationally, but from tourists in the United States. It's wonderful to meet such diverse groups and hear their stories."

I broached the subject of the ghosts at the plantation and her take on them.

"I don't think of them as ghosts," she said, in her slow relaxed way of speaking. "I prefer to call them Guardian Angels. I will tell you why in a moment. I didn't really believe the place was haunted when we bought it! By the time we found out, we had made a financial commitment, and it was too late to back out," she says, laughing lightly. "I was here only two days when someone started calling my name in my husband's voice. I started looking for him. I would ask the staff where he was, and they would say, "Oh Miss Teeta, Johnny went to the bank. He's not here." Then I would hear my name called in my friend Annie's voice, again when she was not here. It may be a way for the ghosts to contact you without frightening you; by using a familiar voice."

As far as her feeling that the resident ghosts are Guardian Angels, she explains why. When she and John were new homeowners at the Myrtles, the owner of an adjacent historic property forewarned the couple that the ghosts at the plantation "will let you know if you are welcome or not." The Mosses were the parents of two young children, at the time they moved into the Myrtles—a two-year-old and a ten-month-old. They were more concerned with physical dangers, such as the open cisterns and pond, rather than the reported hauntings.

"I started to get panicked about the fact that there's this huge open pond behind the house; there are a number of large tour buses arriving daily, where the drivers get out and often leave the diesel engines running; there are cars coming in and out all day— there were so many ways a child could get hurt."

"Guardian Angels" at the Myrtles

Shortly after they have moved into the plantation, Teeta's fears were confirmed. "I was in my office. My ten-month-old, Morgan, was napping, and his nanny was doing the laundry. The nanny had on a baby monitor so she could hear Morgan. All of a sudden, I had this urge that I just couldn't make go away...a foreboding feeling that something was wrong. Then I heard a voice—very deep, like Lauren Bacall's tone—saying, 'Go check the children.' I looked around and no one was there. I went back to finishing up something I was working on, and the voice came again, with a feeling of urgency..."Go check the children!" Finally, I turned off the computer, got up, and walked outside. I looked across the courtyard and there was Morgan about thirty feet from the pond.

"Morgan is only ten-and-a-half-months-old. He has only been walking for about three weeks, and somehow, he has gotten off a large antique bed, and walked across two rooms with enormous heavy doors, walked along a large verandah, and teetered another 50 yards to the pond. I checked later with his nanny, and checked her baby monitor, and found nothing wrong with it; yet she had heard nothing from the room or seen him walking around.

"When I looked over and saw Morgan heading towards the edge of the pond, I froze and began screaming for Nona, his nanny. Then suddenly, with visions of my son possibly drowning in the pond, my fears suddenly vanished. It was like a cape of warm velvet or velour. It was just real soft and comforting, like I was wrapped in something fuzzy. Nothing actually touched me. It was all sensation, but it felt so real. I heard the same voice I had heard earlier, saying, 'You will never have to worry—your children, your family—you will always be safe here.'

"After that I was never afraid to let my sons play on the grounds. We did put up a fence around the pond. The good Lord only helps if you help yourself."

Improvements to the Myrtles' Property

Teeta and John Moss have done much to improve the Myrtles Plantation property, as well as add antiques to the house.

"You have to remember," Teeta tells me in her soft southern drawl, "we lived upstairs in the house when we first moved here. We let the tours go through downstairs and rented out the garden rooms, but for us, this was our home!"

Her love is evident, as she rattles off the plethora of additions and improvements she and John have made to the historic plantation. We were seated at a wrought-iron table on the large brick patio when Teeta looked about her and paused, thinking back to the dreams she and her husband, and staff, implemented.

"This was not here," Teeta says, waving a hand to indicate the large 5,000-square-foot patio. "We wanted an antique brick patio with

French drains. French drains don't hold the water when it rains, so it drains below the surface. We heard about this man who did great work and invited him to come give us a bid. When he showed up, we were surprised to see this small, elderly man. My husband John gently mentioned his concern that the job and weight of the bricks might be a little much for the man. The elderly gentleman promptly dropped to the ground and starting doing push-ups! We gave him the job on the spot!" she says, laughing gleefully. "This is all antique brick," she continued with pride.

The extensive patio area at the Myrtles Plantation. The main house is to the rear of this photo. To your left is the location of the General's Gift Shop, and to the right, you will find Restaurant 1796.

There were many more improvements to the property under the Moss's tutelage. The window air-conditioning units in the mansion were taken out and central air and heating installed.

"*That* was expensive," Teeta says, laughing lightly. "We also replaced and repaired all the copper gutters along the roofline. We put in 4' wide copper gutters! As for the Carriage House Restaurant, we enlarged the kitchen, doubling it in size. The area where we're sitting now used to be a small courtyard with crepe myrtles and an arbor with Carolina jasmine. We created this 5,000 square-foot patio so guests could sit out here and enjoy their food. We took away the former office in the Carriage House and made it an entrance into the restaurant. Arlin Dease added the lovely sunroom in the restaurant; adding more seating and giving guests a choice of views.

"We bought an old slave shack and brought it to the property. It's the Caretaker's Cottage you see out behind the Gift Shop. That fence around it is 210-years-old. The cabin is now a guest suite.

Caretaker's Cottage with 210-year-old fence.

"Arlin Dease bought the house that sits on the back property behind the Garden Rooms. Its original position was over closer to the kitchen in the parking lot. We moved it to where it is today and named it the Coco House, after Mr. Coco, owner of the Coco Mill Works in Baton Rouge. The Overnight Manager used to stay there, but we have since turned it into a guest house that sleeps 10 people…in case a group of people want to stay together while visiting here.

"John and I upgraded all the electricity in the house. When you are renovating a two-hundred-year-old house, and a national landmark, you have a lot of red tape to go through to maintain its integrity. Many eyes are watching what you do," she says, laughing. "We have some great plans for this year," she went on happily. "We are in the planning stages right now for some exciting additions."

The Cottages

The "exciting additions" include the four Cottages named after popular trees located on the property: The Crepe Myrtle, Live Oak, Cypress, and Willow. These guest cottages are made of antique heart pine and cypress. While wrapping you in the rustic charm of the long-past southern plantation days, these rooms offer the modern amenities of a large sitting room with a sofa and farm table, as well as beds in different sizes, and a private bath. You can sit in the hand-hewn rocking chairs on the porch and watch for fireflies in the evening shadows. The pond, restaurant, and plantation house are only steps away.

A cottage guest house at the Myrtles Plantation.

One of the four of the guest cottages by the pond at the Myrtles.
Photo courtesy of Amanda Folce DeVille.

Restaurant 1796

There are few who enter Restaurant 1796 at the Myrtles Plantation, who leave unimpressed. Named for the year the Myrtles is thought to have been built, its inspiration came from owner Morgan Moss, who took over the helmsmanship of the property four years ago from his parents, Teeta and John Moss. It is hard to imagine that the building was ever the rustic location for a carriage house, with tack and saddles, andirons, and horse shoes dangling from the walls.

Today, this location shouts "Home is where the hearth is…"

Centered around a 10' wood-fired hearth, Restaurant 1796 prides itself on fresh Southern ingredients finished to perfection over the fire with a shared experience reminiscent of a family holiday gathering.

"If you haven't been to Restaurant 1796 yet, you're in for a unique treat," Morgan states. "In a reverent nod to the history of the property, most of our dishes have either passed through or somehow been touched by the hearth. Guests are encouraged to choose individual main proteins and then fill their table with small plates and shareables handcrafted from local, market fresh produce. We find the whole experience makes for engaging conversation and brings a relaxed atmosphere to fine dining, with enthusiastic waitstaff, an enviable wine list, and mouthwatering cocktails and desserts."

The exhibition-style kitchen is just the beginning of a dining experience designed to tantalize the senses. Savory aromas of wood-fired cuisine envelope this down-home atmosphere, only steps from the accommodations on the plantation grounds. Here, you can enjoy lunch or dinner on the patio beneath swaying moss, surrounded by the bird calls that inspired James Audubon to paint his famous pieces in the area. Our overnight guests are invited to breakfast here. Flowering shrubs, lazy days, and southern hospitality are at its best. And while we are known as one of the most-haunted homes in America, the "spirits" offered in Restaurant 1796 are of the cocktail variety. A friendly game of bocce ball invites you to linger and make a day of it.

In the Spring of 2017, the existing restaurant called the Carriage House, caught fire and was damaged beyond repair. With an eye to the future, the Moss family designed a new project—one that included an Acadian-style restaurant, six Louisiana-inspired guest rooms, a courtyard, and a nine-acre kitchen garden.

But wait! There's more!

Also, on the drawing board is a walking trail through a future orchard and produce farm. This will enable the plantation to supply the restaurant with fresh fruits, vegetables, and herbs grown right there on the grounds. You can't get fresher food to the table than that. Surplus produce can also be sold in farmers markets and other venues.

"We see this as a big win-win," Morgan Moss says. "We can have access to great produce, and our partner farmer can ride the marketing wave of what we're doing here. Most importantly, our guests will really be having another fun, interactive thing to do on the property."

(My thanks to 225 Magazine for excerpts of their article published in the November 2018 issue.)

Whether you are an overnight guest or just here for the food, tours, or grounds, welcome back to the Myrtles Plantation!

The Myrtles Plantation is open Tuesdays through Saturdays from 11:00 to 2:00 for lunch and from 5:00-9:00 for dinner, with Sunday lunch from 11:00-3:00. We can't wait to welcome you!

Morgan Moss--owner

Main Dining Room of Restaurant 1796 at the Myrtles Plantation.
Photo Courtesy of Amanda Folce DeVille

One of the chefs cooking at hearthside in
Restaurant 1796 at the Myrtles Plantation.
Photo courtesy of Amanda Folce DeVille.

Wall of firewood inside Restaurant 1796 at the Myrtles Plantation.
Photo courtesy of Amanda Folce DeVille.

Smoke in the Night

Myrtles Plantation Fire August 7, 2014.
Photo courtesy of The Advocate

The Advocate. August 7,2014

"Jules Haigler was just finishing dinner with friends at The Carriage House Restaurant, across a small courtyard from the main house at The Myrtles Plantation, on Wednesday evening, when a guest ran in screaming that the house was on fire.

"Haigler, house docent at The Myrtles Plantation, ran outside and saw smoke coming from the roof of the building. It wasn't from the main plantation house but instead from the building just feet away used as the gift shop, laundry facilities, plantation offices and guest breakfast spot.

"As someone called the Fire Department, The Myrtles Plantation staff made sure all of the guests were safely out of the main building.

It was about 8 p.m., and for the next two hours, little could be done as the staff watched as the oldest building on the property burned.

"However, with only about 10 feet separating the smaller building, the firefighters did an amazing job of putting a barrier between the two structures, and by Thursday morning, there wasn't even a scorch mark on the main house.

"Firefighters from St. Francisville Fire Department, West Feliciana Fire Protection District No. 1, and the Zachary Fire Department, responded to fight the fire for about two hours and remained several more hours to make sure all the hot spots were extinguished.

"What has been referred to as the "gift shop" at the plantation has much more historical significance than just selling postcards. The burned building was the original home of Gen. David Bradford and his family while The Myrtles Plantation main house was being built until it was complete in 1796.

"Although there was substantial damage, the most severe damage appears to be in an extension of the building constructed in 2008. Most of the original structure, which is celebrating its 220th birthday this year, is solid."

Beauty Comes to the Myrtles

On July 3, 2015, The Miss USA contestants decided to pay a visit to the Myrtles Plantation. Several of the famous pageant's ladies toured the home, posed for photos, and added their own feminine charm to a property already known for its beauty.

Miss USA contestants at the Myrtles Plantation.
Photos courtesy of Chelsey Blankenship,
The Advocate July 3, 2015

Miss USA contestants at the Myrtles Plantation.
Photos courtesy of Chelsey Blankenship,
The Advocate July 3, 2015

Chapter Twelve

The Journey to Today's Myrtles Plantation

Driveway to the Myrtles Plantation.
Photo courtesy of Jason Phillips Reeser

The Old Woodville Road, marred and rutted from the passage of beating horse hooves and wheeled carriages, was a major artery leading from St. Francisville, Louisiana to Woodville, Mississippi, in the mid-1790s, long before Bayou Sara was obliterated by flood waters. Confederate and Union soldiers picked their way along her dusty, winding curves in search of the enemy, or sanctuary. The American and French Revolutions, the War of 1812, and the Seven

Years War, left their impression as well, stamping into the terrain their infamous mark on history. Riverboats, barges, warships, and pirate vessels, traversed the mighty Mississippi, a mere two miles away, their passengers finding their way ashore and ultimately to Old Woodville Road. From here, they invaded the unsuspecting homes that had been built during the opulent period when Louisiana cotton, sugar and indigo "plantation kings" held sway. French and Spanish royalty manipulated, battled, and bargained over the precious swampland that was Louisiana, finally tossing her to the fledgling territory that was to become the United States of America, thanks to a small document called the Louisiana Purchase.

These tumultuous transitions played out beneath the watchful eye of a modest plantation sitting just a few feet off "Old Woodville;" a home that was to make its own mark in Louisiana history and the world's, when it became known as the "Most-Haunted Home in America."

Today, the name "Old Woodville Road" has fallen beneath the state highway system's nomenclature. 7747 U.S. Highway 61 North, in St. Francisville, Louisiana, is the current address given to a beautiful 220-year-old plantation that still stands facing east toward the main road, just as David Bradford designed it. The rutted thoroughfare is now a paved highway, but its layers of asphalt cannot bury the landmarks made there that played a prominent part in the timeline of American History.

From the moment you turn from U.S. 61 onto the long, winding driveway leading to the Myrtles Plantation, all thoughts of modern day are banished as you are suddenly ensconced in the vestiges of another era. Even without the bronze sign marking the entrance, declaring David Bradford of the Whiskey Rebellion its creator in 1796 (the year the main house was built), you realize you have stepped back in time: a time called the "Antebellum Period," immortalized in movies such as *Gone with the Wind, North and South, Reap the Wild Wind, Washington Square,* and many more. Scenes from the TV movie, *The Long Hot Summer* were shot at the Myrtles Planation.

Movie poster from The Long Hot Summer.

A *garçonnéirre* stands like a guard house at the entrance to the driveway. It served as separate quarters for young men during the plantation days to allow them freedom to come and go at will. Twin white wooden gates await a few feet from this structure, announcing your official arrival at the Myrtles Plantation.

Myrtles Plantation garçonnéirre
Photo courtesy of Amanda Folce DeVille.

Ninety-one live oaks (Quercus Virginiana), dating back over 150 years, line the *allée* and front yard of this beautiful home. Driving beneath their moss-draped branches immediately sets the scene for a gothic mystery, as their gray tendrils move softly in the breeze, as though sweeping away evidence of the real world.   As you make your way along the winding drive you get glimpses of the plethora of plants and flowers surrounding the plantation. Native wisteria, azaleas, sweet olive, catalpa, jasmine, magnolias, mulberry, pines, hydrangea, oleander, red camellias, cypress and, of course, the tree that gave the plantation her name, the Crepe Myrtle, keep the grounds in color and fragrance year-round. An orchard of considerable age, and still bearing fruit, is located in the northern section of the property, and includes peach, pear, cherry and pecan trees.

Myrtles Plantation driveway.
Photo courtesy of Amanda Folce DeVille.

Rising from a circular stand of bushes, is what has become an iconic fixture in most photographs taken of the plantation. A Grecian statue of a fair maiden in a draped gown, holding an opulent garland of flowers, stands in ghostly white, heralding the first glimpse of the Myrtles Planation. Just over her shoulder, where century-year-old oaks stand sentinel, is the home that has captured the interest of historians, ghost hunters, and psychics from all over the world.

The Myrtles Plantation main house.
Photo courtesy of Amanda Folce DeVille.

The Myrtles Plantation circa 1796, showcases the original home. It is an outstanding example of the expanded raised cottage form that mirrored the architecture popular in Louisiana by the mid-19th Century. In all fairness to the Myrtles, however, she stands alone in her unique wrought-iron grillwork, and low rambling style. It is this lack of Greek Revival columns and heavy gables that give the home a lighter feeling and one of total grace. It lends a feminine air to an area of plantations that range from Italianate and Rococo, to Greek Revival. This plantation is also one of the few that has been lovingly restored and is known for its original doors, windows, flooring, mantels, and interior design, placing it solidly on the National Register for Historic Places. Many of these amazing plantations were lost to fire or neglect over the years.

The Myrtles Plantation has been called the last of the "Grand Party Houses" of the original three, which included Greenwood Plantation, and Afton Villa Plantation, both of which were destroyed by fire. It is a rare privilege to step onto her 107'-long front verandah and know you are standing where over two centuries of residents and guests have stood before.

The Myrtles Plantation's iconic grillwork.

Where once stood the front door entrance to the Bradford's Myrtles Plantation.

There is an odd stillness when you first step onto the walk leading to the Myrtles' front door. You glance up to see shutters clinging to the side of the white clapboard second story, allowing a glimpse of laced curtains and moving shadows through the rippled glass. As you step up the stone stairs to her verandah, jalousie shutters flank the floor to ceiling windows along the first story, and have done so for over two hundred years. Muted images of antiques waver in and out of clarity as you walk past these tall windows, expecting to see a dainty hand pull back the opulent draperies to peer out at the unexpected guests. Cypress boards, in subtle cornflower blue, stretch on forever in front of you, as you cast your eye down the long length of the verandah where only white high-backed rocking chairs break the expanse.

The Myrtles Plantation front verandah

Wedding guests in 1852, waltzed through the open windows and out onto this verandah, beneath the glow of moonlight and the hum of cicadas, as the harmonium played from within. The north-facing verandah, was once stained with blood, after gunshots rang out from a stranger's revolver on a still evening in January of 1871, killing William Winter, the plantation owner at the time. The murderer disappeared with the sound of pounding horse hooves and was never charged. Children dressed in pinafores or knickers played on these weathered boards, while slaves swept the planks, hoping for a cooling breeze in the stifling Louisiana heat. The plantation's mistress entertained company here, as they sipped tea while rocking softly in the early evening shadows. It is impossible to pause here and not feel time's soft remnants of the lives that called the Myrtles Plantation home, and still do.

The weighty presence of the towering oaks, shutting out traffic sounds and light in certain areas, gives one the feeling of isolation and having the Myrtles all to one's self, as you gaze from the front door out onto the lawn. An immaculate maze of hedges lends a manicured look to a property that is otherwise left to the whims of nature; allowing the cycle of seasons to dictate the colors and arrival of flowers that are everywhere. Even with the loss of forty trees during Hurricane Gustav's raging winds on September 1, 2008, the grounds are still immersed in fluttering shadows from the different trees and foliage that adorn her grounds.

The quiet is broken only by the sweet songs of birds, and you suddenly realize, they are everywhere. There is a reason for this; Myrtle trees are an evergreen that can grow in the shade of oaks and pines. The tree has a small, fleshy berry that attracts songbirds, and consequently, the famous bird painter, John James Audubon, who was drawn to the area surrounding St. Francisville, due to the wide range of birds found there. Nearly one-third of his famous *Birds of America* paintings, rendered in the 1820's, were from this area.

View from the main doors of the Myrtles looking out to the front lawn and drive.
Photo courtesy of Amanda Folce DeVille.

Audubon's painting of Blue Jays

John James Audubon, 1826

The various rooms at the Myrtles Plantation, carry their own charm, historic design theme, and architecture. They will be discussed in the next section of this book, *The Haunting*. Along with the puddled draperies, antiques, and watchful paintings, these rooms also lay claim to their own ghost stories. For "the Most-Haunted Home in America," would you expect anything less?

The Haunting

Chapter Thirteen
The Rooms of the Myrtles and Their Ghost Stories

The Haunted Mirror at the Myrtles Plantation

The Haunted Mirror

When you speak of the Myrtles Plantation, and the myriad ghost stories surrounding it, the famous haunted mirror that hangs in the main foyer is usually at the forefront. The large shimmering glass has appeared in almost as many photos as the famous Grecian statue out front. It is the only area inside the house where guests are allowed to take photos.

A mirror draped in black during a time of mourning.

What is the story behind this ornate mirror? Why is it haunted? In the early days of the plantation, it was tradition to lay the bodies of the departed out in one of the rooms for a viewing, or wake. Often, they were there for days, awaiting relatives coming from long distances, or for priests, or presiding doctors to list cause of death. A long-held superstition was that the souls trying to depart the bodies were trapped in the house and looking for a place to dwell. Mirrors were thought to house such spirits, and so they were covered with black cloth when someone departed, in an effort to keep the spirit from dwelling there in the silver and glass.

Legend has it, that in the frantic moments following several deaths in such a short span of time at the Myrtles, one mirror was overlooked. It is in that mirror, which now hangs in the main entry of the Myrtles Plantation, that one can see handprints that just will not go away. The mirror has been re-silvered, the glass replaced, the walls and board behind it studied for imperfections, all for naught. The handprints return, and there they remain; a visible testament to souls that have passed away, but not necessarily passed *on*.

Hundreds of guests to the Myrtles Plantation have taken pictures of the mirror hanging in its ornate frame in the entryway of that beautiful home. As the plantation tour guides point out, it is the only place where a photograph can be taken inside the home, resulting in hundreds of images of the mirror appearing online.

When photos taken of the mirror are looked at later, unexplainable images are seen on the staircase reflected in it, as well as faces appearing in the glass. What one finds compelling, is that the mirror seems to age despite the numerous times the glass is changed out to get rid of the handprints. To look at the antiquated striations and discoloring in it, one would think it dated back to the 1800s, instead of within the past two decades.

Close-up of hand print in the Myrtles Plantation mirror.

Southern Superstitions about Death

Covering a mirror with black cloth upon the death of a loved one was not the only superstition of the Old South. If a mirror in your house was to fall and break by itself, it meant that someone in the home would soon die. When someone died in the house, and there was a clock in the room, you had to stop the hands at the death hour, or the family of the household would have bad luck. When the body was carried from the house, it had to be carried out feet first, because if it was carried out head first, it could look back and beckon others to follow it into death. Women wore a veil over their faces in public after the death of a family member. It served two purposes: to shield the mourner's tears from the prying eyes of the public, and to protect the passerby from the grieving person. It was a superstition that spirits of the departed would hover around those they loved. If someone passing by the mourner looked directly upon their face, that spirit might attach itself to that person. So, the veil was a protection for the person wearing it, as well as a protection for others.

A wreath of laurel, yew or boxwood, tied with crape or black ribbons, was hung on the front door to alert passersby that a death had occurred. The body was watched over every minute until burial, hence the custom of "waking." The wake also served as a safeguard from burying someone who was not dead, but in a coma. Most wakes also lasted 3-4 days to allow relatives to arrive from far away. The use of flowers and candles helped to mask unpleasant odors in the room, before embalming became common. Family photographs were also sometimes turned facedown to prevent any of the close relatives and friends of the deceased from being possessed by the spirit of the dead.

Grave robbery by the "Resurrectionist Men," often doctors themselves, was a problem in the 19th century, as medical schools needed fresh cadavers for dissection classes. "Brickingover" a grave was a way of guaranteeing some security after death. The fear of a loved one being buried alive, inspired coffin makers to design warning systems, such as a bell on the grave, which was connected by a chain to the inside of the coffin in cases of premature burial, thus the expression "Saved by the bell." Can you imagine walking through a graveyard and suddenly hearing one of those bells ring?

The fear of being buried alive was a widespread concern during the nineteenth century. This was a superstition that so permeated society, that even Mary Todd Lincoln, the wife of President Abraham Lincoln, and a relatively well-to-do, well-educated woman, shared in her final instructions her fear of this. She wrote, "I desire that my body shall remain for two days with the lid not screwed down." The spirit world held a particular fascination for Mrs. Lincoln, who often held séances in the White House, in an effort to reach her dead son.

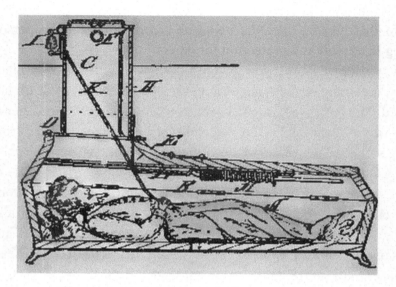

Illustration of elaborate bell systems for graves

Small cakes, known as "funeral biscuits," were wrapped in white paper, sealed with black sealing wax, and given to guests as favors. Lavish meals, or collations, were often served after internment. Burial usually followed four days after death.

Funeral Biscuit

In many cemeteries, the vast majority of graves are oriented in such a manner that the bodies lie with their heads to the West and their feet to the East. This very old custom appears to originate with the Pagan sun worshippers, but is primarily attributed to Christians who believe that the final summons to Judgment will come from the East.

Personal stationery and handkerchiefs carried a black border, with a wide border indicating a very recent death. White was a popular color for the funeral of a child. White gloves, ostrich plumes, and a white coffin were the standard.

The superstitions of the antebellum area were wide and varied. A dog howling at night, when someone in the house is sick, is a bad omen. The people of this era, believed it could be reversed by reaching under the bed and turning over a shoe.

The Haunted Myrtles Plantation—Room by Room

2nd Floor

Cottages

Coco House

Clark Woodruff Suite

John Leake Room

Fannie Williams Room

William Winter Room

Ruffin Stirling Room

Garden Rooms

Pond

Caretaker's Quarters

Restaurant

Fountain

Courtyard Patio

General's Store, Ki

Bradford Suite

Mirror

Dining Room

Game Room

Cistern

French Room

Foyer

Ladies Parlor

Gentlemen's Parlor

1st Floor

Myrtles Plantation House & Grounds

Each room of the Myrtles Plantation has its story to tell. Within its walls, babies were born; news was delivered; weddings celebrated and funerals mourned; grand balls were held; simple dinners tasted; invasions by war, plague and murder trespassed; and generations of families dreamed of happiness and prosperity.

Is it any wonder these antiquated floor boards still echo with footsteps from the past? Shadows pass along hallways and enter through locked doors. Things are moved back into their rightful place by unseen hands, phantom horse hooves clatter up the gravel driveway, and the sound of children at play cease when doors open wide. Her stories of the paranormal continue to this day. Watch for this ghost icon to read some of the recent reports:

Welcome back to the Myrtles Plantation!

The Entry

We have covered the main entry in our chapter on the Stirlings. It is worth noting, that in the later addition of the house—which expands with the entry hall to the south—that this is all the newer addition the Stirlings built. It is in this newer section, you will see Mrs. Stirling's touches in the unique doorknobs and upside-down keyholes. The doorknobs, upon first glance, look like they are made of silver. They are actually made of glass encasing mercury silver. No expense was spared. Off the entry hall, to the east, you will find the Stirling additions on the first floor: The French Room (Day Room), David Bradford Suite (originally the Stirling's Suite), and outside verandah leading from the Suite and along the south end of the house.

Entry chandelier and stairs.
Photo courtesy of Jason Phillip Reeser.

The Chandelier

The chandelier hanging in the main entry is the focus of many haunted stories. It has been seen to sway on its own, even though no one is upstairs above it, and no vibrations are felt. It weighs an imposing 300 pounds. Moving it, let alone keeping it swaying in arcs, would be a formidable challenge. Those who have witnessed it, have performed their own experiments, by going up to the landing overhead and rocking back and forth, stomping around, and basically trying anything to get it to move…all for naught. It would appear the massive fixture has a mind of its own.

The Haunted Staircase in the Entry

While the Author was staying at the Myrtles, in February, of 2012, I had the pleasure of meeting Dianna Montez and her daughters, who were also researching the plantation. They were taking photos all over the property and we compared notes. She came running to find me, while I was in the Gift Shop talking with the staff, to show me what she had just caught on the digital camera she was using. She said she and her daughter were taking shots inside the main foyer of the main staircase. The first photo shows the staircase, with reflections of the wrought iron supports from the front verandah reflecting along the wall where the morning sun had cast them through the windows. It was the second shot, one they had taken literally two seconds after the first, that made my jaw drop. There, on the staircase, its head resting on the seventeenth step, is an oval-shaped shimmering green "blob." I have had dozens of people look at the picture, including professional photographers, who agree with me—the object is not a reflection, as it does not fold into the stairs, but rather lies on top of them, as though floating slightly above the carpeted rungs. One expert told me that carpet does not reflect, so it is definitely not a reflection, and he agreed the "object" seemed to be floating above the stairs. I saw this photo only moments after she took it. It's a digital camera and there is no way to fake that shot. I found it very compelling!

*Please see the two photographs in the following pages.

Photo 1 by Dianna Montez.

The first photo, is slightly out of focus. When you compare the two pictures, you can see by the shadows and lighting, they were taken closely together. The shimmering mass, in the second photo, has its "head" exactly at the beginning of the 17th rung, corresponding to the story of William Winter's murder.

Photo 2. Photo by Dianna Montez.
A color photo is shown on the book's back cover.

Darnelle P., Denver, Colorado. "We had stayed the night in the Woodruff Suite. My husband had made a couple of trips to the car with our stuff. I sat down on the bottom step of the staircase, waiting for him to finish the last run. I was sitting there, checking my emails on my phone, when I heard him coming down the stairs behind me. I slid a little to the left so he could get by. His footsteps stopped on the second rung, right behind me.

"Don't forget the shampoo," I told him, as we often forget stuff we leave in hotel bathrooms. He didn't answer me. I tipped my head back to look at him. There was no one there. Just then, he came in through the back door by the piano, complaining about how hot it was outside. I jumped up and stared at the stairs. Who had been coming down behind me?"

Orbs on the main staircase, close to the 17th step.

The staircase in the main foyer constantly sends EMF readers into a dance. Extremely high readings are reported on the stairway, as well as some unusual photos. People using video cameras have shown orbs going up and down the staircase. Some of the unexplained balls of energy have suddenly veered off the stairs and over the banister at exactly the 17th step. The photo taken of the staircase (shown on page 249) shows what looks like ectoplasm resting on the stairs, its head at the 17th step.

The French Room

As we mentioned earlier, the French Room was originally Mrs. Stirling's domain, and was called her Morning Room, or Day Room. Her writing desk would have been here, along with a couch, dressing area, bed and chairs. The room connected through a door to the Stirling's Suite, but a "day bed" was for the mistress of the house to rest in the afternoon, while dinner preparations were being made.

Once the day began, the mistress rarely returned to her room, especially if it was upstairs, to take the customary nap. The heat in the upstairs rooms was one of the reasons for this. The large suite upstairs, which is today called the Woodruff Suite, was used by their oldest daughter, Sarah Mulford Stirling. The suite Ruffin and Mary used on the main floor, later went through several changes and titles.

Here, in the Morning Room, Mary Cobb Stirling ran her household and had some sense of privacy from what was usually a crowded home. Relatives typically came, stayed long periods of time, or often moved in. Large families were the norm with children running everywhere. Her husband's friends or business acquaintances would be frequent callers, and at the time the Stirlings owned the mansion, there were 50 household slaves! She may have had private conversations here with family members, or counseled her daughters on etiquette and social skills. I find it interesting, that the only private room set aside for the exclusive use of running the household, was entrusted to Mary, not Ruffin. True, he held meetings and conducted some business in the Gentlemen's Parlor, but there was no official office or den set aside for him. This is a testament to the enormous responsibility a plantation mistress took upon her shoulders.

The amenities in the Morning Room (French Room) are truly lovely. Many pieces offer a glimpse of the refined elegance of the reign of Louis XIV and XV. The bed, though not from that era, is an 1850 hand-carved sleigh bed. It is gilded in 24-carat gold. The baldaquin crown above it is a nod to the royalty, whose name, many of the other antiques carry.

Like most of the other chandeliers in the home, the French bronze Doret chandelier in the French Room burned candles until 1970. We have mentioned its cherub adornments, and those of nuns, in the medallion above it as talismans against evil spirits. The pineapple in the medallion symbolizes hospitality and the ears of corn represent prosperity.

The enormous mirror hanging above the fireplace is the oldest one in the home. It is French Regency and dates from 1830. Mrs. Stirling had angels grace its gilded frame…just another little bit of security.

The French Room at the Myrtles Plantation.
Photo courtesy of Amanda Folce DeVille.

In the French Room, you will see an amazing piece of furniture. It is an antique dressing screen, created by nuns.   The dressing screen was designed in keeping with the modesty regulations of the day. A woman's ankles and feet were to be covered at all times. Her bosom, however, could be displayed with as much cleavage as she cared to share. Hence, the top portion of the dressing screen is glass, while the remainder of the hinged paneled piece goes all the way to the floor. You must remember, that women in the 19th century were usually not very tall. Most averaged around 4'10" to 5'2" in height, and weighed around 80 or 90 pounds. The average male was 5'8." Even if you were on the statuesque side, you were still within the required etiquette of the time, as long as your ankles and feet were hidden from view.

An example of a Louis XV dressing screen

All of the furniture that can still be seen today in the French Room at the Myrtles Plantation, is in the same period as it would have been during the Stirling family's stay. They spent an entire year in Europe, shopping for fabrics, rugs, chairs, tables, couches, beds, mirrors, crystal, chandeliers, craftsmen, and artists; sometimes returning more than once. Their wishes were carried out in exquisite detail, similar to the pieces you see in Mrs. Stirling's Day Room. The furnishings mirror France between 1840 and 1850.

A Louis XV 5-piece Aubusson salon set
French Rococo Baroque Royal

The magnificent Louis XV 5-piece Aubusson salon set, which originally graced Doren Palace in Holland, resides in this room. The couch and four matching chairs are covered with what today is called a repaired Aubusson. This is where they lift the tapestry-style material off of the straw-filled bottom and place a white piece of satin down and re-lay the fabric on top. A closer look at the couch reveals it is not one layer, but several. The tiny stitch that created this fabric is 1/16th the size of today's needlepoint and was created underneath magnifying glasses by the small hands of young girls. So many of these young ladies went blind creating the tiny embroidery, due to poor lighting and long hours. The stitch today is called the "Blind Stitch." The couch and chairs in this room were originally intended for the Ladies' Parlor, but were moved into the French Room for safe keeping when the parlors began their use for weddings and receptions.

In the corner of the French Room you will see a wooden table. It belonged to the Woodruff's and it is believed they had their wedding breakfast on it. Woodruff's great-granddaughter was kind enough to give it to Teeta Moss to have on display at the Myrtles. You will also see an antique teapot on the table that dates back to the Napoleonic era. It has Napoleon's crest, and the symbol of French royalty, the bumblebee. The bottom portion would hold a candle, and the middle part, water, to act as a sort-of double boiler to keep the tea warm.

The mantel is impressive craftsmanship using the faux painting technique. It is painted to look like marble. Its base is actually slate.

The French Room at the Myrtles Plantation is also known for its paranormal activity. It was especially active during Marjorie Munson's ownership, with stories of the Lady in Black, frequently coming from this room. It seems the ghosts dwelling here, amid the sumptuous antiques, aren't camera shy.

Vanessa Bolano, a New Orleans news reporter, was putting a show together about the Myrtles Plantation in St. Francisville, La., for ABC-affiliate WGNO, when a strange white light shot by her.

"We wanted to highlight the history of the plantation … so it's sort of interesting that we brought this find back," Bolano told the Daily News, referring to the peculiar image her cameraman recorded in the French Room.

"This thing flew through quickly," said Bolano. "We have the ability to go through frame by frame. … In one of the frames, when you stop it, it looks like the profile of a woman's face."

The link to the YouTube video clip of the report is below:

https://www.youtube.com/watch?v=MyaQ4WsleS8

The white image is at top right in the bed draping.

Photo courtesy of www.WGNO.com.

As the French Room is not offered for overnight guests, the stories reported, are obviously, not as frequent as other parts of the house. This room remains locked when not on tours.

The Stirling Suite

When the new addition to the Myrtles was added, the Stirlings built a suite next to the Morning Room (French Room) that acted as their private bedroom. It was comprised of a large bedroom and sitting area, separated by an imposing fireplace. The fireplace on the bedroom side is painted in a textured red and black faux marble, while the façade in the sitting room area is a travertine faux with white and black featherings. These fireplaces were made of slate and decorated to represent precious stone by talented artisans, including the refurbishment done by Arlin Dease and Stephen Saunders in 1975.

The Stirling Suite's doors led out onto the south and west verandahs. Another door opened into the Morning Room. The windows of the bedroom and seating area overlooked the carriage house and side yard, while the sitting room windows had a view of the back property that is now a large patio. The south verandah wrapped around to the front of the house and allowed the owners to see arriving guests. From this vantage point, the plantation owners could exit their suite, and be out front or back within seconds. Mary Stirling also had convenient access to her Morning Room, where she conducted all her affairs. The windows in both areas also allowed the Stirling's to oversee the working part of the plantation at all times.

With floor to ceiling windows in the bedroom area, the light was lovely as it played upon the lace curtains and threw fluttering shadows from the trees just outside across the polished wood floor. Expensive drapes hung in tasseled perfection, their opulent fabric puddled on the floor to show the world the owners had money to spare. The Mosses replaced the large four poster bed with a gorgeous tester bed, armoire, and dresser that was impeccably restored by Mr. Vernon Guidry. It is snuggled against the west wall, only a foot or two away from the large fireplace.

The sitting area was also used as a dressing area, no doubt, and probably contained a chaise lounge, small table and armed chairs. Both rooms would have sported expensive area rugs.

The General David Bradford Suite

Over the years, the two rooms comprising the Stirling's Suite have changed, based on the current owner's needs. At one point, the French Room became a bedroom, and the Stirling Suite became a sitting area with only a door separating the two. During Arlin Dease's ownership in 1975, the suite was used as a bedroom, and the sitting area next to it was turned into a kitchenette. This set-up remained during John L. Pearce's time in 1977, and was finally turned into the Bradford Suite when Frances Kermeen bought the plantation in 1980, restoring the Suite to its original purpose as a bedroom and sitting area.

The Stirling's Suite today, is l called The General David Bradford Suite, in honor of the man who built the plantation. It is one of the guest suites offered to overnight guests and has been upgraded with a modern bathroom, including a shower. The bedroom is decorated in beautiful shades of red, with the curtains puddled and tied back with tassels just as they were in Stirling's day. The antique tester bed is large and sumptuous with shams, duvet, and decorative pillows, matching the curtains in rich reds and golds. With the red faux marble fireplace, it is truly a room that gives off an air of opulence. The antique chest and table complete the feeling that you are once again living in the 1800s—you can almost hear the sounds of horses just outside the bedroom window, as they return their riders home. The sitting area once again houses a chaise lounge, matching wing chairs and table. A large portrait depicting a lovely lady in period dress hangs above the travertine fireplace. White high-backed rocking chairs wait just outside the sitting room door on the west verandah.

South veranda outside a door to the Bradford Suite.
The cistern can just be seen to the left in this photo.

Guests staying in the Bradford Suite are discouraged from using the door leading out to the south verandah. It is for safety reasons. There is a large cistern in this portion of the property and the owners are simply looking out for their overnight guests. This verandah is 31-feet-long and 4-feet-wide here, and encased in the beautiful grillwork that runs the length of the house and around to the north verandah.

The cistern was used to collect rain water during the early days of the plantation. The location was convenient to the house and the water could be used for myriad purposes. Due to the potential danger associated with it, this area is fenced off, but visitors to the plantation can see it clearly from the walkway.

Detail of verandah railing.
Photo courtesy of Jason Phillips Reeser.

The Bradford Suite seems to have a preference in the guests who people it. Due to the number of emails I received, concerning this bedroom, it seems guests in this Suite often leave between 2:00 am and 4:00 am in the morning. The odd thing is, this typically happens only when a male is sharing the room. It seems the ladies are left in peace…. most of the time!

Just outside the permanently locked bathroom door in the Bradford Suite, sits a 150-year-old baby grand piano. If you were to open the bathroom door, you would literally run into it. Many reports of strains of melancholy music coming from that piano have been reported from people staying at the Myrtles. With its proximity to the door entering into the Bradford Suite area, it is no wonder that many of those stories have come from the guests in this room.

Myrtles Plantation piano in the main foyer.

"It's never very loud," guests have been known to acknowledge. "But it's still creepy. Since that part of the house is locked off to anyone not staying in the Woodruff Suite, you know you are screwed when you hear it playing, and no one is booked into the Woodruff Suite for that night!"

Oddly, 2:00 am seems to be the witching hour at the Myrtles. It is about that time, that people report being awakened by party noises in the entry foyer, piano music, and even the smell of cigar smoke.

One of the more unnerving reports from the Bradford Room, is that of moving bed pillows. More than one occupant has said the pillows on the bed move, sometimes while your head is on them. They have been checked for wires, magnets, anything that would make them jump and slide about, but nothing is ever detected. One woman watched from across the room as the pillows plopped over on themselves, knocking the throw pillows over with them.

Other reports sent to me of paranormal activity in the room, concern the beautiful crystal chandelier going on a dance in the middle of the night. It will suddenly start swaying and dancing about, its stringed crystals tinkling as they play against each other. What makes this interesting, is that the area directly above the chandelier is the small sitting room and bathroom in the Woodruff Suite. It is doubtful someone is waltzing around in those two areas enough to make a 200-pound chandelier pirouette in the night.

Guests have told me closet doors in the room have been known to bang open and shut; they've heard sounds of knocking coming from the empty French Room next door in the wee hours of the morning, as if a ghost is entreating the occupant to let him come in; cold spots; the large four poster bed turning ice cold, while the rest of the room remains a warm constant temperature; and sounds of someone whistling outside on the verandah—just as they did when slaves brought food into the Dining Room from the "whistle walk."

Markus R., Dayton, Ohio. "My friends were staying in the Bradford room. We were talking to them in the sitting area of that room, waiting for one of them to finish getting ready to go to dinner. Right in the middle of the conversation, a big bang sound came from the bedroom part. We went running in and one of their suitcases was upside down in the middle of the floor with the clothes spilling out. My friend looked scared to death. I told her it probably just fell off of the bed. She said, no, it wasn't on the bed, it was still locked and standing over by the dresser. She didn't want to stay the rest of the night, but her husband talked her into it. It was pretty creepy."

Some guests in the Bradford Suite claim to hear horses whinny, which wouldn't be surprising as that room was the closest to the carriage house where horses, buggies, and gear were once housed. Pounding hooves on gravel have been reported, with a snorting animal stopping just outside the bedroom window. This is followed by the sound of someone dismounting, the noise of clanking reins accompanying him. Green orbs seem to turn up in cameras near the bed in the Bradford Suite, and near the iron handles on the closet doors.

A lady wrote to me from my Facebook page for this book, after her stay in the Bradford Suite.

"It's such a big room, with the sitting room adjoining it and two big fireplaces," **Denise F**. wrote me. "My husband felt (ms) right to sleep but I kept looking into the darkness waiting for that Chloe ghost to show up. Something green did float acrost (ms) the room," she wrote. "I thought it was my imagination running away with to (ms) me until I noticed it was reflecting in the glossy sheen of the fireplace surface. I was elbowing my husband, when it floated to the open door leading into the next room, looked back at me and floated through out of sight. I knew from the shape it was a woman in a long dress, kinda tied at the back because the waist was cinched in. She had something on her head that made her head look twice as big as it should have. Her arms never moved, just stayed real still by her side. And there was no sound. That maid (ms) me the most nervous. It was so quiet!"

Marjorie B., Nashville, Tennessee. "We stayed in the Bradford Suite for two nights. I remember being nervous because that room is the only guest room used on the first floor. I was afraid things could tap on our windows and the outside doors. You could hear cars pulling into the gravel parking lot once and awhile, but other than that, it was pretty quiet. Sometime during the night, I felt something on my nose. I freaked because I thought it was a bug. I swiped at my nose, but didn't find anything. A few minutes later, I felt it again. It was really soft, like a feather being brushed across my nose. I wiped it again and noticed how cold the space by my face was, even though it was a hot night. Just then, it ran across my forehead...it felt just like a big feather someone was brushing against my skin. I jumped up and stood there shaking. My friend turned over and asked me what I was doing. Then she shot out of the bed and said something just brushed against her face. We turned on the light and nothing was there. There was nothing on the bed or floor. We were finally climbing back into bed when the door from our room to the sitting room next door slammed shut! We didn't sleep the rest of the night."

David O. L, New Orleans, Louisiana. "Met my friends on the porch outside the door to the Bradford room at the Myrtles. They were staying there for a night. We were drinking beers on the porch, rocking in the chairs, when Glenda comes out of her room there and says the bed is moving. We laughed at her, but went in to look. Nothing was happening. We were headed back out when she screams "Look!" We turned around and that bed slid a good 4 inches sideways! I about lost it! We looked under it, pushed it back, watched it, but nothing else happened. I wouldn't be caught dead sleeping on that thing!"

Patio verandah. Door to General David Bradford Suite is at the end, facing.

Diane R., Baton Rouge, Louisiana. "We had been wanting to stay at the Myrtles Plantation for a long time. One weekend we decided to stay one night. The only room left was the David Bradford Suite. The house is divided so that the only people who can get into the wing where we were staying were the people staying in the Woodruff Suite upstairs. During the night, I kept hearing the door to the entry wing open and close, open and close. I was getting annoyed and wondered why the people staying in the Woodruff room needed to go in and out so much. When I was in the bathroom of our room, I could hear heavy footsteps on the other side of the locked bathroom door. A piano sits on the other side of that door. The door leading out to the verandah just kept opening and closing, and then footsteps. The next morning, I mentioned it to one of the staff during breakfast. She looked surprised, and said the people who were booked for the Woodruff room canceled the night before. We had the whole wing to ourselves!"

The Dining Room

A door leading from the Stirling's Suite into the main Entry Hall is now kept locked. During the Stirling's ownership, this door opened and led into the hallway, and directly across the polished boards to the Dining Room doorway. Again, the situation of the owner's suite allowed them quick access to the outside, as well as pertinent rooms in the house. The door to the Ladies' Parlor is only steps away.

The Dining Room of the Myrtles is an amazing room. This is in the original portion of the house built by David Bradford, in 1796. The large fireplace greets you as you enter from the main hall. As mentioned, the Stirlings took the Bradford's original cypress mantles and moved them upstairs. This fireplace is slate and faux painted to resemble malachite. An enormous mirror resides above it, reflecting the twin Bohemian Crystal chandeliers in its gleaming glass. The medallions, adorning the tops of these chandeliers, are rendered in an acanthus leaf motif. This leaf is commonly used in southern homes and is a symbol for friendship. However, in Greek history, it was a symbol for heaven. Mrs. Stirling worked this acanthus leaf design into each room in the house, whether in medallions, frieze work or other décor. It is evident she wanted her family and friends to feel welcome, and protected.

A massive Chinese Chippendale dining table from the 1850s, stretches out in front of you, set with china, glassware and serving pieces, as though awaiting the dinner party to arrive. As mentioned in an earlier chapter, a fly catcher (the glass dome used to capture flies with a syrup, or sugar water-filled cup inside) is placed at the far end of the table. An authentic shoo fly or *Punka* is standing against the north wall. It originally hung above the table and was operated by a slave during dinner to keep the flies away from the food and guests.

The furnishings in the Dining Room are filled with history. To the left of the door leading to the Ladies' Parlor, is a piece known as a Hunt Board, or Hunter's Buffet. This is one of the English pieces.

During the 19th century, gentlemen spent a lot of time on horseback. They would sometimes develop saddle sores and it would become uncomfortable to sit down at the table and eat, so they would stand at the Hunt Board, or Hunter's Buffet, and dine while standing up.

Typical Dining Room with Hunt Board (rear).

To the right of this same door, is a beautiful table with small mirrors adorning each side, for the ladies. Hester Eby, the knowledgeable docent at the plantation, told this Author, the mirrors were for the women to peek down into and check their dresses before advancing into the Dining Room. As we mentioned with the French Room's dressing screen, a woman in the 1800s was never to show ankle, or petticoat. These mirrors situated at the side, and extending to bottom of the chest, allowed her a quick peek to make sure all was in order before the gentlemen joined the ladies for dinner. It was called a Petticoat Buffet.

As mentioned earlier, Arlin Dease, the man responsible for so much of the restoration work at the Myrtles Plantation, stated that women of the day wore makeup made of wax. Sitting too near the lit fireplaces could prove disastrous to one's appearance.

Once again, we see the opulent puddling of fabric in curtains adorning the twin windows of this room. The rule of thumb, for estimating the wealth of an owner, was sometimes seen in just how much of the curtain material was puddled onto the floor. The bigger the puddle, the more money you had. The standard estimate was one inch of material in the puddle equaled one million dollars. The draperies in the Dining Room today are not original, but they are noteworthy all the same. They were copied from *Gone with the Wind*. You might remember Scarlett O'Hara turning them into a dress under dire circumstances.

A final note about this room—it contains two built-in closets. No big deal? Au contraire! Closets were taxed in the 1800s, as a separate room. To have one closet in a room was lavish, to have two? You were obviously not counting pennies.

Ghostly happenings in the Myrtles Plantation Dining Room tend to center around the outside verandah. Once called the Whistle Walk, it seems the echoes of slaves walking along these weathered boards can still be heard. From footsteps to whistling, tour guides and guests alike have witnessed odd things here, occurring just on the other side of the glass.

Matt D., Boise, Idaho. "I was on a tour at the Myrtles and we were standing in the dining room there. The guide was pointing out the dishes on the table when someone in the group laughed. Since there was nothing funny about the lecture on antique table settings, we all turned to look at her. She was smiling and waving at the window to the left, which overlooks the back. She kept wiggling her fingers and laughing, as though playing with a child. The guide asked her what she was doing. She looked surprised and said she was just laughing at the three little black children with their faces pressed against the glass and making faces. All of us looked at where she was pointing. There was nothing there. She got quite agitated when no one would confirm what she was seeing. She said one had his hands cupped and pressed to the window to see inside. For the rest of the tour she kept looking toward the windows in each room we went through."

Brian H., Ontario, Canada. "Stayed with a friend of mine in Louisiana in a room upstairs at the Myrtles Plantation. We went downstairs to bring in another suitcase from the car. My friend, Steve, stopped at the bottom of the stairs and tried the door to his left. It was open. He peeked in and said it was a dining room. We stepped in to look around. I told him I didn't think we were supposed to be there. He picked up a dish and was looking at the back of it to see if it was expensive. Something smacked him in the back of the head. I saw his head jolt forward and he almost dropped the plate. He swore, put his hand at the back of his head, and looked at me with his eyes popping. I was nowhere near him and he knew it. We got out of there fast. He was rattled for some time after that."

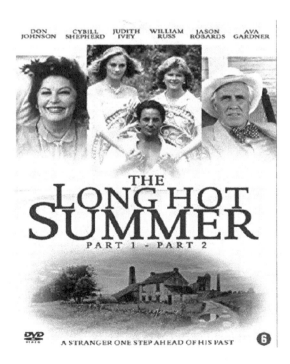

A television mini-series remake of the *The Long Hot Summer*, starring Don Johnson, Cybill Shepherd, Ava Gardner, and Jason Robards, had its share of production problems when a portion of the movie was shot at the Myrtles. One day, the crew moved the furniture in the Game Room and the Dining Room for filming and then left the rooms. When they returned, they reported all the furniture had been moved back to its original position. No one was inside either room while the crew was absent. This happened not once, but several times; even when it had been mere seconds between the time they moved the furniture and when they looked again into the rooms. Although dismayed at the loss of time, and unable to account for the strange phenomenon, the crew finally got their shots. The technicians involved admitted to being happy to move on to other locations for the filming of the movie.

The Ladies' Parlor

The Ladies' Parlor at the Myrtles Plantation.
Photo courtesy of Amanda Folce DeVille.

Perhaps the biggest imprint Mary and Ruffin Stirling made on the Myrtles Plantation, with the possible exception of the wrought-iron grill work that surrounds the verandahs of the house, was their renovation on the Ladies' and Gentlemen's Parlors. By combining the two rooms, they created a 60-foot long ballroom when the pocket doors separating the two areas were open. Some of the finest open frieze work in the nation crowns the ceilings of these two beautiful reflection parlors. Matching Italian Carrara marble fireplaces sit exactly 55-feet apart, anchoring the two parlors. Though the chandeliers are different in their design, they are equally spaced from each other, continuing the feeling of a cohesive unit.

Jib window raised to access verandah.

The windows in these two rooms are called "jib" windows. They can be easily lifted up into the ceiling recess, opening the rooms to the verandahs outside. The hinges allowed the doors to be completely removed. You now have a 10,000-square-foot pavilion, created by combining the two rooms and bringing the outside verandahs into the space. Mrs. Stirling wanted her home to be considered the party house of the Feliciana's, and she spared no expense in its design and appointments.

The Ladies' Parlor houses some amazing antiques. The room, which originally featured the 5-piece Aubusson salon set that now resides in the French Room, has an elegant feel with a beautiful white winged settee and four matching chairs. A dark walnut entry table takes center stage in the room, sitting atop a beautiful antique area rug. A cut-glass vase of flowers is usually reflected in the polished wood.

An antique writing desk now sits next to the floor-to-ceiling window in the Ladies' Parlor. It is a dainty piece with cubbyholes for stationary and a place for an ink well and pin. The chair is a Louis XV, with the typical cabriole legs and arched padded back.

A Louis XV Writing Desk and Chair

John L. Pearce, the former owner of the plantation, purchased a beautiful sewing chest that graces this room. As mentioned earlier in the book, sewing consumed copious hours at the plantation and was a never-ending pursuit, whether for pragmatic reasons or for crafts and decorative items. The sewing chest at the Myrtles is made entirely of papier-mache and has a mother-of-pearl inlay. Small sewing items are housed within. It is flanked by two antique chairs, just waiting for the ladies of the plantation to sit and pick up their needle work.

The armed chair in the corner of the room is a classic Louis XV walnut fauteuil, c. 1750, with a molded frame carved with scrolls and cartouches; the upholstery is covered in a needlework fabric with flowers. Again, we have the classic cabriole legs. This style of chair was so popular that it has been emulated ever since.

Against the soft, pastel peach walls, sits a beautiful Louis XV kingwood table. This style of table showed a much higher leg than the XIV period. Above this piece is a large portrait of a biblical scene encased in an elaborate gold-gilt frame. Another large portrait with a biblical theme hangs above the ornate Louis XV commode, whose twin is just outside in the foyer beneath the "haunted mirror."

The feeling of both parlors is very light, thanks primarily to the soft pastel wall and ceiling color, offset by white frieze work, doors, trim and baseboards.

The faux bois workmanship is evident everywhere throughout the Myrtles. Windows and door frames were painted to look like granite, the doors to resemble antique oak, the two staircases to look like walnut, and the baseboards in the game room to look identical to the fireplace's faux marble. Even the cypress floors were painted to look like heart of pine. This art form, which has made a huge comeback in the 20th and 21st centuries, is a highly accomplished skill. Layers of translucent paints are often used, along with beeswax, oils, and varnishes, to create an astonishing replica. To have the ability to hire artisans, such as the ones featured in the Myrtles Plantation's décor, required a great deal of money. It is testament to the talents of Arlin Dease and Stephen Saunders—who hand-painted the damaged faux painted areas—and the generations of owners that cared for the home later, that the faux painting is in such remarkable condition.

In the 1800s, games were often played in the parlors of great homes. They were typically a form or charades, guessing games, cards, and other light entertainment. They became known as "parlor games" and offered a respite from the day-to-day tedium of work, and often, isolation.

One such game was called Snapdragon. A bowl was filled with brandy and several raisins, or prunes, were dropped in. These sank to the bottom. The brandy was then lit on fire. The guests had to try and snatch the fruit from the blazing bowl, without getting burned. During a time when fires were highly feared, it is an interesting idea for a parlor game.

Agatha Christie features a game of Snapdragon in her book, *Hallowe'en Party*.

Playing Snapdragon in the 1800s.

Hide and Seek Parlor Game

The number of people who find their way to the Myrtles Plantation every year is formidable. The tours run at a fever pitch during the peak seasons. The Myrtles Tour incorporates the plantation's rich history along with the continuing mystery and intrigue of this antebellum home. The daily daytime tour is 45-mintues long. The evening tour is an hour which allows an additional 15 minutes in length for discussions concerning the paranormal activity here. After all, the plantation is called the "Most-Haunted Home in America" for a reason. Please see their website for reservations: www.myrtlesplantation.com.

The usual stories of cell phones, cameras, and video equipment malfunctioning is prevalent.

"A friend and I spent the night there in the slave quarter rooms a few years ago," a woman wrote in. "No strange happenings, but our cameras and cell phones wouldn't hold a charge on the property—but worked fine when we stepped outside the gates."

Unsolved Mysteries at the Myrtles

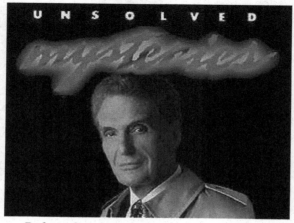

Robert Stack with Unsolved Mysteries

When *Unsolved Mysteries* shot their one-hour segment at the Myrtles Plantation, they reported an inordinate amount of problems with their electrical equipment. Cell phones, video cameras, lighting, and other equipment, constantly malfunctioned.

A local TV anchorman and crew were sent to the plantation to film a segment for a Halloween presentation. Everyone on the crew was joking about the ghosts and inviting them to join the program. The anchorman was live on the air and taunting the ghosts, while relaying the history of the plantation to the television audience. He was standing in the Ladies' Parlor and telling the spirits to show themselves. He had been animated and upbeat, when suddenly his expression changed, and his voice became monotone. His face suddenly drained of color, and at the same time, all the equipment and transmission failed. Although they tried for almost an hour to continue the program, the equipment refused to work. They finally had to leave the Ladies' Parlor and continue the telecast outside on the front verandah. Later, reports flooded in from the television audience, who had been watching the live production from the Ladies' Parlor. The viewers reported seeing a ball of light flying from a corner of the room and *through* the host, just as his voice and expression changed, and all transmission was lost.

Many reports, turned in from tour group members, come from the twin parlors. Janet Roberts, a psychic who is the treasurer of the Louisiana Society for Psychical Phenomena, is certain the Myrtles is "crawling with ghosts." She was reported as saying, "Walking into the parlor was like walking into a crowded cocktail party. We were literally bumping into people. You wanted to say 'Excuse me' though no one was there."

300-lb. Baccarat Chrystal Chandelier in the foyer of the Myrtles.

Frances Kermeen, former owner of the plantation, said she found a warning about the ghosts in a book published in 1882.

"The lights are never extinguished at the plantation," the book admonishes. "When the lights are all out, something always happens." To this day, the large baccarat crystal chandelier hanging in the main entry is always ablaze at night.

Guests on the tours, whether in the daytime or evening, have reported hearing muffled conversations when everything is quiet. These stories almost always generate in the twin parlors.

"It sounds like a conversation is going around you, yet there is no one talking in your group," a woman wrote to me. "I've had friends tell me they have heard them as well, and even heard the sound of a party, where you can hear clinking glasses and music coming from the Ladies' Parlor and Gentleman's Parlor. Our tour guide stopped and told us to listen. We did and we all heard it! Soft, unmistakable voices conversing with one another. It was very muffled and sounded like it was a great distance away. It was hard to make out the words. It was when one of the voices laughed, that I got the goose bumps. Really, really creepy!"

The Double Parlors, separated by a pocket door. The Ladies' Parlor is in the foreground with the Dining Room to the left. Through the pocket door is the Gentlemen's' Parlor with the Game Room to the left. Photo courtesy of Amada Folce DeVille.

As mentioned earlier, it seems the Myrtles has a rhythm to it. 2:00 a.m. seems to be the witching hour, reported by more overnight guests than the staff can keep up with. Many guests staying in the main house have been awakened at 2 a.m., myself included.

The sounds of parties in the twin parlors ramp up in the Spring and Fall seasons when balls and galas were typically held at the plantations. During the Stirling's rein, the Myrtles was known as *the* party house in the English Plantation countryside. The Confederate soldier's ghost in the John W. Leake Room is more active in May and June, when he was reportedly housed in that room while recuperating from a leg wound. People hearing the sound of drums, coming from the distant corner of the property at night, typically report the disturbance in the summer months. Drums could be attributed to both the Tunica Indians who roamed the property, or the method of communication the slaves used when talking to neighboring plantations...sort of like smoke signals in percussion. And, there's voodoo rituals.

Hester Eby told me that the parlors house yet another phenomenon. "The guides have stepped behind the couches in the past to address their tour groups, so that they could face everyone, and give them a clear view of the rooms," Mrs. Eby said. "While standing behind these couches, many of us have had the sensation that someone small, like a child, is pulling on our clothing, trying to get our attention." Perhaps the children of the Myrtles used to play hide-and-seek behind these couches. We do know that sacks of salt were kept behind the curtains flanking these couches, in an effort to ward off spirits from entering in through the windows.

When this Author visited the Myrtles Plantation, in August of 2011, I rented a car at the Baton Rouge airport. When I had finished my work, I returned to the airport and stood at the rental car check-in, waiting for them to process my bill. The young man behind the counter was friendly and asked if I was in Baton Rouge for the first time. I responded to his questions and he eventually found out I had been staying at the Myrtles Plantation. He lifted his eyes from the paperwork with a look of awe on his face.

"I had a really weird thing happen to me at that place," **Timothy Walton,** the car agent told me. "I was on the tour and listening to the narrative. I was at the back of the group when suddenly I feel someone push me a little in the back. When I turned around, there was nobody there!"

Reports of feeling touched, or the sudden smell of cigar smoke, sweet perfume, a voice at your elbow and, of course, the missing earrings and hair adornments, have all been told to the staff at the Myrtles. Some children actually buy small hair ribbons and clips and wear them on the tours so that the ghost of Chloe can take them. Many believe it is she who is responsible for the missing jewelry and accessories.

Ghost photo taken of a young girl looking out Myrtles'
parlor window.

Tour guests have relayed seeing faces of children standing outside on the verandah peering into the twin parlors, Game Room and Dining Room. Others see children from another era looking *out* from the parlor windows.

The Gentlemen's Parlor

The Gentlemen's Parlor at the Myrtles, has its own bragging rights, when it comes to beautiful furnishings. Twin walnut Louis XV chairs, with tufted back and sides, flank the Italian Carrera marble fireplace; a small table is situated between them to hold the occasional brandy snifter or cigar. A beguiling black statue of cupid shooting a bow and arrow sits in the right-hand corner next to them.

Typical Gentlemen's Parlor.

The fireplace, it is said, still shows scars from a Union soldier's sword, when the plantation home was under attack during the Civil War. The fact that the area plantations were looted, is no mystery. News that the enemy was advancing toward their beloved homes sent more than one plantation mistress hurrying to gather the family heirlooms and jewels, and secret them in some very creative places. The able-bodied men were all away from home, trying to defend their land and families, and beat back the advancing soldiers. Women, children, and the elderly, were left to try and defend their possessions as best they could. Arlin Dease, former owner of the Myrtles, said it was common knowledge that the plantations in the area were looted by Union soldiers, and that they probably camped out on the Myrtles property. Many plantation owners, living mere minutes from the Myrtles, have written notes in their diaries about the loss of possessions and damage done to their properties.

It was said that Mary Catherine Cobb Stirling's heirs sued the Federal Government for damages incurred in the Civil War.

Against the east wall of the Gentlemen's Parlor, is a large bookcase in burled wood. Next to it, sits a small armless chair with tufted back and cabriole legs. A camel hair sofa sits between opulent draperies overlooking the front verandah on the east wall. One of the most beautiful pieces in the room, is an antique rocking chair with padded back and arms. The room combines Chippendale and Louis XV pieces in a harmonious blend of exquisite taste. A brocade Aubusson rug anchors the room in warmth, while the polished cypress floors peek from beneath. The north end of this room has the dubious distinction of being a murder site. The door leading out onto the north verandah, to the left of the fireplace, was where William Winter was gunned down, in 1871.

It is here, in this room, that the master of the plantation conducted business, entertained friends and colleagues, and relaxed. This was the masculine domain, where topics concerning politics, commodities, crop sales, slavery issues, current events, wars, and plagues, were discussed in baritone voices. These topics were considered outside the realm of feminine sensibilities. The pocket doors separating the two parlors would be closed to allow for privacy, and to, no doubt, spare the fairer sex from the overpowering smell of cigars and pipe tobacco. The door leading out onto the north gallery was conveniently located next to the fireplace to allow for an evening stroll onto the property, or along the verandah, while discussing the needs of the day with a neighboring planter or business associate. The east-facing windows also overlooked the front of the property, so arriving visitors were always within view. If the evening turned into one where a friendly game of cards or chance might be welcome, the Gaming Room was only a few steps away through an adjoining door.

One of the more chilling accounts I received, about the phenomenon happening during certain tours, came to me from Mark Leonard, Tour Guide at the Myrtles.

"I had taken a group of Catholic schoolgirls from Rayne into the Gentleman's Parlor and I was in the middle of the room talking about Mr. Winter's murder, and when I got to the part where 'an unknown horseman rode across the front lawn, and stopped just outside this door,' I turned back to them and all twenty-four of them, students and teachers, were staring intently out the front windows.

"I knew that something had happened. I had seen that stare before. I asked them if something was wrong. A girl at the front asked me if that always happened when I talked about the horse.

"What happens when I talk about the horse?" I asked her. "The horse sounds," she said. "The neighing just outside the window."

"You heard the sound of a horse neighing?" I tried to keep the skepticism out my voice. There were no horses within miles of the Myrtles. Twenty-four heads nodded up and down! I had not heard a thing."

Mark Leonard also told me that "the candelabras with dangling pieces of crystals occasionally do a thirty-second boogaloo during tours, and then suddenly stop dead still."

"I had a thoroughly believable bus driver tell me he had a long conversation with a woman in a purple and black dress in the foyer right before she seemed to evaporate," Mr. Leonard told me. "A seven-year-old and her engineer father also told me that they heard Mr. Winter climbing the foyer stairs at 1:46 in the morning. As for me…I regularly straighten furniture pieces in the French Room, and put them back in the place, even though that room is bolt-locked. Dozens of photographs people show me, have captured people wearing antiquated clothes staring out of windows, or from the haunted mirror. Every week there are new stories, new digital images, and new sounds, that reshape our weekend mystery tours."

Haunted Mirror courtesy of HauntedAmericaTours.com

Miki M., Newport, Rhode Island. "So, there are four of us on the ghost tour at the Myrtles Plantation. Some lady was giving the tour. She was very soft-spoken and nice. We were enjoying the tour and loved all the furniture. We stepped into the gentlemen's parlor and she was pointing out the fireplace. Just then, a lady next to me gasped. I turned to look at her, and she leaned over and whispered that the statue of a guy with an arrow in the corner just turned slightly. I stared at the statue, but didn't see anything. I figured most people on ghost tours are looking for something to happen. Two minutes later, a guy by the couch pipes up, and says the statue with the arrow is moving. This time when I looked, I noticed the statue's face was facing out toward the group, when before he had been angled toward the window. That's a pretty spooky place."

French bronze Louis XVI cupid statue, 1880

*Photograph of ghosts of Revolutionary Soldiers taken
by Jamie Miles, on the Myrtles Plantation property.*

Some tour guests have shared their stories of seeing soldiers through the parlor windows, that suddenly disappear. The most prevalent report is that of children in period clothing playing on the grounds. Usually they are reported as small blond girls with ringlets and dressed in long dresses, or pinafores.

Little girl ghost.
Photo courtesy of AmericanGhostStories.com.

The Gaming Room

The smallest room on the first floor was used for various purposes. During the Woodruff's time, it served as the children's dining room. When the Stirling's renovated the plantation home, they had other plans for that area. It would serve as a room to entertain guests.

Painted in the deep green of Ruffin's native Scotland, it is a decidedly warm and masculine room.

A portrait of a young child in a tartan plaid dress hangs against the west wall. It may be a painting of one of the Stirling children. Mark Leonard, one of the head tour guides, told me that each Scottish Clan had their own design in the plaid fabric, which indicated what part of the country they were from. The youthful face adds a touch of whimsy to a room designated for the playing of cards, and joviality.

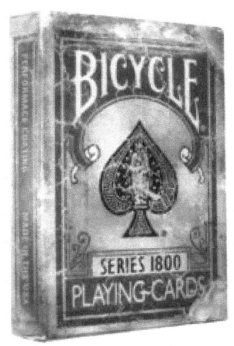

Vintage 1800s playing cards.

Myrtles Plantation Gaming Room.
Photo courtesy of Amanda Folce DeVille.

An antique Chippendale game table takes center stage in this room. It has been said that many a plantation and fortune have been won or lost over a friendly hand of cards. Rumors that Lewis Stirling, Ruffin's oldest son, was shot in this room over a card game, still linger. We do know he died at the age of 23 on the same year, and only three months after, his father died of consumption. Perhaps tempers flared over something trifling, and in his grief, it escalated. I was unable to ascertain the details of his death, although the prevalent reports are that he died of yellow fever.

Arlin Dease, former owner of the Myrtles, was kind enough to show me the original four chairs that went to the gaming table when the Stirlings owned the plantation. They are in his private collection, and he took a photo of one of them for me. It is shown on the next page. This chair is not at the Myrtles Plantation.

Two arm chairs, in exquisite Napoleon detail, flank the faux painted fireplace in the Game Room. Their distinctive swan legs are hard to miss, as an iconic design of that era.

Original chair from the Stirling's Game Room
Photo courtesy of Arlin Dease

Two antique tables placed about the room are also in mint condition. A portrait of, what I have been told is, David Bradford hangs above the table on the east wall, while a Confederate soldier looks out upon the room above another table along the south wall. An authentic sword from the Civil War, that was found upon the property, is lying upon its polished wood.

The fireplace is hand-painted by Mrs. Stirling's French artisans in a decidedly masculine tortoiseshell façade. Its dark black and amber detailing is repeated in the room's baseboards. Once the shiny lacquer is applied as an overcoat, it is difficult to tell the fake from an authentic piece of stone. Arlin Dease told me that most of the faux painting had worn away on the fireplace, and that he and Stephen Saunders studied the matching baseboards in the room to create the original faux design.

1850s Gasolier

Hanging above the game table is a rare find—an 1850 German gasolier crafted in brass, bronze and pewter. It is the only lighting fixture of its kind in the home. It originally burned carbide gas, but Arlin Dease told me it never burned gas while in the Myrtles home. I noticed how many elements are included in this massive lighting fixture. Small heads of dogs, cherub heads, cherubs sporting spears, and elaborate scrolling, all fuse together into an expensive piece of craftsmanship. If you get a chance to see this beautiful fixture, take a close look at the amazing amount of detail.

The molding in this room is much simpler than the pierced frieze work in the parlors, entry, and dining room. The reason for this, is that a Stirling family plaid was hung as a border up along the top of the wall at the ceiling level. In the 1980s, when the room was restored, they found evidence of the plaid design in the old plaster, and recreated the pattern in a wallpaper border, which has now been removed.

Children's Dining Room with smaller table and chairs.

During the Bradford years, as well as the consequent ownership, the Game Room was also used as the Children's Dining Room. Here, the table was smaller, as were the chairs. The door between the main Dining Room could be left open between the two rooms, and the adults could enjoy their conversation, while the little ones had dinner nearby.

The Photograph of Chloe in the Game Room

The tour given at the plantation typically ends in this room, but they have saved something special for you as you depart through the door to the outside verandah. Leaning against an easel, is an enlarged photograph of what many believe to be the image of Chloe, the Myrtle's famous ghost. Mrs. Moss inadvertently captured the ghost's figure in 1992, while taking photographs of the property for insurance purposes. When the pictures were developed, it was noted two of the photographs contained what appeared to be a slave girl, her hair wrapped in a tied turban, standing in the space between the original Bradford building (today's Gift Shop) and the main house.

Wanting to make sure what she saw in the picture was indeed that of a human form, Mrs. Moss set out to have it authenticated. The disconcerting element in the photograph, is that you can distinctly see the slats of the clapboard siding of the main house through the figure, as though it was transparent. First, a National Geographic filming crew studied the photo, and confirmed that the apparition appeared to be a nineteenth century slave girl. In May of 1995, a researcher named Norman Bourgeois, was given permission to enlarge the photograph 170%. He discovered that the measurements, such as the width of the head, the length of the shoulder to the elbow, and the length of the elbow to the wrist, were all human proportions. He also did what is called a "shadow density" analysis of the photograph. This is when an even bigger surprise surfaced. Two small children are seen sitting along the roof line just above where the shadowy figure of the slave girl is standing below! There were no children at the plantation that day; in fact, Mrs. Moss chose a time without guests to take her photos for the insurance company. The roof of the Myrtle's plantation has a wide gutter running the length of it, and it would be not only painful to sit upon it, but I know from experience, the windows looking out onto the roof from the upstairs rooms are painted shut; so, access to the roof from that avenue would be impossible. The limbs from nearby trees that reach the roofline are too fragile to support anything other than a bird.

Mr. Bourgeois said this in his report about the photograph:

"A closer image of the figure in question appearing to be of a person standing at a slight angle of approximately 20" towards the right, from a square front position. The image at this point shows some very unique comparisons of prospective sizes to a normal adult human figure with a total height of 5'1" tall.

"Taken while increasing shadow density to study more closely the apparent ghostly image appearing to be translucent at this time. Showing the boards or siding of the house through the image in question."

It goes on to mention seeing images of two children during the shadow density review. The odd thing, is that when Mr. Bourgeois tried to make copies of the original, the children had disappeared!

Chloe's ghost is circled here.
Photo courtesy of Teeta Moss.

The location of the mysterious photograph in the Game Room is appropriate. The moment you exit through the door next to it, you are standing on the verandah overlooking the location where the ghost was standing in the photograph—the space between the two buildings that comprise the Gift Shop building and the main house. Copies of the amazing photo are for sale in the Gift Shop as post cards.

Another unique feature is presented at this location. If you look up at the north side of the Gift Shop building exterior, you will see a small window. Arlin Dease placed the window there, in the 1970s, to show the original building materials and design from 1794, when Bradford first built the outbuilding. Mr. Dease thoughtfully allowed a piece of history to shine through the more modern renovations.

Mark T., New Orleans, Louisiana. "This may not be a big thing, but while I was on a tour at the Myrtles Plantation, we were in the game room and this strange tapping sound kept coming from the other side of the locked door in that room. We were told the door led to the back staircase on the other side. We thought a guest staying upstairs had come down and was probably standing on the other side of the door, knocking to scare us. A few seconds later, it sounded again, but this time on the window looking outside. Just a tap, tap, tap, like fingertips tapping really softly. When it started tapping on the painting hanging over the side table, the tour guide started looking a little nervous."

The Verandah

Ruffin Gray Stirling and his wife Mary Cobb Stirling created much of the iconic look that people today associate with the Myrtles Plantation. No other home in Louisiana has the Myrtles' signature grillwork, that runs the length of four verandahs, wrapping this plantation home. The delicate grape and vine motif give this Wedgewood cast iron railing and supports an almost fairytale look.

Some have compared it to the detailing on the Haunted Mansion at Disneyland. That isn't surprising since the Imagineers came to New Orleans to garner images for their popular attraction at the "Happiest Place on Earth." The townhomes of the Crescent City have similar detailing along their upper galleries and the Stirlings no doubt wanted to emulate that beautiful lacy façade.

The railing is an impressive 120'-long and is in remarkable shape. Its color is hard to pigeonhole. To me, it is a blend of soft turquoise and sea foam green. It has also been called aqua. Against the blue-painted cypress floor boards, and white clapboard siding, it gives the large house a loftier feeling, and some have said in the right light, it almost appears to be floating. Whether that has to do with the fact the house is actually four feet above ground to protect it from flooding, or due to the trick of moonlight, it sets the Myrtles apart from the neighboring Greek Revival plantations.

Another element of the grillwork, that became a bonus during the shifting light of the day, is that the upright supports along the verandahs cast delicate shadows of their lacy design through the windows of the Myrtles, playing upon the interior walls like expensive wallpaper. Photos taken during the morning and late afternoon hours show the delicate pattern running up the main staircase as though it is not content to be kept outside.

The Stirling's love of their plantation home is evident. Their desire to maintain the integrity of the original building, while expanding it and putting their own stamp upon it, is also plain. Thanks to the careful integration of these two structures, generations have been able to enjoy the vision of two families who had a dream of an amazing place to call home.

Many ghost stories have surfaced concerning the verandah that virtually wraps the Myrtles Plantation. Most concern hearing small children laughing and running along the antiquated boards, when no children are in sight. Some have reported hearing music, conversation, laughter, and even chickens clucking, coming from different locations on these 120'-long porches. Photos of orbs abound, and some have captured strange light anomalies. Even the white rocking chairs move under their own volition, without a wind, or soul in sight.

Strange lights near the Myrtles Plantation verandah.

Chapter Fourteen
The Myrtles Plantation:
The Upstairs Stirling's Addition & Ghosts

Upstairs gallery of the DuBois Plantation, Bostwick, Georgia

Upstairs, on this wing of the house, are the Woodruff Suite (Sarah Mulford's Suite when the Stirlings were living there), and the upper gallery. You can see across from the Woodruff Suite a door, that is now padlocked. That once led into the Ladies' Dorm where visiting guests would stay, or rest, during and after parties. The Dorm was doubtlessly used for other things when the parties were not in session. Today, this locked door leads to the Fannie Williams room.

The Stirling's new expansion of the home did not just include the downstairs Morning Room, Bedroom Suite, and entry hall. That addition afforded a matching foyer upstairs that could be used as a formal sitting area, as well as a large bedroom suite, that took up the entire south wing of the house. During the Stirling's ownership, the suite was given to their daughter Sarah Mulford Stirling, as she was the oldest girl. Lewis, her brother, was two years older, but may have had quarters in the garçonnéirre outside, as was the custom for males of a certain age, to allow them freedom to come and go. The smaller children were all grouped into the Nursery wing in the original upstairs area of the house.

Sarah Mulford's Suite (The Woodruff Suite)

Sarah's new suite was quite lavish, with its own fireplace, dorm windows and sitting room. The fireplace was one of the original fireplaces to the plantation that Mrs. Stirling had moved upstairs. The cypress wood was now a glistening white with matching doors and trim. An elegant chandelier dangled from the ceiling, filled with candles. Her bed would have been a four poster with a canopy.

The windows flanking the fireplace looked out over the south side of the house and the winding entrance road to the plantation. Her dormer window, on the east wall, overlooked the front of the house and the towering oaks outside.

Typical Plantation Bedroom, 1800s

An armoire, or wardrobe, would have been in service to house her clothes. A wash basin and pitcher would have graced a special chest, and a "chamber pot" was probably secreted beneath the bed. Some bedrooms had portieres (curtained areas that hid chamber pots and slop pails).

Her sitting area would have had chairs, a table, possibly a writing desk, and perhaps a small couch, or chaise lounge. The dormer window in this area overlooks the back property. Here, she had privacy from the ubiquitous noise of the house, with children dashing around and slaves going about their chores. She was entering adulthood and learning the social graces, as well as sewing skills, and other accomplishments that would prepare her for marriage someday.

Today, Sarah Mulford's Suite is called **The Woodruff Suite,** in honor of Judge Clark Woodruff, who owned the plantation prior to the Stirlings. Mr. Woodruff never slept in the room, as this portion of the house was added after he sold it to Ruffin Gray and Mary Cobb Stirling. It has been beautifully restored, with a reproduction of a Zachary Taylor wallpaper in soft pewter colors and floral bouquets. The opulent drapes are in matching pewter with pink trim.

A large four poster bed with a lace canopy is nestled in the corner of the room to the left of the white fireplace. Its satin duvet, with matching shams, is in a diamond pattern, and continues the feeling of freshness in the room with its white doors and trim. A small round table sits next to the bed, draped in a flowing floral fabric. A nod to the 21ˢᵗ century sits atop this table in the guise of an electric table lamp.

In the Woodruff Suite, a giant mirrored wardrobe is against one wall, with a high back antique chair with a green brocade cushion, seated next to it. A lovely dresser with drawers sits near the door to this room. In the corner, near the dorm window, is a 5-shelf display table with small figurines and bric-a-brac. The chandelier, dripping with cut crystal, is reflected in the large gold mirror over the fireplace. Today, it is electric with small white lamp shades, but it originally housed candles. Anchoring the room, is a beautiful antique rug in floral design with soft blue trim.

A sunken sitting area is off to the right of the entrance in the Woodruff Suite. It was originally used as such, and today houses two wing-back chairs and a table. Off of this small room, is a modern bath with a tub, sink and toilet, all in a feminine pink color.

The views from the windows of these two rooms have the same vantage point as they did in Sarah Mulford Stirling's time, but the view has changed a bit. The south-facing windows now overlook a large courtyard with a central fountain, wrought-iron tables and chairs, and potted plants. The original Bradford home is still there, but it has been turned into a whimsical gift shop. The view from the window to the left of the fireplace now commands a view of Restaurant 1796, instead of the stables.

This author had the pleasure of visiting the Myrtles Plantation, in August, of 2011, and again, in February, of 2012. On my visit in 2011, I was given the Woodruff Suite. As it was my first visit to the Myrtles, I was not familiar with the layout of the house, or the guest room situations. I arrived at the plantation after the staff had gone for the day, and was shown to the main house by James, the caretaker and overseer at the Myrtles. He unlocked the back door to the newer wing of the house, from the back veranda, and led me into the central hallway of the house. I saw the mirror hanging above the opulent Louis XV commode to my left and felt a feeling of awe to see the area featured in so many photographs and videos taken of the entry foyer. I knew the mirror's reputation for giving up images of faces and figures when guests took photographs of its aged glass. I caught a quick glimpse of the handprints in its mirrored surface, that were famous for their tenacity in returning to the mirror's face, no matter how often the glass and backing were changed out. Walking beneath the enormous chandelier, looking much too heavy to be anchored overhead by a ceiling dating back over 172-years—when this newer portion of the house was built—was surreal. Light glinted off the smoky amber crystals and played across the polished cypress wood floor. A tall, banjo-style grandfather clock was off to my left against a lovely fragile wallpaper of birds and delicate tree branches. A glimpse of the Ladies' Parlor winked from behind white lacy sheers as we passed the door leading into the original section of the plantation.

James carried my bags up the main staircase toward my suite. The eyes of a man in a large portrait watched us pass beneath him from his perch on the wall above the red-carpeted rungs. I knew the reputation of the staircase I was climbing. Somewhere, up ahead of me, would be the seventeenth step; the place where William Winter supposedly died in his wife's arms, after being gunned down on the north verandah. I hadn't counted the steps, but I was pretty sure, as I neared the landing, that I had probably just crossed over it.

The upstairs gallery was huge, furnished with just enough pieces to give you a sense of its purpose in another lifetime. The floors groaned slightly beneath our weight and gave off a vibration that sounded like metal rattling. I must have looked like an awestruck child as I stared at everything around me, reminding myself over and over, that I was in a plantation whose original structure was built over 216 years ago! Not only that, but I was about to spend the night in what has been called the Most Haunted House in America! AND, I was sleeping alone!

As if James could read my mind, he said quietly to me, as he set down my bags and inserted the room key into the lock, "You get this whole side of the house to yourself. There are a couple of ladies in one of the rooms in the other wing, but you have the only key to this side of the house. Nobody else is here." Just as images from a B-Movie began running through my head, he added, "I got a place over there," (he waved vaguely toward the back of the plantation) "in the Gift Shop part, if you need anything in the night."

He swung the door to my suite open, and my view of the gorgeous room took over my fear...temporarily. The room truly was beautiful, and I felt like I had stepped through a time warp into another century. James handed me the key, reminded me to let him know if I needed anything, and left, closing the door quietly behind him.

I stood in the middle of the Woodruff Suite, looking about me and trying to get my bearings. I faced the windows flanking the fireplace, which showed only the darkness from outside through the sheers, and oriented myself. My white rental car should be just outside the window to the left in the parking lot below. Somehow, the thought that a car awaited me gave me some comfort. I walked to the edge of the step leading into the sunken sitting room and peered at the *small twin bed there. Swallowing, I stepped down and turned to the left, hurriedly flicking on the light switch to the bathroom. The ceilings were so high! The window above the bathtub seemed to climb up forever.

Finally, I walked back up into the main bedroom and sat on the bed. It felt very comfortable and plush. I saw my reflection in the large mirror adorning the front of the wardrobe and felt as if I was trespassing on someone else's memories. This room had been the main bedroom suite for so many owners after the Stirlings were gone. Sarah Mulford had spent years of her life in this room, mourning her husband who had been murdered outside the Gentlemen's Parlor. She probably died in this room, at the age of 44, after becoming a recluse. Other owners, who lived and died at the Myrtles, no doubt used this as the master bedroom, including Fannie and Harrison Williams, who purchased the Myrtles in 1891. Fannie was widowed during her stay at the Myrtles as well, and sorrow once again stained the walls in this room.

* Today, the small single bed in the sitting room of the Woodruff Suite has been replaced with chairs and a table.

I thought about the great joy that also permeated this room. So many children were born at the plantation. Sarah Mulford planned her wedding to William Winter here. There was romance in these walls as owners held each other and made plans for their beautiful home. It was so surreal to sit here and wish I could peek through the veil that shrouded all those years, and hushed all the footsteps that had walked across these floorboards...well, hushed *almost* all.

And then, came the time to go to bed. I will be honest. I do not scare easily. My movies of choice are usually psychological thrillers, or ones with a supernatural bent. I have no problem with entering a dark house and walking around, before finally turning on a light. I typically fall asleep with a book about the paranormal resting across my stomach. I took one last look out the bedroom window to the lights of the closed Gift Shop, and was reminded of staring out the windows of the Manor House at the haunted Stanley Hotel.

Myrtles Gift Shop at night. Photo Jason Phillip Reeser.

While writing *The History and Haunting of the Stanley Hotel,* I stayed for five nights in the Manor House, at the Stanley Hotel complex, all alone. When I say all alone, I mean I was the only one in the entire Manor House! Three floors of suites and I was the only one in the entire building for five nights. The staff stayed in the main hotel a few feet away. Going into that building at night, after I finished interviews for the book with the staff and guests next door in the main hotel, was a little daunting. Riding the elevator up three floors to my room, without a sound from another soul, was a bit unnerving, and sleeping in Room 1301, next door to the haunted room of 1302 was, again, a bit heavy. But I did fine. I even watched *Ghost Lab* at night before I went to sleep. Snow was falling outside and I could hear the ethereal bugling of an elk in the night. It was not lost on me, that this was the exact setting that inspired Stephen King to write *The Shining,* after his stay at the Stanley Hotel. Still, I slept like a baby.

The Stanley Hotel at night. Estes Park, Colorado.

Not to say that things didn't happen to me at the Stanley Hotel. My watch stopped every morning at 1:17 am, only to start again later in the day, and be on the correct time. The ghost of Lord Dunraven blew a blast of cherry blend tobacco smoke into the faces of myself and seven others, during an investigation on the 4th floor of the main hotel. The closest encounter I've ever had occurred on the landing between the 2nd and 3rd floors at the Stanley Hotel.

I had stopped on that landing to ask the tour guide, Scary Mary, a question after the rest of the group went up to the 3rd floor and waited at the balcony. Suddenly, something burning pressed into the bare shoulder of my right arm. I jumped and gasped. As I did so, several of the people in the tour overhead heard me and looked down; they snapped several photos. When they looked in their camera view finders, they were shocked. Depending on where they were standing along the upper landing, each camera showed a giant green orb, the size of a soccer ball, coming over my right shoulder. In one photo, it left a tendril trailing across my throat.

When I looked at my shoulder, there was a 4-inch square red mark, like someone had pressed a giant ice cube into my arm. It remained for several hours. The tour guide said the landing was where a ghost named Sarah was known to frequent, and that she had been a fourteen-year-old nanny back in the early 1900s, when the hotel opened. She was very tall for her age and that era, and the guide felt she may have had an affinity for me, as I am 6'2"! Those experiences made me realize, there is so much more to our world than we know, and what happened in Louisiana only intensified that knowledge.

Enter the Myrtles Plantation! The atmosphere one feels in this plantation home is "thick," for better choice of a word. You feel the history and the impressions that over two hundred years of people living here leave on a place.

When I finally settled beneath the covers that night, and sank into the soft pillows of my four-poster bed, I could not bring myself to turn off the lamp that was within reach to my left. I kept looking around the room…at the corners, at the glimpse of the twin bed in the sunken sitting room across from me. I watched the reflections in the mirrored wardrobe. I thought of all the emotions and events to which this room had been privy. Finally, I reached over and shut out the light. It was so quiet here. It was August, and I guess I expected the sounds of bugs outside in the Louisiana heat. The bed linens smelled so fresh, as if they had been air-dried in the breeze. It was comfortable in the softness of the bed, but I couldn't bring myself to shut my eyes. "The most-haunted home in America!" kept running through my head.

I must have finally fallen asleep, because something jolted me wide awake in the darkness. A loud BANG had sounded from below; from what I knew to be the area of the front doors leading from the main hallway to the front lawn. It was so loud that the wall shook. My heart was pounding, and I sat there in the darkness with the covers pulled up to my chin, shaking. I kept hearing James, the caretaker's, words in my head, that I had the only key to that section of the house, which happened to contain the main front doors. When nothing else happened, I picked up my cell phone from the night table next to me and flipped it on. The light from the phone face nearly blinded me.

The time read 2:12. It was 2:12 in the morning! Who would have been coming in the main doors at that hour, let alone slamming them?

Then I heard it! The unmistakable sound of someone climbing up the creaking stairs leading up to the landing, just outside my bedroom door. All the stories I had read, and heard, about William Winter's ghost climbing that staircase, only to have the footsteps stop on the 17th step (where he supposedly died), came flooding into my head. I started counting the steps I could hear mounting the stairway.

One. Two. My heart was pounding out of my chest. I had the covers up to my eyes, and was whispering over and over to myself, "I'm an idiot…. I'm an idiot! It was my idea to come here alone!"

Three. Four! Just as I was about to have a full-blown panic attack, the steps stopped. I could hear my heart beating in my ears, and I wanted it to quiet down so I could listen. If that piano sitting in the alcove beneath the stairs began to play, I knew exactly how long it would take me to grab my bags, throw on a pair of Levi's, and make it to the afore-mentioned white rental car outside in the parking lot. I waited, but there were no other sounds.

Lying there was too hard. I flipped on the table lamp and swung my legs over the side of the bed. Grabbing up a robe I had draped over the end of the bed, I slipped it on and walked as quietly as I could to the door leading into the foyer. I knew just outside that door was the balcony overlooking the main staircase, and at the bottom of that staircase were the front doors. It took all I could do to open that door.

I pulled it open a couple of inches and peered out into the lit gallery of the upper foyer. When nothing out of the ordinary appeared, I opened it the rest of the way and stuck out my head. Still nothing spooky. Swallowing over and over, I stepped out into the gallery, and felt the shuddering that I had witnessed when James took me up to my room. A soft vibrating sound, like a metal frame rattling against the wall, sounded. I had to walk the length of the balcony to peer down the stairs and see the front door. I was afraid every step I took was alerting something of my whereabouts. Finally, I leaned over, and peered down the main staircase, its deep red-carpet runner absorbing the light from the chandelier.

Looking down the stairs to the front doors.

There were the front doors…soundly shut. I saw nothing broken. No pictures were hanging askew, as they would be, based on the force of the slam I heard. The man in the portrait looked stoically out over the staircase, as if to say, "I understand the things that happen here. I see them every night." I stood there a moment and listened. The house seemed to be listening with me. My nerves got the better of me and I hurried back to my room, and locked the door. I slept with the bathroom light on the rest of the night, sure that James, the caretaker, could see it from his room at the back of the property, and was probably laughing about the silly guests that stayed here.

The next morning, over a wonderful breakfast of ham slices, eggs, grits and juice, I got to know the amazing people who ran the plantation. I felt silly telling Teresa, the General Manager at the time, and Hester Eby, the Director of Tours, I had heard slamming doors and something creeping up the stairway. Instead of raised eyebrows and bemused glances, I received the somber look and nodding heads of those who had heard these stories, and so many others, all too often. Hester, who has the most wonderful way of making you feel like one of the family, with her soft-spoken voice, motherly tenderness, and the words "Baby" and "Honey" sprinkled throughout her sentences, simply looked at me fondly, and said, "Baby, it's OK. It happens here all the time." Teresa smiled at me, and said in her delightful southern accent, that she was "so happy I got to witness something, since I was writing a book about the plantation." Happy…yeah…. that's what I felt… 'happy.'

In February, of 2012, I returned to St. Francisville, Louisiana, to do more research for the book. I was anxious to meet Teeta Moss, the owner of the Myrtles Plantation, as she had not been there on my prior visit the summer before. I also had appointments with libraries, museums, newspapers, historical societies, and a university. It would be a hectic few days.

I was booked into three different rooms for my three-night stay at the Myrtles. I had offered to stay at a local hotel, to leave the rooms for other guests, but Teeta wouldn't hear of it. Teeta Moss is southern hospitality personified. She is called "Miss Teeta" at the plantation, and it evokes the civility and charm of an era that is still alive and well at the Myrtles. She graciously gave me two full days of her time, including giving me a tour around St. Francisville, and of her beautiful new estate, called Ridgecrest.

When I was told that the staff had once again booked me into the Woodruff Suite, I felt my heart thud. I tried to wrangle for a different room, assuring them that other guests should have the pleasure of sleeping in the master suite. I was outvoted. So, once again, I mounted the steps, took a long hot soak in the tub, looking over my shoulder at all times at the darkening corners, and finally slipped into the protective shelter of fluffy covers, plump pillows and crisp linens. Ok, I had been here, done this. I had survived before and I would do it again. I got up and took off my earrings and laid them on the mantle next to my bed. Just to make sure I wouldn't forget them the next morning, I placed my room key on top of them. Then I nestled into the covers, turned off the lamp and watched the room for several hours.

The morning light, through the window just over my shoulder, surprised me. I had slept through the night! No terrors…no slamming doors, or creaking stair rungs. Feeling very happy with myself, I got up and dressed. I packed my bags, checked my camera, and, remembering my earrings, crossed to the fireplace to retrieve them.

1800s white marble fireplace.

The room key, which was where I left it the night before, was still sitting on the left-hand corner of the fireplace mantle. The earrings, however, had managed to come out *from under* the room key, and move the entire length of the mantle to the other end! I stood staring at them, not really wanting to pick them up. I ran it all through my mind again to make sure I was not mistaken in my placement of them the night before, but I knew I was not wrong. I had deliberately put the room key on top of them, so I wouldn't leave them behind. That makes the score 2 for the Woodruff Suite.... Rebecca—0!

There are many stories from guests, of things moving about in the Woodruff Suite. A delicate 5-tier display cabinet sits in the corner by the east-facing dormer. Beautiful little boxes and figurines from a bygone era catch the light in their bone china and painted porcelain. Reports of these innocuous-looking little trinkets moving around the room, are not uncommon.

Sometimes, they switch places on the cabinet shelves, at other times, they are found clear across the room on a chair. Perhaps the ghost is dusting, but it does leave one a little unnerved. One of the stories I received, I will admit, made me nervous to stay the night in the Woodruff Suite again. Anyone who has stayed there, knows that a few feet from the large four poster bed, is a small sunken sitting room, that you step down into. A twin four poster bed was nestled into the corner beneath a door that once led out onto the gallery. At one point, the sitting room had been closed off to the master suite, and was a small room attached to the modern bathroom the Michaud's put in, during their ownership of the plantation in the 1950s. People in the Woodruff Suite, needing to use the bathroom, would have to go out to the foyer, and enter through the door there at the top of the main staircase. When Frances Kermeen took over the house, she tore down the plastered-over door separating the two rooms, returning the Suite and sitting room to its original condition. It is the small bed in this sitting room, that could be clearly seen from anyone sleeping in the master bed, that prompted the story told to me by someone visiting the Facebook page I set up for this book. (The small bed has been replaced with wing back chairs and a table.)

Lori R. said she was staying in the Woodruff Suite and having trouble sleeping. Her mother was terminally ill, and thoughts of more visits to the hospital, when she returned home to Oregon, kept going through her mind. She was tired and feeling hopeless. The trip to the Myrtles had been her friend's idea. That same friend was staying out in one of the Garden Rooms behind the Carriage House Restaurant (now Restaurant 1796).

Lori lay there in the semi-dark room. She had left the bathroom light on, not so much from fear, but so that she could find her way around if she awoke in the night and needed to find the bathroom, without falling down the step into the sitting room. Her eyes were fixed on the small twin bed in the next room for no particular reason. Her mind was elsewhere. *Something is wrong with the bed*, a tired voice murmured from the back of her mind. Lori blinked a few times, certain the bathroom light was playing tricks with the shadows created by the soft duvet on the little bed. But as she watched, the blanket rumpled, and the lower edge came up, as though someone had just turned over, taking the blanket with them.

Rising to one elbow, she stared wide-eyed at the twin bed, her breathing coming faster. Moments passed, and all she could see was an un-kept bed. Then it happened again. The little bed moaned, and the blankets pulled toward each other, as the unseen guest turned again in its sleep.

1800s single bed.

"I had the most absurd thought go through my mind," she wrote me. "Seriously, the first thing I thought was, 'Ok, you didn't leave anything in the bathroom, so you don't have to go past that bed to get anything.' That fast, I was planning my escape! I got out of bed, snatched up my purse and overnight bag, that were on the big chair next to the step going down to that haunted bed, not at all happy that I had to get that close to it! Then I got on my cell phone and called my friend, who was sleeping out in one of the outside bedrooms, noticing as I did it was 2:40 in the morning! —and told her to unlock her door and be ready for me to come stay with her. For some odd reason, she didn't ask why…just mumbled 'OK,' in a husky voice, and that was it. I left. The next day, she reamed me for checking out of a room that had cost her quite a bit of money. It was her present to me, as a means to get away from all that was going on with my Mom. I did feel badly, but I really doubt anyone could stay in that room, when you are sharing it with some*thing* in the next bed!"

Hester Eby, tells of one of her favorite stories pertaining to the ominous goings-on in the Woodruff Suite. "When a Chicago policeman and his wife spent a night in the Suite," Hester said, smiling, "the officer awoke to a knock on the door about 2 a.m., and found a woman walking the hallway outside in a wedding gown! She walked right through the window!

"The officer woke his wife and said, "We're leaving. Now!"

While I was staying at the Myrtles, and interviewing the staff, the guest's stories were a common amusement among the people there who are in charge of checking guests in and out of the plantation. "It's always the big, tough guy, who says he doesn't believe in ghosts, who is the first to come high-tailing it out of here in the middle of the night," Teresa David, the former General Manager said in her wonderful, honey-laced Southern accent. "It just tickles me. They check in and he's all, yeah, right, real spooky place…whooo hooo…and sure enough, next morning, he's either too scared to eat his eggs, or he left sometime in the night. Usually, the girlfriend or wife is teasing him about it."

Oprah Winfrey Show at the Myrtles

Oprah Winfrey. Photo courtesy of wmbfnews.com

The Myrtles Plantation has been in the media spotlight for years. It has graced more magazines, TV documentaries, and newspaper articles, than most venues with a haunted reputation. Oprah Winfrey, not to be left out of the media circus, chose the Myrtles for her upcoming Halloween show. She sent her production staff to the infamous plantation to shoot footage and report back. The crew and producer toured the home, and made notes for an evening taping to be added to the footage they had from earlier in the day. The producer went up to the Woodruff Suite, upon hearing the room had a history of extraordinary paranormal activity.

She walked into the antebellum bedroom and set her 35mm camera on the dresser near the door. As she crossed the room to check her lighting, the camera flashed. There was not an action sensor on the device, and it should not have gone off without someone pushing the camera button. Finding this a little unnerving, especially after hearing all the stories about the room, she rushed to the door, which refused to open. As she struggled with the door, she said she felt icy cold fingers grab her shoulder. She screamed, and the door suddenly released its hold.

The producer grabbed her camera and rushed down the stairs, announcing to the startled crew that the program was complete, and they had all they needed. It was time to pack up and go! When the TV segment about the Myrtles aired, Oprah talked about it in first person, leading some to believe she herself visited the plantation for the shoot, but she was not there. The producer may have relegated herself to safer topics in the future, such as Easter Egg Hunts at the White House or Fashion Shows.

Upstairs' Gallery in Newer Wing

In the Stirling's day, Sarah Mulford Stirling's door led from her room and out into the large foyer. Couches, tables and reading materials were, no doubt, arranged here, with a possible hurricane lamp and candelabras sitting on polished tabletops. The cypress wood floors gleamed in the daylight that penetrated the sheers, hanging on the windows at each end of this room, or from the twinkling candlelight in the evening. It would have been too hot to use the room during the summer days, but the other seasons, and evening, would have been lovely here.

As mentioned, there is a padlocked door on this foyer across from the door leading into Sarah's Suite. The wing was turned into two guest suites during the 1980s. The door, which if functional, would now lead into the Fannie Williams suite, was closed off and locked to allow the guests in that suite their privacy. For the Fannie Williams Room, guests use the door leading out into the upstairs gallery in the older part of the home. There are no other doors, leading from the gallry in the newer part of the house, into the older section on the north side.

For the purpose of collecting reports for this book, I posted two websites online, asking for credible stories of paranormal activity happening to people while staying at the Myrtles Plantation over the years. One site was at Paranormal 9 (which retired two years ago), and the other is on Facebook at *The History and Haunting of the Myrtles Plantation/Facebook.*

I received an email from a young woman, who stayed in the Woodruff Suite (Sarah's Suite), in 2009. She was there with her husband and was fascinated with the house. Her spouse was not as enamored with ghosts, and said he wanted to sit out on the rocking chairs and have a beer while she looked over their suite. He made good on his word, and the young woman began opening drawers and cabinets in the Woodruff
Suite, thrilled to have it all to herself.

After about half an hour, she told me she ventured out into the gallery outside their suite door and sat in a chair there, trying to imagine what life had been like in the house. She set a half-full plastic bottle of Coke down on the floor by her feet and leaned her head back. There was definitely a feeling of isolation here in this part of the house. She knew this section was shut off from the rest of the rooms. Her nerves began to get to her, and she sat upright and reached down for her bottle of Coke. She would join her husband out on the porch. Her fingers closed around air. She looked down at her feet. The bottle was gone. Her first instinct was panic, she wrote to me. Not from fear of some ghost with a sudden desire for caffeine, but she feared she had accidentally kicked the bottle, and it may have overturned under the chair, spilling the syrupy liquid all over the antique floorboards. She got down on her knees and looked under the chair. There was nothing there.

Just then, something brushed against her ankle, and she froze. She described it as the feeling of a soft gauzy curtain floating over her bare skin. Goose bumps erupted along her leg. She finally looked over her shoulder and stopped breathing. The Coke bottle was now sitting next to her leg and it was empty! She wrote that she jumped up and ran from the gallery, taking the long main staircase two steps at a time. When she slammed out onto the back verandah, where she found her husband chatting with another couple—who were also having beers as they rocked languidly in the late afternoon sun—she spouted out the entire story before anyone could get a word in. The other couple was on their feet. They wanted to see for themselves. The young woman reluctantly led them, along with her snickering husband, inside, after unlocking the door into the main entryway. She waited at the bottom of the stairs, however, as the other three went up. Moments passed, and finally her husband came down, with a smirk on his face. The other couple was behind him and laughing.

Not getting the joke, the young lady glared at him for not believing her. "What's so funny?" she fumed.

Without a word, he held out the object he had been secreting behind his back, as he descended the stairs. It was her Coke bottle, completely full!

"Maybe next time you should leave out the rum. It was sitting on the floor next to a chair by the window," he quipped, as he and the other couple returned to their rocking chairs.

In her letter, she swears the bottle was half-full when she set it down. She had been drinking from it the entire time she was searching the Suite...rum-free. Her husband never did believe her.

Chapter Fifteen

The Myrtles Plantation:
Original Upstairs Section & Ghosts

When David Bradford built the Myrtles, in 1796, the main house was a simple design of four down, four up, with a central staircase. This staircase leads to the upper gallery and what are now four guest suites and new bathrooms. In the Stirling's time period, the upstairs in this section of the house, was divided into two wings with a central gallery in the center. Bathrooms had not been installed in the 1800s, and chamber or bed pots, were probably in use, as well as a privy somewhere nearby on the property. Bradford's original staircase was now called the servant's staircase, as a grand main staircase had been added in the newer expansion of the house.

The upper galley in the original wing had two raised platforms; one on each end. These were used for Sunday services and schoolwork. Today only the raised platform on the east end of the gallery remains. This was the School Room area and a desk was situated on the platform for the "teacher's" use. This teacher may have been either parent, or someone hired to tutor the children. The other end of the foyer had a matching platform where the patriarch of the family, or a priest, would stand and deliver the Sunday service. This platform has today been turned into two modern bathrooms for the use of two of the guest rooms on this floor. These bathrooms house all the modern amenities a guest could want. The step has been removed.

Today, a large wooden table is seated near the remaining platform, surrounded by large overstuffed chairs in mauve fabric. Soft pastel green satin curtains adorn the window; once again their lush fabric is puddled onto the floor showing wealth. Antique portraits grace the walls of the gallery, but I have been told they are not related to the home's ancestry.

I received a few stories concerning the table and chairs that sit at the east end of the upper foyer. People staying in the four guest rooms on this landing have reported hearing the chairs move in the night. Their stories are identical, in saying the sound of furniture scraping across the cypress wood floors of the gallery are heard, usually around 2 or 2:30 in the morning. That time period interested me, as it was 2:12 in the morning I heard the front doors slam, and footsteps on the main staircase, during my stay in the Woodruff Suite. It seems the active hour at the Myrtles is of the 2 a.m. variety.

One couple said they peeked into the gallery after hearing the scraping sounds and saw nothing out of the ordinary. The overstuffed chairs were in place. Another gentleman was not to be put off so easily. He had booked a room for two nights. After hearing the furniture move about on the first night, he put small pieces of tape by the chair feet the following day to monitor their placement. Sure enough, at roughly 2:20 the next night, he heard the scraping sounds right outside his door. He was staying in the Ruffin Stirling Room, which was the original nursery. The table and chairs are right outside his door. He threw open the door and marched over to the innocent-looking chairs. Upon close inspection of the chair feet, he found three of the four sitting within the tape markings he had put down. The chair that sat closest to the open gallery however had moved! He said it was a good two inches outside of the tape marking! He had witnesses as to the chairs' placements, and was very excited that he had proven some kind of paranormal activity.

You will notice a slight sloping of the floorboards as you walk across the gallery expanse. This may be due to the Stirlings raising the upper floor a foot during their renovation, or there have been rumors that a fire may have broken out in this part of the house during the Bradford/Woodruff era. Perhaps this section was rebuilt after some minor damage was done. Stories from guests have circulated as to a strong odor of smoke on occasion permeating the William Winter Room, and then suddenly disappearing.

The staircase leading to the upper foyer is very steep. During the Stirling's day, it was mainly used by the servants, with the family primarily entering this section of the home through the door in the dorm room which is now the Fannie Williams Room. I especially like the door leading out to the back verandah at the bottom of these steps. It has one of Mrs. Stirling's original upside-down keyholes.

The Fannie Williams Room

At the far end of the upstairs foyer, on the right as you come up the staircase, is the Fannie Williams Room, named for one of the plantation owners that came after the Stirlings. This room is half of the original dorm room used by the ladies for rest time during the Stirling's reign. It was created by former owner Frances Kermeen in 1980, when she renovated the upstairs and turned the two wings on this floor into four guest rooms. The Fannie Williams Room was originally called the Blue Room. Today it goes by the formal name of Fannie Williams and is a decidedly feminine room.

This room is beautifully decorated with blue wallpaper in a dainty gingham design with periodic vertical stripes and lace trim. A matching scalloped border adorns the ceiling. The wooden bed is truly interesting. Unlike the other four poster beds in the home, this bed is known as a "tester bed" and dates back to 1820. Made of dark oak, these Elizabethan beds are rare. Another antique in this room is a wash stand, still housing the porcelain wash bowl and pitcher, with an octagonal pivotal mirror adorning its spindle top.

This room has often been called the "doll room." At one time, there were several dolls with porcelain faces standing prettily along the mantel. Guests reported that the dolls would move during the night, sometimes all the way across the room. One antique doll now resides on the mantel, flanked by a stand of books, a porcelain music box, and a floral plate that matches the bedspread in the room. The fireplace is painted a crisp white, complementing the wallpaper and giving the room a fresh feeling. An oval gold mirror hangs above the fireplace reflecting the chandelier and throwing light into the corners of the room. A private bath is only a few steps away in the hallway.

As mentioned, the Fannie Williams Room has a history of things moving about. Tenacious guests have set up video cameras to record the movements of the dolls at night. One such video shows a doll lying upon the floor with her dress moving as though being lifted by currents of air. Her original position had been atop the mantle. The film does not show how she ended up on the floor.

Hester Eby has been part of the staff at the Myrtles longer than anyone. She is considered the resident expert on the stories that have evolved over the years. I found her to be truly unflappable, with a kind, soft-spoken demeanor, and a person who holds steadfast in her beliefs. She has had enough unexplainable things happen to her at the plantation to stand the test of any skeptic daring to throw down the paranormal gauntlet in front of her. I found her totally trustworthy and without rancor toward the non-believers.

During one of the many tours Mrs. Eby had given at the plantation, she mentioned the Fannie Williams Room and an incident that happened there.

"One evening," Hester related, "a woman and her husband were lying in bed asleep in the Blue Room (Fannie Williams Room). The woman woke; an old lady stood over her. 'My name is Mrs. Woods,' the old lady stated. 'Brenda is OK.' And the old lady vanished."

'Brenda' was a friend of the people staying in the Blue Room and had been involved in a tragic accident. The guest called Brenda's husband and was told Brenda had emerged from a coma and was doing well. He handed the phone to Brenda who listened to the frightened friend's story of the lady standing over her bed, claiming to be a Mrs. Woods.

"Mrs. Woods raised me," Brenda told her friend. "She's dead."

"The guests left," Hester Eby told the fascinated tour guests.

The rooms upstairs are not on the official tour. It is to respect the privacy of the paying overnight guests. Many photos and videos of the guest rooms have made their way online in today's ever vigilant need to document everything. Nothing replaces the thrill of actually staying overnight in one of these beautifully appointed rooms, and I encourage you to visit the Myrtles Plantation, if you have not already done so.

One of the stranger stories that came my way, via my website, is that told by a woman in her early 60's. Her name is **Mary Ann Freeman** and she was visiting the Myrtles in 2005, from Austin, Texas. Ms. Freeman was not booked into the plantation, but was merely visiting her friends, who were staying overnight in the Fannie Williams Room. Ms. Freeman, after hearing the many stories concerning the paranormal activity at the plantation, had opted to stay at a local hotel.

When she met her friends for dinner at the plantation restaurant, they insisted she at least come up to the room and see how lovely it was. Being a huge antique buff, Ms. Freeman could not resist the temptation to peek at the furnishings in the room. As they unlocked the door to that wing of the house, and began their ascent up the steep staircase, Mary Ann commented that she must be getting old, as the stairs proved challenging. Her friends teased her good naturedly, but they did have to stop twice for Mary Ann to catch her breath and flex her right knee, which had been damaged in a car accident years earlier. Wincing a little from the climb, Mary Ann followed her friends along the gallery, until they reached their room door.

"I may need to sit down for a moment," Ms. Freeman commented, a sharp pain radiating from her knee.

"I'll clear you off a space...," her friend began as she swung the door to the room open wide. She stopped in mid-sentence, and stared in surprise at their room. Her husband also let out a gasp.

When the couple left the room to go downstairs and meet Mary Ann for dinner, they had hurriedly unpacked several bags, and tossed things onto chairs and the bed, in their hurry to find cameras and change into other clothing. They both distinctly remember putting a small overnight case on the chair and tossing two parkas over the top of it. Now, the chair in question had moved from its place against the wall, and was sitting in the middle of the room, quite empty, facing the door in readiness. The small overnight bag was now on the bed next to the larger suitcase, and the two parkas were lying neatly beside it. Mary Ann, not knowing the condition the chair had been in before, limped over to it and sank gratefully onto the soft cushion.

"Don't mind if I do," she said with a grateful sigh. Then looking about at the room, she said, "This really is lovely! I can't imagine anything scary ever happening here!"

Her friends merely stared at her in disbelief.

Tales of guests being tucked into their beds at night by a kindly presence are a popular theme at the Myrtles. Perhaps a benevolent spirit, witnessing Mary Ann's pain, had pulled the chair to the center of the room and removed the clutter, allowing Ms. Freeman a place to rest.

Reports of cameras, cell phones, recorders, and other electronic devices having a hard time functioning at the plantation, are prevalent. While interviewing Mrs. Moss, the plantation owner, for this book, my small recorder would function at one minute and stop dead the next, refusing to work. She laughed gently at me, as I tried over and over to get it to record our conversation, as we sat at a table on the patio courtyard, saying, "Darlin', it happens all the time around here." Pulling out my notebook and pen, I hurriedly took notes for the rest of the interview.

When I returned to the Woodruff Suite to get ready for a meeting I had in St. Francisville, I once again pushed the "record" button on the tape player. I would give it one more chance before putting in new batteries. It started immediately, the little wheels mocking me as they turned around and around. I stood there fuming. I turned it off and pushed the "record" button again. Once again, it whirred with its soft little hum as it recorded the silent room. In exasperation, I muttered, "You've got to be kidding me!"

I went to my meeting, and when I returned to the plantation, I stopped and had dinner at the former Carriage House Restaurant at the Myrtles. I had the tape recorder with me. I was going to use it to interview a few of the restaurant staff. Picking it up I rewound it a little way to where I thought I had left off before. But when I pushed the record button, nothing happened. Now I was ticked! It would rewind but not record. It had worked fine in my room!

For the next hour, I talked with the owner of the restaurant, Beth Pace, and some of her staff. I madly took notes and asked her to repeat a few things. I kept silently cursing the recorder. Finally, back in my room, I went over the notes and added some details from memory. The small silver recorder winked at me in the soft light of the chandelier in the Woodruff Suite, where I was staying. Biting my lip, I picked it up and pushed the record button. The little wheels began to turn. I almost threw it across the room! I pushed "rewind" and heard the speedy humming sound as the tape backed up. Finally, I pushed the" play" button to see where I was on the tape. There were several seconds of dead space, so I knew I had not rewound it back far enough. The last interview I recorded on it was a small fraction of Teeta Moss's statements from the day before. Just as I picked it up, to rewind it back a few seconds, I heard my voice saying "You've got to be kidding me!" followed by what sounded like a laugh on the tape. It was muffled and far away. Surprised, I rewound it and immediately hit the "stop" button. When I pushed "play," there it was…a man's muffled laugh!

Had I recorded his laugh in this room? It had to be. The only time it was working that day was in this room. In my mind, I felt the ghost of some male was laughing at his clever joke of messing with my recorder when I needed it most.

Ori S., New York City, New York. "We stayed at the Myrtles Plantation, in 2015. My wife wanted the Fannie Williams Room, so we booked it. During the night, something kept pulling on my feet through the blankets. I finally sat up and turned on my cell phone light to shine it at the end of the bed. I didn't see anything, and my wife was sound asleep. It happened three more times during the night. I can tell you, that is quite frightening."

Mary L. T., Des Moines, Iowa. "Several of my friends and I booked two rooms at the Myrtles. They got the Ruffin Stirling Room and I got the Fannie Williams Room across the hall. We ran back and forth between the two rooms, laughing, and probably annoying the other guests. I had set out a doll I brought with me in my room, to see if it would move, since I'd heard that dolls move around in that room. I kept checking on it. Nothing. We were in the Ruffin room when one of my friends started laughing and pointed over to the dresser in that room. The doll I had set out in the Fannie Williams Room was now sitting on the dresser in the Ruffin room. She accused me of staging it there; I accused her of the same thing. We both swore we didn't move it. It bothered me so badly that I locked it away in my suitcase for the rest of the trip. Even when I got back home, it freaked me to look at it, so I gave it to a neighbor's kid."

The Ruffin Stirling Room (Former Nursery)

The guest room, with the number 9 on its door, has been christened the Ruffin Stirling Room. This area was once half of the nursery wing during the Stirling's ownership. The Bradford's may have used the wing that now houses the Fannie Williams and John W. Leake Rooms as their master suite, as the Fannie Williams Room has a fireplace and the Leake Room does not. We do know that the nursery wing had a connecting door between two large rooms.

Due to the large number of children, and the fact that many families in the 1800s had the help of a governess or nanny, a separate area was typically used for the smaller members of the family. In the Victorian era, the mother was often a remote figure who deferred many child raising duties to a hired caregiver. The movie *Mary Poppins* is a factual depiction of the role the mother and nanny played in the household. Children had a large room that comprised their beds and play area.

During the Stirling's era, several children lived at the Myrtles, although only one, Mary, was actually born there. Stephen, Clarence, Lewis, William, Ruffin Stirling III, Sarah, Henry, and Mary all lived at the Myrtles. Young Ruffin Stirling Jr. had been born in North Carolina, and died the same year at 5 months of age. Sadly, Clarence died at the Myrtles at the age of 13; Ruffin Stirling III died at the age of 1; Mary died at the plantation at age 18 of typhoid fever; and Lewis Stirling died at age 23. The other children, Stephen, William (who died at age 36), Henry, and Sarah, lived to adulthood and married.

Mary was probably still living at the Myrtles after her sister Sarah married William Winter and the two of them took over the plantation, following Ruffin Stirling's death from consumption, in 1854. It was common for an extended family to live together, especially if a female member was not married, and had no means of support.

So, we know that for a time the nursery was filled with children. In 1850, when the Stirling's major renovation of the plantation was taking place, Stephen was 3, William had just been born, Henry was born three years later, and Mary was 5.

Lewis was 19, and probably living in the *garçonnéirre* outside. Sarah Mulford Stirling was 17, and had her own room according to the floor plan of the house. Clarence Stirling died, in 1849, and it is not clear if he died at the Myrtles, or back home in North Carolina.

Rare 1800s Double-Seat Rocking Horse.

Typical 1800s Nursery

Today, the room in the northeast corner of the upstairs is the Ruffin Stirling Room. It is a beautiful suite painted in soft greens. The tall windows are encased in peach draperies. A fourposter bed dominates the room, its off-white satin bedspread and sham pillows giving an opulent feeling to the room. Unlike the other rooms, the Ruffin Stirling Room has an antique game table with four matching chairs; an area rug in blue trim sits beneath them. A portrait of a small child riding a pony, with dogs playing happily alongside, gives a nod to the original purpose of the room. It hangs above the white painted fireplace with the original cypress wood. This room has a private bathroom, just a few steps down the hallway, in the area that was once the Sunday School platform in the gallery.

Sadly, many children died in the nursery wing. Yellow fever and typhoid fever were common during the late 1700s and throughout the 1800s. Children often died young from other causes, perhaps due to the lack of immunization during those times, or weak immune systems. James and Cornelia Gale died in the Ruffin Stirling Room from yellow fever during the

Woodruff's time at the plantation. The old nursery saw both happiness and sadness.

It is ghost stories concerning young children that tend to permeate this room. Guests frequently report hearing the sounds of children's laughter and cries in this area of the house. People taking photographs from outside the house report children peering down at them from the dorm window in this room, when no children are in residence at the time. The small angular closet space that sits near the dorm window, has also seen its share of disturbances.

"We had been asleep for about an hour, when my husband poked me in the side and told me to wake up," **Mrs. Jane A**. told me in an email. "He was sweating and clearly rattled. When I asked, what was wrong, he said someone was knocking on the inside of the small closet door off to the left of the bed. I listened, but heard nothing. I told him old houses make noises. I plumped up my pillow and turned away from him to go back to sleep. I had barely closed my eyes, when I heard it as well. It was the sound of a small fist knocking on the inside door of the closet, as though wanting someone to open the door and let it out. I grabbed my husband's arm to let him know I heard it too. We were both too scared to move. It came again several times during the night, but neither of us had the courage to get up and look. Twice the sound of scuffling noises came from the closet as well, sounding very much like shoes moving around if someone were seated on the floor."

Other guests in the Ruffin Stirling Room have claimed to have seen a pale blue, wispy form hovering about the bed. It is usually at this time they feel themselves being tucked in.

"You don't feel like anything is there to hurt you," one man wrote me. "But, come on...it's unnerving to feel the blanket tighten in around you by something you can't see!"

Hester Eby told a tour group that "a male guest woke in the

*Twin Room and couldn't move. His covers had been tucked in tightly around him. The same had been done to his two sons, though they hadn't done this before going to bed." (*At one time, the room contained two beds and had been nicknamed the Twin Room, when James and Cornelia Gale Bradford lived there.)

Another prevalent occurrence in the Ruffin Stirling Room, is that of missing makeup. The spirit children seem to enjoy taking lipstick and hiding it. Most of the missing articles are later found hidden under the bed. It is the mischievous prank of little ones still wanting to play.

I received the following story, from a woman visiting the plantation, from her home in Georgia. She asked to simply be called **"Sylvia."**

"I was in the Stirling Room with my sister. We had always wanted to stay overnight at an old plantation. Neither of us knew of the place's reputation for being haunted. Our first clue, was when we pulled into the driveway off the highway and saw a big sign saying "Mystery Tours." I just thought it was like those Murder Mystery dinners people are so fond of having.

"After eating at the restaurant on the place, we went to the room and started taking out toiletries and stuff for the night. We were jabbering on about the plans we had for the next day…seeing other plantations, that kind of stuff. I put out my toothbrush and toothpaste, and told her I was going down the hall to the bathroom to get ready for bed. When I turned back around to pick up the toothbrush and paste, they were gone. I checked my bag, all over the room and they were simply not there. I finally left for the bathroom to wash up, racking my brain for where they could possibly be. When I entered the bathroom, I had the shock of my life. There they sat, on the sink, just waiting for me. I am not nuts…I am not crazy. Even my sister comforted me by saying she was sure I left the room without my toothbrush, and I had not gone to the bathroom before that time. I found out later that the place has ghosts. I think that makes my story more credible, as I did not go in there expecting anything abnormal to happen. Did anyone else tell you about losing a toothbrush when they stayed in that room…or any of the other rooms?" Sylvia

That was the only toothbrush story I had told to me. Several people mentioned missing cosmetics. Some were recovered, some were not. One woman mentioned losing one shoe for an entire day only to have it surface outside in the gallery under the table. People have taken small toys into the room to entice the children to play with them. This doesn't seem to work. It's as if the spirits refuse to perform on demand, and prefer to play with their own objects of choice.

As mentioned before, many people staying in the guest rooms throughout the mansion have reported experiencing the sensation of being "tucked in" at night. They will feel the bed sheets and coverings close in around them, until they are nice and snug. The nursery rooms turn in more stories than the other guest rooms of a presence hovering about in a protective manner, and the feeling that one is being cared for. While it may be unsettling to feel unseen hands plumping the pillows and pressing the blankets along your sides, it's never a sense of malice associated with the experience, but one of care, and sometimes…playfulness.

Beth Pace is an effervescent, lovely woman who was part owner of the Carriage House Restaurant on the Myrtles property. It was replaced by Restaurant 1796 in 2018. Everyone who meets Beth feels her love for the place, and her fondness for making everyone feel welcome and coddled. While interviewing her for this book, she related a story that happened to her while spending the night in the Ruffin Stirling Room, along with a friend who was visiting at the time.

"I was staying in the Ruffin Stirling Room and was sleeping on my stomach with my pillow fluffed up under my head," Beth told me. "Sometime in the night, something started jerking on the pillow. I looked over at my friend, but she was sound asleep. I put my head back down, and a few minutes later, it happened again; something tugging on the pillow. This was away from my friend, where she would have had to reach across me to do it, and once again, when I checked on her, she was sound asleep. Now feeling a little nervous, I re-plumped the pillow and put my head down. Several minutes passed and suddenly the pillow was ripped out from under my head and tossed across my friend's face. I punched her and yelled 'Stopped doing that!" but she was in a dead sleep.

"Later that same night, after finally managing to fall asleep, I was awakened by the sound of a loud party going on. I couldn't place what part of the house it was coming from—but it was really loud. I knew no one in the mansion was having a party, let alone one that sounded like a herd of people. It was pitch black and I couldn't see anything. After the pillow incident, I was too nervous to go and check it out."

Ghost Adventures **and the Ruffin Stirling Room**

In Season 9, Episode 2, of the popular reality TV series *Ghost Adventures*, the paranormal team visit the Myrtles Plantation. During the show, the lead investigator, Zac Bagon, interviews Myrtles tour guide, Mark Leonard, concerning paranormal activity reported in the Ruffin Sterling Room. Mr. Leonard recants an experience where he was reading a book in the room, when the bed he was seated on began to violently shake. He said he looked up at the chandelier, and found it was not moving, thus ruling out the probability of an earthquake. The cameraman zooms in on the deep gouges shown around the bed's feet, evidence of its extreme movement.

Photo of floor gouges in the Ruffin Stirling Room.

The William Winter Room

A connecting door from the Ruffin Stirling Room leads into the William Winter Room, named for the plantation owner, and son-in-law, of Ruffin Gray Stirling. While Mr. Winter is the most famous death at the Myrtles, his ghost does not haunt this room. It was originally the second half of the nursery and was called the Peach Room.

This room has an antique poster bed with a white satin comforter trimmed in a patchwork quilt fabric. The colors are repeated in the area rug and reflected in the pale green walls. A large armoire and chest of drawers anchors the room, their dark burled wood reflecting the soft light from the brass chandelier overhead. The fireplace is, again, the original cypress wood that was present downstairs during the Bradford's stay. It is painted white to match the doors and trim in the room. A portrait of white magnolias hangs above it, giving the room a decidedly southern feeling.

The addition of a private bath lends an air of modern refinement to the room. Its window overlooks the patio courtyard below and the original Bradford outbuilding.

The William Winter Room, was the room used by young Kate Lyle Winter, daughter of Sarah Mulford Stirling and William Winter. Kate was born September 28, 1858, in West Baton Rouge, Louisiana, at the Arbroath Plantation. She later lived at the Myrtles Plantation, and died there, at the age of three, of typhoid fever. Reports of the sound of a child crying in the William Winter Room are mentioned by guests, time after time. These stories are usually told when no one is booked into the room. While many children stayed in that portion of the house, the story of young Kate's illness and death carry with it one of the more intriguing stories of the plantation.

In the time of plantation owners and slaves, many cultures were thrown together. The African Americans, that tilled the earth, scrubbed the floors and dressed the children, had migrated to the area, either under their own power, or were brought in by boat to act as labor. Many of these people came from areas where medicine took on a different form than was typically practiced.

New Orleans was renowned as the home of "Voodoo" or "Voudon". When other more practical methods of treating a patient's illness had been exhausted, some families, desperate to save a loved one, turned to something a little more otherworldly.

VOODOO at the Myrtles

In the 18th century, voodoo was the most dramatic symbol of division between master and slave, and it loomed as a sinister threat to the ruling class. Plantation owners were aware of the eerie drums they heard beating at night somewhere in the distance on their properties, but it was like the elephant in the room. No one wanted to acknowledge it was there or talk about it. It was bewildering to the planter and the priest. Away from the plantation house, in the secluded woods near river and bayou, booming drums summoned slaves to torch-lit ceremonies in the night. Men and women, often dressed in mysterious masks gyrated to the percussive rhythms, as the cult priest or Voodoo Queen, chanted, filling the night with spirits and magic.

In 1782, the governor of Louisiana, fearing rebellious uprisings of the cults, put a clamp on voodoo-worshipping slaves imported from the Caribbean island of Martinique. But it was the equivalent of shutting the barn door after the horse had escaped. Voodoo had taken root and was growing.

Voodoo was actually a religion that had journeyed to the New World in overloaded slave holds of African slaves who had been uprooted from the animist culture of their homeland in Dahomey and Yorubaland. The religion involved dance, masks, rituals and evoking their dead ancestors, or *orishas*. The word Voodoo comes from the word vudu, the Dahomean "spirit," an invisible mysterious force that can intervene in human affairs. Followers of Louisiana Voodoo, believe in one God and multiple lesser, but powerful spirits, which preside over daily matters of life, such as family, the sky, and judgment.

Marie Laveau MarketPlace.SecondLife.com

In the 1800s, when the Stirlings and the Winters lived at the plantation, waves of planters, free Creoles of color, and slaves, reached New Orleans, many via Cuba, scattering seeds that sprouted new voodoo cults. As the antebellum era wore on, the voodoo sensibility—adaptive to the culture in which it found itself—worked its way into the thoughts and culture of aristocratic white society. Many white people sought the spiritual advice of Voodoo Queen Marie Laveau in New Orleans. She worked as a hairdresser in white homes, where she gathered secrets of the Creole elite by utilizing domestic servants to spy on whites. She introduced strange rituals to the affluent society, including sticking pins into a voodoo doll to provoke trouble for someone's enemy, or magical gris-gris dust (spell-casting powder) as a curative or protective hex.

The knowledge of herbs, poisons, and the ritual creation of charms and amulets became key elements of Louisiana Voodoo. The *ouanga*, a charm used to poison an enemy, contained the poisonous roots of the figure maudit tree, brought from Africa and preserved in the West Indies. The ground up root was combined with other elements, such as bones, nails, roots, holy water, holy candles, holy incense, holy bread, or crucifixes. The Voodoo doll is a form of gris-gris, and an example of sympathetic magic. Contrary to popular belief, Voodoo dolls are usually used to bless instead of curse. The purpose of sticking pins in the doll is not to cause pain in the person the doll is associated with, but rather to pin a picture of a person or a name to the doll, which traditionally represents a spirit. The gris-gris is then performed from one of four categories: love; power and domination; luck and finance; and uncrossing.

The administrator of the ritual frequently evoked protection from Allah, the Christian God, and Jesus Christ. This openness of African belief allowed for the adoption of Catholic practices into Louisiana Voodoo. This integral component may have added comfort to the minds of Louisiana plantation owners when they turned as a last resort to a practicing Voodoo Priest or Queen.

When little Kate Winter became consumed by fever, in 1861, Sarah and William Winter were desperate. Stories of miracles wrought by the Voodoo medicine, so prevalent in New Orleans, reached their ears. They sent for a priestess to cure their child. As told in an earlier chapter, beneath the cloak of night, a woman dressed in strange clothes and an elaborate turban is secreted up the back staircase, and into the room closest to the top of the stairs on the left. Rumors have reported her name as Cleo and that she came from the neighboring Solitude Plantation, but that has not been substantiated. Mark Leonard, assistant tour guide at the Myrtles, told this author that a young man on one of his tours said he was related to the people at Solitude Plantation and he had heard stories of a slave from Solitude being taken to the Myrtles to perform voodoo on a dying child. He said his family's stories reported the "priestess" was indeed killed when she was unable to save the child.

Gris Gris ingredients.

A compelling story was sent to me concerning this room. I was told at one time a rag doll sat on the mantelpiece in the William Winter Room and has been reported to fly, or jump to the chandelier in the room. Several people staying in the room swear they have seen the doll hanging from the light fixture, when it had been seated securely on the fireplace mantle only moments before. Rumor began circulating that perhaps the doll contained gris-gris or simply contained a protective spirit left over from the visiting Priestess. Others have heard someone mumbling the Lord's Prayer in this room, possibly a remnant from the parents of young Kate praying over her sick body.

Henry W., San Diego, California. "A friend of mine stayed at the Myrtles in the William Winter room. She told me she didn't sleep all night because she kept hearing these heart-wrenching sobs coming from the walls. At times, there was a child crying as well. She said the room made her very sad, and she felt like death had visited that area."

Valerie B., Detroit, Michigan. "The Myrtles has a lot of atmosphere. It's old. It's got stories. I stayed a night in the William

Winter Room. There's a sense of sadness in that room. I felt depressed, but I didn't anywhere else at the plantation. During the night, I kept feeling like someone was bent over me…watching me sleep. Twice I smelled this strange "earthy" odor, like a damp garden. Really weird things go on at that place."

The John W. Leake Room

In the Southwest corner of the north foyer, in the older section of the house, sits the John W. Leake Room. The room was named after a gentleman who owned a portion of the plantation at one time, and is a direct relative of the current owner, Teeta Moss. It is the room's history of housing a wounded Confederate soldier, however, that has most people requesting to stay there.

The Leake Room was originally called The Green Room, due to its soft green accents. Though the walls are in a pastel pink, the opulent green curtains that grace the dormer window, and the sage green dust ruffle circling the bed, give the room its nickname and the feeling of Spring. The bedspread is a complimentary pink and cream floral design. What makes the bed unique is that the four poster is crowned with a cream- colored tufted canopy that radiates out from a large self-covered matching button. It immediately evokes thoughts of the Colonial south. The oval portrait of a southern belle that hangs over the bed completes the atmosphere of a genteel era.

The antiques in the room are also period pieces, in both the large armoire and the marble-topped dressing table. A dainty lamp and French Cross statue grace this piece, and are reflected in its large mirror. A pink overstuffed chair sits in the corner next to the door. This room comes with a private bathroom and a claw-footed tub. The dormer window overlooks the courtyard with views of the pond and gazebo.

The Story of the Confederate Soldier

In 1863, when Port Hudson, only a few miles down the road from the Myrtles Plantation, was being fired upon by Union soldiers, residents of the opulent plantations in the areas began scurrying to reinforce the security of their homes. Able-bodied men were called out to try and thwart the enemy before they could encroach on their home turf. Ruffin Stirling, along with his oldest son Lewis, had died in 1854, nine years before the Civil War broke out.

I would like to clarify something at this point. Many reports exist that seven of the eight Stirling sons went off to fight bravely in the war and only one, Lewis, returned alive. As mentioned above, Lewis died before the Civil War broke out, in 1861. The War lasted until 1865. Stephen Stirling, who was 16 when the Union soldiers began bombing St. Francisville, at the far corner of his property, could have, and probably did go off to fight and halt their advancement. His brother, William, was 13 at the time, and again, could have helped in the fray. The sad truth of the war, is that many young men, barely into their teen years, and some as young as 12, were enlisted to fight. Those are the only two sons in the Stirling household that could have fought in the Civil War. Clarence had died in 1849 at age 13; Ruffin Stirling III died in 1844, at the tender age of 1; Henry was only 10, when the soldiers came calling; and Ruffin Gray Jr. had only lived 5 months, and died in 1840. We do know Stephen returned from the War and lived to be 79-years-old. William also returned and died in 1886, at the age of 36.

Sarah Mulford Stirling had married William Winter in 1852, and along with Ruffin's widow, Mary Cobb, and other relatives, was still living at the Myrtles. The far-off sound of shells exploding over the ramparts at Port Hudson grew closer until the towns of St. Francisville and Sara Bayou, only minutes from the plantation's door, erupted in shattering blasts from the *Albatross,* docked just outside their border on the Mississippi River. The War had come to the Myrtles Plantation.

The story of a Confederate soldier hiding out at the Myrtles, after his leg was seriously injured, has circulated since the Reconstruction Years, following the end of the Civil War. Some say his name was John W. Leake, Private 1st Lieutenant of Company C, 1st Louisiana Calvary Infantry. The compassionate souls at the Myrtles put the bleeding soldier in the upstairs room, that was originally part of the Ladies' Dorm, and hid him there for two months while dressing his wounds and caring for him.

The legend goes, that a member of the family at the neighboring Rosedown Plantation, heard of the soldier hiding out, and was appalled that he had deserted his brothers-in-arms. They notified a Confederate unit at Port Hudson and the soldier was removed. Rumors that he was hanged on the property circulated, but I could not verify that. He may have been court martialed, or executed for deserting his post. We do know he has an affinity for the room, and the people that cared for him.

Emails I have received, from people staying in the John W. Leake Room, show an interesting pattern. Most men who sleep in this room report disturbing dreams and images of war and being chased. Their confusion upon waking arises from the details the vivid dreams include of an era and battle they know little about. Most were able to describe the small details of the uniform they were wearing in the dream, and could correctly recall locations and events known only to someone who had actually been in the midst of the war-torn area. As mentioned earlier, a Civil War sword was found on the Myrtles' property, and is now on display in the Game Room. There is no doubt the famous war marched across the fertile grounds of what was once David Bradford's Richland.

The letters sent to me, state that the hallucinations experienced by a number of male residents in the room seem to escalate in May and June, two of the months the soldier reportedly hid out in the room. It is ironic that, today, the guest suite is decorated in the soft pinks and greens of the Spring season. Some of the people reporting the dreams say they have seen a glimpse of the solider reclining on the bed, his leg bandaged, or crouching in a corner, looking as solid as someone real and present.

One couple wrote to me about their experience. They had been unaware of the Myrtles' savory reputation. They left the plantation in the middle of the night after their stay in the John W. Leake Room. The wife had settled in to read a book as her husband showered. A noise sounded in the room, and laying the book aside, the woman called to her husband, only to be "shushed!"

Irritated at being told to "Shush," she called out that she had heard a strange noise in the room. Once again, she heard a male voice saying "Shush!" The woman leapt from the bed and crossed the room to confront her husband on his rudeness, only to find him still in the shower with the water running, unable to hear her, much less tell her to "Shush." Grabbing her purse, she fled the room. When the husband finally located her later, waiting outside, she refused to return to the room. Reluctantly he climbed the steep back staircase to collect their luggage. Walking over to the chifforobe (a large wardrobe), he opened the door to remove the clothes they had previously hung there. Their clothes were not there, but someone else's was. A single gray uniform hung in the shadows of the closet. Confused, the gentleman closed the doors, stood there a moment surveying the room, to see if perhaps his wife had already taken the clothes from the wardrobe and laid them out across the bed. Finally, not seeing the missing items, he opened the door to the chifforobe again, and the uniform was gone. Their own clothes, once again, hanging in place. Unsettled, he grabbed the clothes and the suitcases, and turned to leave the room. An apparition of a soldier, dressed in a gray uniform blocked his exit from the suite.

Many, many reports of people seeing a soldier in this room have circulated over the years. Sometimes, he is staring at them silently from a corner of the room. Others have seen him limping about like a caged animal, tired of being secreted in the small space. Numerous guests of the room have told the staff that they feel something touching their leg, as though wrapping it in bandages. And still others say their feet are touched, as they lay in the canopy bed in the dark.

Another story I received, were of two brothers coming to the Myrtles with their companions and booking the Fannie Williams Room and the John W. Leake Room. During the night, the brother in the Leake Room felt like something was sitting on his chest and he couldn't get up. When he was finally able to move, he fled to his brother's room next door. The next evening, the man's girlfriend, who was also staying in the Leake Room, felt the same pressure of something sitting atop her, pinning her to the bed. She began to pray and heard a voice say, "No pray...no pray!"

People staying in this room, have reported feeling something pressing upon them, to the point they were unable to move. The sensation passes and they are freed, but rattled none-the-less.

I mentioned earlier, that I had the pleasure of staying as an overnight guest at the Myrtles, in August of 2011, and again in February of 2012. On both occasions, I stayed in the Woodruff Suite for an evening. In February, I also had the opportunity of staying one night in the Bradford Suite, and the last evening in the John W. Leake Room. While nothing occurred during my night in the Bradford Suite, I cannot say the same about the hours I stayed in the Leake Room.

When I had finished all my meetings in Baton Rouge and St. Francisville, researching every archive I could find (while gathering information for the 1st Edition of this book), I collapsed into the welcoming softness of the canopy bed in the John W. Leake Room. Compared to the other two rooms I had stayed in the previous two nights, this room was much smaller and very cozy. The Woodruff Suite and Bradford Suites are huge, both with sitting room areas and large bathrooms. I got the immediate feeling that tonight I would sleep well, instead of watching corners from clear across the room. I turned on the lamp at my right elbow and settled back to read for a little while. I could hear people walking around in the hallway outside my door, as they checked into the Ruffin Stirling, William Winter, and Fannie Williams Rooms. This also added to my sense of security, as in the Woodruff and Bradford Suites, you are isolated from nearby neighbors.

Finally, the pace of the day's running around overtook me and I laid the book on the marble top of the dressing table. I flipped off the lamp and lay on my side, watching the door that led into the hallway, as I listened to other guests leaving their rooms, entering the hall bathrooms, returning to their rooms, and one guy who must have made twelve trips up and down the back staircase to get something from outside. After what seemed like hours, the house was finally quiet. It is at those times, that you feel the presence of the plantation. The walls seem to advance a little toward you, the ceiling lowers just a touch, and you are acutely aware of the sounds, or lack of them.

I turned onto my other side, the creaking of the antique bed sounding like thunder in the quiet room. Curling into my customary fetal position, I felt the bedspread pinned beneath my left knee. Cradling the plump spare pillow, I drifted off to sleep. I have no idea what time it was. My mind was still happily ensconced in the dark fuzziness of sleep when I felt something tugging on the bedspread. Since it was still pinned beneath my knee, I could feel it acutely, like a fish pulling on a line. It tugged again, and in my foggy state, I had forgotten where I was.... or *when* I was. In my dreamlike awareness, I was still married, and my husband was trying to hog the blankets. When the tugging motion came again, I fumed and muttered, "Just take it!" It was then that my eyes flew open, as I remembered I was no longer married, and no longer at home. I was in the most-haunted home in America! I sat straight up in bed, my heart pounding. Part of the comforter was still beneath a section of my leg. As I sat there, hearing my breath come in ragged bursts, something pulled on the blanket again, this time freeing it from my leg.

My hand shot out and flipped on the bedside lamp. Ok, this is where the bright glare of reality is supposed to halt all paranormal activity...right? In my horror, I watched as the bedspread moved jerkily across my legs, heading for the side of the bed closest to the door. It was angling toward the right bed post at the end of the mattress, as though something seated on the floor was pulling it off in that direction. With every ounce of courage I had, I leaned out and peered over the edge of the bed, thinking, "Please don't let me see a hand.... please don't let me see a hand!" What I saw was the edge of the bedspread crunched into a ball, as though enclosed in a fist, as *someone* continued to pull it across the bed. The fabric finally caught against the bed post and the movement stopped—so did my heart at this moment! I was too frightened to put my bare feet on the floor. What if it was under the bed waiting for me? I lay there, my eyes transfixed on the now motionless blanket.

Only after I saw the first glimmer of morning light, threading its way through the thick green curtains in the room, did I find the courage to leave the bed. I still stepped out as far as I could from the uncertain realm beneath the bed frame. I hurried into the bathroom and shut the door. This area is rather cramped, as the bathroom was an addition added much later to the house, when the guest rooms were added. At the time, it felt like a sanctuary.

Now I had a decision to make. Do I tell the staff when I go for breakfast, and look like an idiot, or do I keep it to myself, at least for now? I chose the latter, opting for a professional author demeanor. After all, I had published several books. I owned two successful businesses. I was not going to run in there like a ghost-hunting newbie and blubber all over the eggs and grits! It only took hearing one other guest describe what happened to them in the night, while staying in the Fannie Williams Room, that had me spilling my guts! In Hester Eby's calm, mothering cadence, she said, "Oh Honey, isn't that just wonderful that you got to be part of that! I am so glad!"

Well, at least I wasn't the only one there with bags under my eyes! As I talked to the other guests, and wrote down their excited accounts, I had to admit--the lack of sleep was incidental compared to the story I had to take away with me!

Renee B., (anonymous). "My boyfriend and I were staying in the Leake Room, during the summer.

We were lying in bed talking about our plans for New Orleans the next day. All of a sudden, this big bang sound came from the closet in the room. It's this big piece of furniture I guess people used to hang clothes in. He got up and went over to it. When he opened the door to it, some hangers were swinging back and forth. He stopped them with his hand, and turned to look at me, like "What's going on?" Just then, they started swinging back and forth again, real hard. He freaked out, slammed the closet door, and then grabbed a chair that was sitting up on a ledge in front of the dormer window. He put the chair in front of the closet, like that was going to keep a ghost from coming out. I was scared, but I still laughed at how ridiculous that looked."

Chapter Sixteen

The Haunted Grounds and Outbuildings

The Myrtles Plantation at night.

The ten acres comprising today's Myrtles Plantation is but a small portion of the original 250 acres David Bradford purchased in 1794. Yet, these lush grounds have witnessed over two centuries of history. When one walks her pathways, they are in the company of ghosts— from plantation slaves to antebellum debutantes, soldiers of war to voodoo priestesses, pirates and Cotton Kings. You have but to stand still…and listen.

The Patio

The 5,000-square-foot antique brick courtyard anchors this delicate plantation and offers a respite to those who visit here. White wrought-iron tables and chairs encircle a large fountain, with views across the back property and pond. To the north is the General's Store gift shop, and to the south is Restaurant 1796 and the French Quarter with its Garden Rooms. Behind you, to the east, looms the two-story plantation manor house, its dormer windows always watching.

View of the patio & house looking north.
The General's Store gift shop is to the left.

The patio area of the plantation is no stranger to ghost stories. Guests roaming the grounds at night, peering from their guest room windows, or rocking languidly on the verandah, have tales to tell.

Patio fountain at night. Photo by Jason Phillip Reeser.

Stories have circulated around the plantation about an elderly man, who appears to people from time to time, dressed in overalls and a straw hat. Many believe him to be the ghost of a caretaker that was reported murdered on the property in 1927. For the Moss family (current owners of the Myrtles Plantation), he became all too real when their young son, J.G. saw him on the courtyard next to the former Carriage House Restaurant.

"Our family was in the restaurant eating near the large windows that overlook the back courtyard," Teeta Moss reported, "when J.G. looked out and said, 'Oh, Mommy…there's my friend!' I looked out the window and seeing no one, I asked him, 'Who, Baby?' J.G. pointed emphatically at a place on the courtyard, and said, 'Him! Him!' It was obvious that he saw someone, though no one else could. I bent over my three-year-old, and said, 'Well, I don't see who you are talking about, Sweetie. You're going to have to show Mommy where he is.'

J.G. sighed, and said, 'Mommy, he's right there! He looks like Popa.'"

Teeta goes on to explain that J.G. calls her father, "Popa." Whatever J.G. was seeing, was an older man like his Grandpa.

Could it be the caretaker Clark Woodruff hired to look after his property, when he took his only surviving daughter Octavia to New Orleans, after the loss of his wife Sarah and his two young children, James and Cornelia Gale? Was this the man who was murdered on the property during a botched burglary?

"I was trying to humor my son, so I asked J.G. if he thought his friend would like to eat with us," Teeta continued. "J.G. jumped up and ran out to the courtyard patio. We could see him looking up and talking to someone we couldn't see. When he rejoined us, I asked him where his friend was. He simply said, 'He not hungry.'

Mr. Guy, the maintenance man at the Myrtles at the time, told "Miss Teeta" that he sees J.G. talking to "someone" all the time. 'He's forever talking to him and telling me to look at him too,' the maintenance man told Teeta. Others saw the little boy walking along, chatting happily with someone they couldn't see, tilting his head back to look up to someone much taller, and holding his little hand high in the air as though holding onto a tall figure.

With her academic background, Teeta decided to put her inquisitive nature to work. She delved into the subject matter concerning children who interact with ghosts. What Teeta found during her studies, was very compelling. A three-year-old, such as J.G., may be able to fib, but at that age they are incapable of conjuring up images and events that are not there. They simply can't create stories with such vivid detail. You can ask them if they took their sister's doll, and they can deny it, while holding the doll behind their back, but they cannot fabricate something from their imagination, especially something outside their realm of knowledge.

Larry Armstead is a handsome young man who was part of the staff at the Carriage House Restaurant during my visits. He was the person to seat me on my first day at the plantation and was wonderfully attentive. His quiet demeanor and warm smile made you feel relaxed and welcome. As he filled my water glass, I told him I was writing a book about the Myrtles and asked if he had any "experiences" while working there. He looked surprised at the question and then got very quiet. "No, Mam, I haven't had any ghost stuff happen to me here." He hurried away and I felt he was either nervous to talk about it, or was just taken off guard by the direct question. As he continued to bring wonderful dishes to my table, I smiled each time and thanked him. Finally, when he returned to refill my water glass, as I was finishing my lunch, he glanced around, and when he saw no one was near us, leaned over and whispered, "Miss Rebecca? You've seen all the cats around here?" I nodded and said, 'Yes.'

"Well," he continued, looking around again. "Out there on the patio...," he motioned to the courtyard just outside the sunroom window near my elbow, "sometimes, I will be looking out the window at those cats, and they start acting like someone is petting them! You know, squatting down with their backs in the air...like this." Larry mimicked with his hand the way a cat's back will slink under the pressure of someone petting it, only to rise again, and repeat the process as the person continues caressing it. Anyone owning a cat will recognize the movement, and knows a cat only acts that way when someone is running their hand along its back. Larry continued, "Then...the cats will circle in and out of someone's *legs*, rubbing against them, their tails in the air, and look up at the person, and then someone starts petting them again, and their backs go up and down! Only there is nobody there…nobody I can see!" He paused, looking out the window at the several cats lounging near the fountain. "I don't like it when they do that," he said simply, and walked away.

One of the black cats at the Myrtles Plantation patio.
Photo courtesy of Jason Phillip Reeser.

Guests at the plantation have also reported seeing the cats acting as though some unseen person is petting them. The cats' backs will rise and fall, their heads up to receive the caress, as their bottoms finally rise in a type of ebb and flow. It is typically in the courtyard area that people have seen the cats act this way, and it is unmistakable. James, the plantation's former Night Manager and Groundskeeper, says he has seen the cats on many occasions "acting strange."

A mother wrote to me saying her little girl kept bothering her to let her go and play with the other kids. "We were sitting in the rocking chairs on the back verandah by the courtyard at the time," the woman told me. "I looked around and asked, 'What children?' My daughter got very agitated and thrust out her arm, her finger pointing determinedly toward the white fence surrounding the pond area.

"I looked and saw no one. She sighed and jumped up from the chair and ran across the courtyard, waving and laughing, as though signaling to someone she was on her way over. I watched in total disbelief, and not a little horror, as she began "interacting" with people I could not see. I saw her bend over as though picking something up from the grass and handing it to someone. She frolicked and ran around, looking over her shoulder and waving for someone to follow her, only to fall down laughing on the grass. She has never acted like this in her life. I finally called to her to come to me and she reluctantly did so, but not before yelling back over her shoulder to someone that she would be 'right back.'

"What?" she blurted, when she reached my chair, clearly annoyed at being interrupted.

"Who are you playing with?" I asked, the hairs on my arms already rising.

"Geez, Mom," she said, placing her hands firmly on her hips. "You need glasses! Those four girls over there with the black faces...," she began, and went to point over at them. She paused, looked around, and stuck out her bottom lip. "Great! You scared them off!" she said hotly.

She ran to the pond and looked around, but clearly could not find them. When she finally returned, and plopped down dramatically in the rocker next to me, arms folded tightly and fuming, I asked her what the girls had been wearing.

"Old stuff," she said, still upset. "I think maybe they were poor."

"That's all I could get out of her. She continued looking for the "playmates" off-and-on throughout the morning, until we had to leave. She is five-years-old and very smart. Believe me, this is very uncharacteristic for her, and she spent far too much time looking for the "girls" for it to have been made up."

Louise B., Baton Rouge, Louisiana. "I was sitting on the patio at the Myrtles Plantation with a group of women who were touring the state. We were enjoying the sunshine, and watching the tour groups coming and going.

One of the women in our group commented on how nice it was that they had the staff dressed in period clothing. I hadn't noticed this, in fact I had just seen another tour guide go by leading several guests. She was dressed in slacks and a blouse. "What staff are you referring to?" I asked.

"The lady over there sweeping the courtyard," she said, and turned in her chair to point her out. When she turned, she looked about with a furrowed forehead, and said, "That's odd, she was just right over there." She pointed past the fountain toward the restaurant. "She was wearing a turban, long simple dress, and an apron."

I was seated facing the direction she pointed to, and there had been no one there sweeping. The woman became clearly agitated and suggested we go over to St. Francisville a little early.

View of the Myrtles house from courtyard at night.

Myrtles' patio at night with orb.
Photos courtesy of Jason Phillip Reeser.

The Generals' Store Gift Shop

The past is never far behind at the Myrtles Plantation. Today, guests can step into the original building David Bradford built in 1794, when he began his dream as a plantation owner in West Feliciana Parish, Louisiana. This building, which once housed David and his young family, while construction ensued on the main house, is today a multi-purpose domain.

Entrance to The General's Store
Photo courtesy of Jason Phillip Reeser.

Stephen Saunders did extensive research on the plantation in order to present it for consideration for the National Register of Historic Places. His keen eye for detail gives us a wonderful insight into the wealth of architectural and historic detail in the old Bradford home…today's Gift Shop and The General's Store. Words in parentheses are inserted by the author for clarification.

In Mr. Saunders words:

"This building at present possesses much of its integrity with its original 12/12 window panes with shutters, the original fireplace in the Overseer's Office (just inside the gift shop door and to the left), and its original 6-panel doors.

"The northern wall of this room contains a 12/12 window. The eastern wall is solid with no openings. The southern wall contains a 6-paneled door to its east, and a 12/12 window to its west. This wall of the room, is in fact, still "smoked up" from the fires of the original open-hearth fireplace. The eastern-most door on the front of this building leads into the original food storage room or whose northern, eastern, and western walls are solid, and whose southern wall contains the door connecting it to the front gallery of this building.

"The 6-paneled door to the east on the front of this building, leading into the original pantry or storage room, shows many holes above and below the present doorknob from the changing of many locks over the years. The middle door has its wooden threshold below the door worn completely in half by many footsteps by slaves during the plantation days passing in and out of the original kitchen.

"Reference to the kitchen, storeroom, and overseer's office is mentioned in the probate sale by Elizabeth Bradford in the Monday, December 2, 1816 partitioning of David Bradford's estate amongst his heirs."

Today, the Gift Shop and General's Store is a delight to the senses. Everywhere one looks, are wonderful displays of gifts and cooking enticements. From jewelry, books, clothes, DVD's, magnets, scarves, pillows and candy…all the way to Voodoo dolls, pottery, Chloe dolls, canteens, sauces, dry goods, ceramic roosters, plaques, and even miner's helmets, the array of tempting souvenirs is a shopper's paradise.

Postcards and cold beverages are found in this area, and visitors entering in through the ancient doorway are met with a warm smile. This is where tours check in, as well as overnight guests.

Ornamental brass hand for notes
outside gift shop door.

The Caretaker's Quarters

Behind the gift shop, sits a large cabin. Wood for this building was gleaned from three slave shacks from neighboring plantations. The Moss' built it as a playhouse for their children when they moved into the Myrtles. It now acts as a Guest Suite, and is listed as Room #5 at the plantation's check-in office. Surrounding this structure, is a 210-year-old fence, also carefully moved to this location. The Cottage is for overnight guests only and is not on the tour.

The Caretaker's Quarters offers two queen size beds and a private bathroom with a shower. It has a rustic atmosphere and offers a true sense of seclusion from the plantation's main house.

Caretaker's Quarters.

Many ghost stories have come from within, and without, the rustic boards of the Caretaker's Quarters. Some have reported hearing the rhythmic droning of drums beating off in the distance, supposing it to be tied to the Native American Indians that once roamed these acres. Others have said they could hear faint chanting coming from the direction of the Mississippi River at the far corner of the property, giving them the impression that Voodoo was alive and well in the woods. Even gunshots, and sounds of a war reenacted in the tall trees, have been reported by those staying overnight in the Quarters.

According to Hester Eby, Myrtles Plantation Assistant Manager and Director of Tours, many guests staying overnight in the Caretaker's Quarters have reported seeing an elderly man dressed in overalls standing in the corner watching them. This is not the original caretaker's cabin where a man was reportedly killed, in 1927, during a robbery. That shack has been replaced by the one you see today. Still, the caretaker seems to have an affinity for the location. He has turned up in photos, looking out the windows of the cabin, as visitors snap shots from outside.

The cabin has an extreme feeling of isolation as its location is separate from the other buildings. Though only a few feet from the gift shop and main house, it is quite dark during the night when all the lights have been extinguished. Trees close in and the moss sways slowly in the evening breeze. Hester Eby has reported that many times people booked into the Quarters will ask to change their room and move to other accommodations.

In this area, the report of clothes being rearranged while the guests sleep, is also prevalent. You have to hand it to the spirits of the Myrtles Plantation...they are hospitable and tidy.

Kim H. from Omaha, Nebraska, stayed in the Caretaker's Quarters in 2011. She was there with a group of people who were, in her own words, "totally nuts!" She claims that the others acted like a bunch of teenagers, running around the property at night with cameras, video and tape recorders, trying valiantly to capture something of evidential value to take home. "We were in our mid-30's, for gosh sakes," she wrote to me. "I finally tired of it, and told them I was going to bed. I could hear them running around outside giggling, and every few minutes a flash would go off, as they took pictures.

"I was dozing off, when I heard the doorknob rattling at the front door. I blinked and looked at it, thinking they had locked themselves out and were trying to get it to open. After several minutes of this, I sighed, got up, and opened the door, a scowl plastered on my face. A flash went off on the other side of the pond and I made out my three friend's silhouettes, racing about and still taking photos. There was no one standing on the porch! They did not have time to rattle the door and then run clear over to the other side of the pond. The doorknob was still shaking right before I put my hand on it! That freaked me out. I put on my shoes and jeans, and ran out to join them. When we finally got back to the cabin, it was around one in the morning. I was so tired, but I didn't want to go in. I let the others go in ahead of me. When I walked in behind them, I froze. My bed…that I had been sleeping in, was freshly made up, as though I had never even slept in it! It took all I could do to stay the rest of the night, and if the Myrtles staff had been there, other than the overseer, and it wasn't so late, I would have asked to be moved somewhere else."

Dennis F. from Salt Lake City, Utah, sent me an email saying he thought the Caretaker's Quarters was cool, but he didn't sleep all night. Something kept poking him. "I felt something sticking me in my feet…something sharp like a pointed stick. I vaguely remember kicking at it the first time, then rubbing my feet together, thinking it was a nerve or something. When it happened again, I threw off the blanket and shone my cell phone light on my feet. The right one had three little red marks where I had felt the poking. Fearing a bug had gotten into the room, I turned on the lamp and took the bedding apart…no bug…but a long-pointed piece of metal fell out of the blanket, and landed with a clank on the floor. In case you think I had rolled over on it and it poked me…I was lying flat on my back, and had been the entire time, not moving except to respond to that thing poking me on the soles of my feet. I kept the thing. It's still sitting on my desk at home. I have asked people what they think it is, and some have said it looks like an old-fashioned prod, used for cleaning horse hooves. I didn't show it to the owners because I wanted to keep it, but it makes me wonder who was poking me with it."

Mitchel W., Lodgepole, Nebraska. "My wife and I stayed in the Caretaker's cabin. I liked that it was off by itself a little. We were reading brochures of some places we wanted to see in Louisiana, sitting on the two beds, and just talking. Something tapped on the window. She looked at me, kinda scared. I looked out and didn't see anything. It was pretty dark and hard to see much. A few minutes later, something tapped again, on another window. This time I ran out onto the porch, thinking it was some guests running around trying to scare us. I still didn't see anybody. I was walking around the cabin when my wife comes running out onto the porch, saying something is tapping on all the windows at the same time. I was right there. There was no one around. Later that night, the toilet kept flushing on its own. Next time, we'll stay in the big house."

Harold S., Rapid City, South Dakota. "My son and I were staying in the Caretaker's cabin several years ago. My wife and daughter were staying at a hotel down the road, too scared to stay at the plantation. My son said there were handprints on the sink in the bathroom that looked like someone with big hands, covered in mud, had put them there. Surprised, I got up to look. Sure enough, there were two huge, muddy prints that had not been there a few minutes before. I washed them off. A few minutes later, my son peeked in to see if anything was happening with the sink, and he yelped. The two muddy prints were back, in the exact same place. I left them, afraid I would get something mad at me if I kept cleaning them off. The next morning, they were gone. Later, after we were safely on a plane home, we told my wife, who was upset that we thought it was cool."

Side view of the Caretaker's Quarters

Audrey R., Lansing, Michigan. "Some friends of mine were staying at the Myrtles Plantation. I was on the phone to one of them about 11 o'clock at night. They were staying in the slave cabin at the plantation. I was joking with her about ghosts and slaves coming to get her in the night, when she screamed. She said a pillow from another bed just came flying at her head. I would have thought she was joking, but all the girls in the room screamed at the same time, and I could hear them freaking out."

The Ghost Hunters Come to the Myrtles Plantation

Many paranormal reality shows find their way up the treelined *allèe* leading to the Myrtles front door. When the *Ghost Hunters* made an appearance in their second season, there was much made of their time spent in the Caretaker's Quarters. It was known as the Caretaker's Cottage at that time.

Grant Wilson and Jason Hawes of the Ghost Hunters
visit the Myrtles in Season 2, Episode 1.

Jason Hawes and Grant Wilson, the two lead investigators for the *Ghost Hunters*, were seated inside the cabin. Jason was reclining on one of the beds, while Grant was hunched down in a chair near a round side table. On the table was a lace tablecloth and a lamp. As the two sat talking over their roles as paranormal investigators, the lamp began sliding across the table toward Grant. The movement was replayed several times, and the two tried to reenact the lamp's actions, while checking its cord. Of the footage taken during the show, this incident garnered the most attention from fans. You can watch the episode on YouTube   at https://www.youtube.com/watch?v=ZWbaadhFDZk&list=PL0B 89K3ZdovNnsdi2XRrV39iWpK6loRuS.

The Coco House

The Coco House, once the Overnight Manager's residence, is now a large guest house that will accommodate up to 10 people. With its two bedrooms, bathroom, and sitting area, it is a perfect retreat for a group or family. It is the only accommodation on the property offering a television. Sitting 50 yards from the courtyard, it is nestled in the trees with views of the pond and back acreage. Its white clapboard siding, mirrors that of the main house.

The Coco House
Photo courtesy of Morgan Moss.

Only a few steps away, are the Garden Rooms and Restaurant 1796. Although the rest of the plantation buildings are nearby, there is a sense of having the property to yourself in this removed location.

Many stories concerning the supernatural swirl about the Coco House, as guests report things out of the ordinary happening during their stay there. Several people have reported the doorbell ringing only to find nothing is there when they answer the door. The staff is forever putting toilet paper in the bathroom, as it mysteriously disappears over and over again. Jewelry tends to go missing at the Coco House, and many guests have left theirs locked in their cars, after hearing the stories. One such story was told by a group who booked the Coco House for a friend's birthday.

Six women reserved the guest house for a birthday celebration for one of the ladies present. One of the guests, a 47-year-old woman, began talking to Chloe, the slave girl who was reportedly hung on the property after attempting to poison Clark Woodruff's family with a tainted cake. The woman was telling Chloe how sorry she was that she was killed and was sure the slave didn't mean to harm anyone.

At that point, the birthday girl's daughter came out of the Coco House bathroom and asked, "Mom, did you lose your earring?" She held up a small diamond earring. The woman put her hands to her ears, touching the two gems and said, "No, I have both my earrings."

One of the other ladies, recognizing the earring the young girl was holding, raced out to her car where she had locked her own diamond studs in the glove compartment. One of them was missing!

Returning to the guest house, she looked at the earring that had been found in the bathroom. It was indeed her missing diamond from the car. The group believed the ghost of Chloe had brought the earring to the kind woman who had been trying to contact her.

Many stories circulate around the Myrtles of jewelry that are reported missing, especially earrings and hair adornments, only to turn up elsewhere, or not at all.

Barbara Longley from California, wrote to me online and said that while she and four others were staying in the Coco House, they kept hearing something tapping at their windows. It would circle the house, tapping at each window. Two of the guests got up from bed and followed the tapping as it circled the house. Even though they were looking out the windows where the tapping was occurring, they could see nothing there. This went on for hours--something circling and tapping. None of them got any sleep that night.

The second night they heard someone walking around outside whistling. It was an old tune; *I've Been Working on the Railroad.* The "whistler" circled the house and once again the guests peered from the windows trying to locate the source. There was no one there. They also reported hearing loons crying out on the pond, although loons have not been reported there. The doorbell rang, on several occasions throughout the night, until the group wearied of answering the door, only to find an empty porch.

A small family was staying at the Coco House and reported that their clothes were moved about the rooms constantly. Each morning when they woke up, they would have to go in search of the things they had laid out the night before. One small boy's baseball cap, that he had tossed on the floor when he climbed into bed, was actually found outside, sitting neatly on the front stoop. He also reported that the book he was reading when he went to bed, had not only been moved to another room, the pages were folded in half, so that he had to straighten them all out.

Rick D. S., Colorado Springs, Colorado. "We had a wedding party at the Myrtles Plantation. A bunch of us rented the Coco House the night before the wedding. The next morning, all the groomsmen's silk boutonnieres were missing. They had been laid out on the table, ready for the next morning. We searched the whole place. Finally, we had to get outside for the final rehearsal for the wedding. When we stepped out the door, the boutonnieres were stacked on top of each other in their plastic boxes on the bottom step! One of the guys refused to put his on."

Alex W., (anonymous). "I stayed at the Coco House with my wife and kids. All night long we heard the chairs moving around in the living room area. When we looked, they were where we left them. As soon as we got back in bed, we could hear them scraping across the floor. Since the house is off by itself, there aren't any other sounds going on out there. It was pretty scary."

David T., Chicago, Illinois. "We were visiting the Myrtles Plantation in Louisiana, and stayed one night at the Coco House there on the property. The sound of furniture moving around in the area with the couch kept us up all night. Nothing was out of place when we looked, but we kept hearing sounds like someone shoving heavy furniture around...even thuds on the walls."

The Garden Rooms

The six guest rooms, just south of Restaurant 1796, have been nicknamed the Garden Rooms. They reside in the area of the Plantation called The French Quarter and include a lovely patio area where bocce ball is offered. This area of the property was said to be where the stables were and there are rumors that a fire broke out in the 1800s, burning the stable and carriage house to the ground. Only the floorboards of the carriage house remained. It was perhaps this same fire that also spread to a part of the main house, as reports of a mother and two children dying in a fire, during that time period, were circulated.

With New Orleans only an hour and a half away, it's only fitting that the Myrtles Plantation gives a nod to its famous architecture and culture. The French Quarter next to Restaurant 1796 does just that. While maintaining the plantation's façade, the patio area and two-story guest quarters offers a respite for travelers in a way befitting southern charm and hospitality. These rooms offer a private patio with views of the grounds and pond area. The rooms feature queen-sized bed with bathrooms en suite and custom showers.

Restaurant 1796 and the Garden Rooms in the French Quarter.

The Bridge and Gazebo

A lovely bridge and gazebo were put into the pond area during Frances Kermeen's ownership of the plantation. The bridge's boards were painted blue as a nod to Claude Monet's famous painting *Bridge Over a Pond of Water Lilies*. It leads to a lovely gazebo with a stone cherub nestled near its side. Large butterflies and native birds are seen here.

The cypress trees here are eons old. Their knobby knees protrude from the still waters and anchor the area that was originally a buffalo wallow when the Native American Indians once roamed the grounds.

Monet's "Bridge Over a Pond of Water Lilies"

Most stories coming from the pond area of the plantation are of people seeing reflections in the water of strange lights that seem to have no origin. They hear footsteps crossing the bridge when no one is there, and many EVPs have been picked up in this area. Sightings of small children running about in clothing from a different era are also reported. When guests try to intercede, the children vanish. This is also the area where an amazing photo of soldiers bearing a coffin was taken. Many people persist in saying they have seen a young Native American Indian girl sitting by the pond. She turns to look at them and disappears.

Bridge and Gazebo at the Myrtles Plantation.

The Cottages

The four Cottages near the pond at the Myrtles.

With an authentic nod to the past, the Myrtles Plantation offers four cottages located on the south side of the property. Reminiscent of the early plantation days, the Crepe Myrtle, Cypress, Live Oak, and Willow Cottages, rim the pond with rustic charm. Inside, the furnishings are more modern, complete with private bath, couch, beds and area rugs.

Many of the ghost stories reported from the Cottages pertained to outside the buildings. Oddly, the several I received, had a common thread.

Rob M., Banff, Canada. "Several of us were staying in the Cypress Cottage at the Myrtles Plantation. During the night, we heard a low moaning sound coming from outside. Two of us went out on the porch and listened. There was no wind, which was my first reasoning for the sound. As we stood there, it came again, off to the north past the pond.

It was this low moaning noise, that rose and fell. It didn't sound like an animal or bird. It gave you goosebumps."

Juan P., Albuquerque, New Mexico. "My girlfriend and I were staying in one of the cabins at the Myrtles Plantation. There are four of them in a row. We were sitting on the porch at night and talking with guests staying in the other cabins. This really loud wailing sound stopped everyone from talking. It was like a woman crying. Kind of a high wailing. Then sobbing. This one guy in the cabin next to ours says "That's coming from over by that big barn." I said, "What big barn?" He says "There's a big barn over there for equipment and stuff. I saw it today when I was walking around." The wailing went on for about five minutes. I dared him to go look, but he wouldn't. It wasn't no animal. Animals don't sob."

The Myrtles Grounds

Strange lights, floating orbs, unexplained sounds of phantom conversations and parties…it seems these ancient grounds have absorbed the memory of feet pressed upon them, blood spilled, and a litany of families playing out their lives here.

Many people report issues with photography going haywire throughout the property. In some areas, the photos are blurry, upside down, and even black. During one of my stays at the plantation, this author could not get a clear photo of one of the small statues near the front step. After six tries, all of which were blurry, as if the little guy was moving during the shot, I moved on to the statue next to him. The pictures of that statue were clear and crisp. I went back and tried again with the statue that refused to focus. I took five more photos and none of them would come out clearly. It was the only place on the grounds that this occurred.

See photos of the two statues on the next page.

Blurry image

Clear image of 2nd statue

The positioning of the many statues throughout the Myrtles Plantation grounds, gives one the feeling they are there to keep an eye on the people traversing their grounds. Their stone eyes follow you, their faces amused and animated. You almost get the feeling they are whispering amongst themselves.

Myrtles Plantation statues, as if whispering to each other.
Photo courtesy of Jason Phillip Reeser.

Guests to the Myrtles, whether booking a room or a tour, report interference with their electrical devices, moving furniture, rapping, shadows, and yes, ghosts.

The Allure of a Haunted Bed and Breakfast

As John L. Pearce had done before them, Frances and Jim opened the plantation doors to guests wanting to tour the house and learn about its history. It quickly became clear that the topic of ghosts was expected to be on the tour guide's agenda. It was during Ms. Meyers' time at the plantation, that magazines and TV shows began turning up on her doorstep. Word was spreading fast that the Myrtles Plantation, just outside the small hamlet of St. Francisville, was offering more than a night's stay with all the antebellum accoutrements; you also got to visit with past residents long after their demise. When rumors began to circulate that the Smithsonian Institute had been out to the mansion, and formally named it "the most-haunted house in America," the dance with the media hit full force. You will find a comprehensive list of magazines, books, TV and radio programs that ran feature stories on the Myrtles Plantation at the back of this book.

If you have that much public focus on you, and you are in the hospitality business, your bottom line is always factored in. Playing up the spotlight that was shining brightly upon her antebellum home, Ms. Meyers began writing and staging Murder Mystery Weekends in 1985, based on the unsolved murder of William Winter and other legends surrounding the Myrtles. Everyone was in period costume and guests were encouraged to dress accordingly to feel a part of the gala from the past. Although local plantation owners were appalled at the overt sensationalism of a man's murder, and the exploitation of the ghost stories that they felt were, quite honestly, unbecoming the demeanor of a true southern plantation owner, the coffers filled as the buying public demanded more.

Today, the Myrtles Plantation is listed in the Top Ten Most-Haunted Homes in practically every paranormal survey. Her continued appearances on television, radio programs, and in print, leaves little doubt that this antebellum plantation will beckon to visitors for many years to come.

"No matter where one goes on the Myrtles Plantation property, there is always a feeling of *someone* watching over your shoulder." Teeta Moss, owner.

Myrtles Plantation Grecian Statue
Photo courtesy of Jason Phillip Reeser

Myrtles Plantation from the front drive.
Photo courtesy of Amanda Folce DeVille.

Myrtles Plantation front entrance. Photo by Morgan Moss.

Louisiana's Gumbo Pot of History

Chapter Seventeen

An Overview of the Creation of Louisiana

Gumbo is a stew or soup, and has been called the official cuisine of the state of Louisiana. It originated in Louisiana, in the 18th century, and became widely popular, in part, due to its transitional ability to feed as many people as there were ingredients to dump into a cast-iron pot measuring anywhere from 2- feet in depth and diameter, to 3-feet deep and 5 feet in diameter. Everything could be tossed into the pot; from chicken or turkey, to seafood, such as oysters, crawfish or shrimp. A thickener was then added, and seasoning vegetables, which typically included celery, bell peppers, and onions (a trio know in Cajun cuisine as the "Holy Trinity"). The thickener depended on the chef: the African vegetable okra, the Choctaw spice file powder (ground dried sassafras leaves), or roux, a French base made of fat and flour.

Creole gumbo usually contains shellfish, tomatoes, and a thickener. Cajun gumbo's recipe is harder to pin down but typically has a dark roux with shellfish, or fowl, and the tomatoes are eliminated. The Cane River Creoles make a gumbo based more on file. Sausage or ham could also be added. The seasonings are varied and range from mild to "I-had-a-tongue- there-once" in intensity.

The mixture of components, that led to the creation of Louisiana, has been accurately compared to a *cultural* Gumbo, and for our recipe we start with French ingredients. Louisiana is the only state where the French cultural influence is as strong as the Anglo-Saxon. French refugees poured into the region during a slave revolt in Haiti, and large numbers of immigrants from France continued to settle in Louisiana into the mid-1800s. The other side of the French franc are the French Canadians, notably the Acadians or Cajuns. They fled to Louisiana and created a culture all their own when England kicked them out of Canada (Nova Scotia), in 1755. Longfellow's epic poem, *Evangeline* captures their story. Over time, the pronunciation of "Acadian" was watered down to "Cajun." Some Cajuns still speak the Cajun-French language; a delightful blend that is very hard to understand. They are known for their *joie de vivre*, a joy for life. The Acadians reinvented themselves to the extent that they can only be called native Louisianans.

The Gumbo now consists of two types of French ingredients: French immigrants and refugees, and the Acadians, or Cajuns. We now add other cultures that found their way to this varied landscape of swampland and bluffs: American Indian, Spanish, German, Scottish, Irish, African, Hispanic, Anglo-Saxon and others. Each brought with them their own heritage in the forms of music, cuisine, superstitions, and traditions. We stir the "stock" and begin adding the "seasoned vegetables" in the form of diverse religious practices.

The French colonists brought Roman Catholicism from Europe to Louisiana, which was later underscored by Spanish rule. Protestantism was gaining a foothold before the signing of the Louisiana Purchase, when Americans began settling in the Florida Parishes. This area became predominantly Baptist, with the second largest Protestant denomination being Methodist. Episcopalian missionary, Leonidas Polk, served as the first bishop of the Diocese of Louisiana, establishing that religion in both Catholic-dominated French districts, and Florida Parishes, that were primarily Baptist. When the Jewish population entered the Pelican State, they became some of the most-influential leaders in cultural, business, and political arenas. We add, finally, a religion that has left an indelible stamp on Louisiana: the practice of voodoo. There is no exact definition for the strange amalgamation of animal beliefs that were brought to the New World by slaves from Africa and Senegambia. Local Indian beliefs and even Roman Catholicism all blended into this strange religion.

The Louisiana Gumbo is now seasoned with the spices that make this state famous—her music and her food. The cacophony of notes that have filled the humid air on any given day, or evening, range from blues, ragtime, Dixieland, Native American drums and flutes, to "swamp pop." New Orleans gave birth to jazz and it is no surprise that greats such as Louis Armstrong came from here. Festivals abound, and pretty much any occasion is a reason to host one. Mardi Gras is, of course, the most-noted gathering, but by no means the only one. The Zydeco Festival in Plaisance is huge, and Morgan City's long-running Shrimp and Petroleum Festival gathers large crowds. St. Francisville's own Audubon Pilgrimage, in March of each year, is not to be missed! This blend of music and celebration gave New Orleans the nickname, "The city that care forgot!" and is it is well-earned!

The final zing to the recipe—what is arguably the best food in the United States! Barbeque, catfish, pan-seared foie gras, crab and sweet corn bisque, etoufee, pompano *en papillote*, softshell crab in sherry sauce, oysters, smoked salmon with tasso, Po Boys, crème brulee, crayfish, and beignets are offered next to jambalaya and gumbo. It is said that Creoles and Cajuns don't eat to live, but live to eat. With the influence of the South, Creole, Acadian, and haute French, is it any wonder most vacations to

Louisiana result in larger pants' sizes?

You now have only a portion of what goes into creating the fascinating culture of the state of Louisiana. Its turbulent history with wars, pirates, slavery, politics, hurricanes, and epidemics, could be the roux that adds the final flavor to the cultural gumbo of the most diverse heritage in the nation.

So, in the words of the locals, *"Laissez les bon temps rouler!"* Let the good times roll!

The Mississippi River

Louisiana is here for one primary reason, the Mississippi River. The "Father of the Waters" literally created Louisiana over time, as it carried silt downstream, building up land around its mouth as it flowed into the Gulf of Mexico. It is this location that continued to insure the state's value, as America's history evolved. At first glance, Louisiana was nothing but a large swamp, although its landscape is much more diverse. It was wanted for its strategic location rather than for any economic resources it could provide.

Before the Europeans considered her as a tool to be used for their lust for gold, a fur trading route or as a battle stronghold, Louisiana was home to interrelated Indian tribes back as far as 3400 BC. Watson Brake, what may be the oldest large-scale mound culture in the Western Hemisphere, can be found in northern Louisiana near Monroe. From 2000 to 1000 BC, an evolved culture once lived in northeastern Louisiana West Carroll Parish. It is now the Poverty Point State Historic Site and has some of the largest prehistoric earthworks in North America. We are still unclear as to the identity of the people who created it. The Great Mississippi Mound Culture existed here in AD700. This tribe was known for its strains of fast-growing corn that produced not one, but two harvests a year. This crop, along with squash and beans, became known as the Three Sisters. This maize-based diet gave birth to many of the Southern standards, namely hush puppies, grits and corn bread.

Other tribes, who found their way into the diverse landscape of Louisiana, were the Chitimacha, Tunica-Biloxi, the Jena Choctaw, Coushatta, Houmas, Adais Caddo, Choctaw Apache, Four Winds and others. Many plantations, towns and attractions bear the name of these early founders.

It was De Soto, who left Florida in 1540, and trekked across Louisiana in his futile search for gold, who begins our story. After De Soto died two years later, the region was pretty much ignored by Europeans for over 150 years, until a French explorer named La Salle sailed down the Mississippi from the Great Lakes. When he reached the Gulf of Mexico, on April 9, 1682, he claimed the entire Mississippi Valley for France and named it for his King, Louis XIV. Without a single Re/Max agent, or due diligence period, Louisiana was now French territory. Its location at the mouth of the Gulf of Mexico, acting officially as the entrance to the Mighty Mississippi, gave the owner complete control of the fur trade ongoing inside the vast interior of the still forming American states.

Louisiana's enormous commercial potential was still untapped; in fact, the coastline was still a steamy cypress swamp. It was her location at the mouth of the Mississippi that was her only bargaining chip...so far.

Louisiana Ping Pong

Louisiana was now in an interesting position. For France, her location at the mouth of the Mississippi and Gulf of Mexico made her an integral blockade, keeping Spain and their territories from gaining access to the fur-laden interior, and to the back door to French Canada. The problem was, Louisiana also sat at the doorway to Spain's sliver-mining region in what is now northwestern Mexico. While the haggling continued, Louis XIV sent La Salle back to Louisiana to establish a province, and erect a port. LaSalle, unfortunately, landed in Texas by mistake and was murdered by his own men.

King Louie sent the Le Moyne brothers, sons of a Canadian family, with titles of nobility as lords of distinguished estates. Pierre, the older brother, was the Sieur d'Iberville, and his brother, Jean-Baptiste, was the Sieur de Bienville. They left France, on October 28, 1698, and began their voyage down the Mississippi, on March 2, 1699, sailing up past present day Baton Rouge. Along the route, they passed two large lakes. Iberville named the larger lake in honor of Louis de Phelypeaux, Count of Pontchartrain, due to the Count's support in the past. The smaller lake was named for Pontchartrain's son, Jerome de Phelypeaux, Count of Maurepas.

Iberville built a fort on the lower Mississippi, at what is now Biloxi, Mississippi, as other areas they had considered were in constant danger of flooding. He left his brother Bienville behind with a handful of colonists and returned to France. Iberville returned in 1700, to fortify the region. The War of Spanish Succession put the process on hold. In 1706, Iberville died of yellow fever, and his brother Bienville, assumed the governorship of the struggling area. The colony was plagued with fever epidemics, food shortages, and the constant threat of Indian attacks. In 1712, King Louis, finding himself strapped for money, decided to consign the providence to Antoine Crozat, as a proprietary colony. Antoine de La Mothe Cadillac was appointed governor. Cadillac was not popular and he and Bienville constantly butted heads. The colonists were also unimpressed, especially when Cadillac sparked an Indian uprising with the Natchez. He was eventually recalled, but not before he ordered a Canadian fur trader named Louis Juchereau de St. Denis to open trade with the Spaniards in Texas. St. Denis did so, and established the first white settlement in Louisiana at Natchitoches, in 1714.

Meanwhile, back in France, Louis XIV, who had outlived two generations of heirs apparent, died after a seventy-two-year reign, in 1715. A small, five-year-old boy, the great-grandson of the King, was now crowned Louis XV. Due to his age, his uncle Phillipe, Duke of Orleans, would oversee the French government as prince-regent.

King Louis XIV

In Louisiana, meanwhile, things were not going well. Bienville kept the little colony hanging on, while administrators came and went. Crozat had had enough, and asked to be released, which Orleans did, in 1717.

The beleaguered colony was now passed to yet another hopeful, who had a shrewd plan in store for the swamp-laden territory at the bottom of the great river. Enter, one John Law, who convinced Orleans to give him a charter for the province. This clever entrepreneur was a member of a large community of Scottish expatriates, who were known throughout French society as fugitives, mercenaries, political exiles, and pretty much any label you could bestow on people out to milk any opportunity that would profit them. Law landed a gold mine, when the charter gave him the green light and title to practically the entire Mississippi Valley, which also included Illinois. With the package, France tossed in trading privileges in Santa Domingo, Africa, China, and the Spanish-owned province of Argentina. For this, Law promised to settle 6,000 colonists and 3,000 slaves within ten years.

John Law

The new venture was called the "Company of the West" and Law issued shares at 500 livres. However, Law had only just started. In a huge advertising campaign that sent Europeans reaching for their wallets, Law touted the province as rich in mineral resources and unlimited opportunities. Suddenly, the little swampland was now being seen in France, southern Germany, and Switzerland, as the best thing since dark chocolate! The shares shot to 8,000 livres! The Company of the West merged with other French Colonial companies, and the Company of the Indies, or the "Mississippi Bubble," as it came to be known, was born.

Law was sitting pretty. His colonists were a strange blend of rich investors, sons of nobility, German and Swiss farmers, and other not-so wholesome contemporaries. The wealthy investors grabbed up the larger sections of land, with grants of thousands of acres. Some of the giant plantations of Louisiana sprouted from the ground, seemingly overnight. Descendants of the German farmers still live along the river above New Orleans in a region known as Cote des Allemands (Coast of the Germans).

Legendary author, Ann Rice rose to fame with her blockbuster book *Vampire Chronicles*, which spawned several other books in that genre. It seems that Ms. Rice got her inspiration from some very real people living in the new colony Law had created. Because the ratio of men to women was overwhelming, the French government shipped over orphan girls to become brides of the new settlers. They garnered the nickname "casket girls" because each girl was given a trunk of clothes and linens, issued by the French government, as her trousseau. Unfortunately, France also saw this as a chance to get rid of some undesirables, such as female convicts and prostitutes, and shipped them over as well. The practice was finally banned in 1820, by Orleans, but the damage had been done. These outcasts permeated the new region, and legends of their undead forms, still roaming the streets of New Orleans at night, have given the present-day "Crescent City" a reputation for harboring a large community of vampires. New York City lays claims to the Vampire Capital of America.

Illustration of Casket Girls arriving in New Orleans.

The Mississippi Bubble finally burst, in 1720. Epidemics such as malaria, swamp fever, and other tropical illnesses, brought in largely by the mosquitoes infesting the ever-prevalent swamp areas, took the lives of many of the settlers. Food, created by the German and Swiss farmers, began to dwindle as the crops were inadequate; due primarily to the farmer's unfamiliarity with the Louisiana environment. Finally, the mineral-laden earth, that John Law had sold the Europeans on, was, quite frankly, nonexistent. Tensions with Spain came to a head as colonists found themselves in the middle of Spanish-owed Texas and Florida. The colonists struggled on, planting tobacco and indigo, but they proved inferior to the crops produced by the British provinces along the Atlantic Coastline. These factors converged to cause the fall of John Law's shrewd business plan. Shares in his company plummeted, and thousands of investors lost their shirts. Law barely made it out alive when an angry mob cornered him on the streets of Paris. The Company of the Indies was reorganized, and focused now on India, where the settlements were more lucrative. John Law passed out of the spotlight and died in obscurity, in 1729.

The game continued, with Louisiana becoming a territorial ping pong ball, as it was served back to the French crown in 1731, when the Company of the Indies transferred its Louisiana assets back to the royalty.

The Spanish Take Over the Game

After the Mississippi Bubble burst, and Louisiana was once again under the French government's whims, nothing much happened. By 1762, only three settlements of note had been established as trading centers: Kaskaskia (now in Illinois), Natchez and New Orleans. The growth tabled off to about 5,000 whites and 3,000 blacks, along with a host of Native Americans. These small colonies were breaking the French piggy bank, at the astronomical sum of $1.75 million a year.

The Treaty of Paris was instrumental in turning the tides of Louisiana rule. The Treaty ended the Seven Year's War, in 1763, and French Canada was handed over to the victorious British, leaving the French influence in Louisiana non-distinct. Great Britain was now on a roll, and took over Spanish Florida, and eastern Louisiana. Spain, however, had already received the region west of the Mississippi, and the district between Lake Pontchartrain and the Gulf of Mexico, which just happened to include New Orleans. The area was still considered by the Spanish to be valuable only as a strategic route to Mexico, and one that needed to be watched. In a final move, that clearly defined the boundaries between the territories, Spain moved the administrative seat from Los Adaes to San Antonio. There was now a boundary and a distinction between Texas and Louisiana. Spain proved to be a good overseer. They began a program of bringing in settlers to the Louisiana area from diverse areas. Americans, refugees from Europe, and the Acadians, who were fleeing Canada and its now British rule, headed for the Pelican State, in 1764. The once sparse population of 8,000 shot to 50,000, and the cost to keep the area flush, dropped by two-thirds, making Spain a much better governor than its rival, France. During the Spanish rule, the state was divided into parishes, rather than the customary counties, and Louisiana is still organized as such.

Although the newborn territory of Louisiana was beginning to prosper, she was a still a "ho-hum" step-child to the Spanish. They controlled her colonies for four decades, but basically let her thrive on her own. Most of the population was European and Catholic, and Spain was content that the area was "civilized." The Creoles (French descendants born in the New World), were unhappy with the Spanish dominion. Revolts took place as the Creoles ousted the governor, Antonio de Ulloa. It was the first uprising of the New World against a European patron. It did not end well. The leaders of the revolt were executed by the Ulloa's successor, don Alejandro O'Reilly, an Irishman in Spanish service, who came in and overhauled the administration. After that, the colony began to prosper and was finally in the black. The French influence was further diluted when Spain brought in settlers from Malaga and the Canary Islands, planting them smack dab in the middle of the Creole and Acadian heartland. Under the tutelage of King Charles III, Spain sat back and kept a tight rein on the newly established territory.

In 1793 and 1794, about the time David Bradford, of the Whiskey Rebellion fame, ran from Pennsylvania to Louisiana to escape indictment, an insect infestation destroyed Louisiana's indigo crops. Mr. Bradford had just completed construction on the original structure that was to become the Myrtles Plantation, and had planted indigo in the rich farm land he found there. Planters, including Mr. Bradford, were forced to look to something else to make their profit. While the southern areas of Louisiana turned their attention to sugar, "Whiskey Dave" planted cotton, as did other plantation owners in the area. However, in 1795, a creative entrepreneur developed a way to process the sugar cane that had been growing in the area for some time. It revolutionized the sugar crop industry. With the signing of the Louisiana Purchase in 1803, Louisiana was suddenly in a position to export their newfound commodity. It was only a matter of time before sugar's cash registers began to ring!

The Louisiana Purchase

Thomas Jefferson

Louisiana, by 1803, had been passed back and forth between the different governing powers of France, and now, Spain. The confused province didn't know whether to order *pisto manchego* (a Spanish soup made from red and green peppers, tomatoes and squash) or French truffles. It was at this pivotal time in American history, that Thomas Jefferson, who assumed the presidency in March 1801, made a record-breaking purchase, one that literally doubled the size of the infant United States in one transaction.

Little 'ole Louisiana had gone from an unimpressive swampland to a highly desirable location, due again, to its creator, the Mississippi River. During the eighteenth century, the population that was to one day become the United States of America, had grown. Americans were moving into new territories, such as Ohio and Tennessee. The Mississippi River was now a major force to be reckoned with, in terms of transportation for the exportation of valuable crops. Always regarded as precious for her meandering passageway from Lake Itasca in Minnesota to the mouth of the Gulf of Mexico—a mere 160 km from New Orleans—the Mississippi is the second longest river in America, at 2,348 miles long. Her value doubled as ports began to spring up, needing a speedy and strategically located means to do business. Jefferson realized the importance of the river and its locale as being one of imminent value. The only problem? The area's government was speaking Spanish, not American.

The Spanish possessions in the Western Hemisphere had been in Jefferson's cross-hairs, since 1786. Louisiana was his first move in acquiring the now valuable Mississippi region. He felt Spain could be dealt with. To his consternation, Spain, ready to be done with the Americans pushing into its provinces, and bowing to pressure from an equally pushy Napoleon, signed the Treaty of San Ildefonso, on October 2, 1800, effectively serving Louisiana back across the net to the French.

Jefferson realized he would have to ally with his enemy, Great Britain, if he was to have a chance at forcing France out. He appointed

Robert Livingston, minister to France, with instructions to try and buy New Orleans for $2 million. Jefferson thought the deal would also include West Florida (the area to the north of Lake Pontchartrain), but he was mistaken. That area had not been part of the land ceded to France by Spain. If Jefferson's purchase went through, America would own everything from the Mississippi to the Atlantic coast.

When France stalled on the offer, Jefferson threatened to make an alliance with Great Britain. He gave the French one more chance before siding with the "Brits," and sent James Monroe with an offer of $9,375,000.

Napoleon, knowing he was spread too thin financially, and dealing with a massive revolt of Haitian slaves in the French- owned island of Santo Domingo, began to waver. War was rearing its ugly head in Europe and he was overwhelmed.

Getting into a fight with Jefferson over one city was not worth it, and he could use the money being waved beneath his nose. Knowing if he sold New Orleans, Louisiana would be without worth, he sent an agent to meet with Livingston only a few days before Monroe arrived, and said basically, "Take it!" Livingston took the deal.

The ping pong game of "Louisiana, Louisiana, who gets Louisiana?" was not quite over. Spain had not totally relinquished control of New Orleans. It had delayed implementation of the Treaty of San Ildefonso, retaining de facto control of Louisiana, in an effort to keep the Americans from getting their hands on her. So, when the treaty with France was signed by the Americans, on April 30, 1803, delivering 828,000 square miles to the United States for $11.25 million, Spain still had temporary control. On November 30, Spain finally volleyed the province back to France. A ceremony marking the transfer was held in New Orleans in the Place d'Armes (now Jackson Square). Thanks to Jefferson's Louisiana Purchase, a mere eight weeks later on December 20, the French sent the spinning state back across the net to a new opponent. Louisiana was now an official property of America! Game...Set...and Match!

Louisiana vs the Creoles

The Haitian revolt, that had played a part in Napoleon giving up his hold on Louisiana, sent a surge of white and black refugees into the region, ramping up the French Creole culture there. In 1804, Louisiana was divided into two halves: The District of Orleans and the District of Louisiana, both under U.S. domain. The Creoles wanted more control, reminding Jefferson that he had promised the new territory would be self-governed. Federal authorities relinquished some control and allowed a semblance of local government.

Jefferson's choice for Governor to the new area met with popularity. William C. C. Claiborne quickly won over the Creoles with his youth and handsome countenance. He gained further favor when, two years after his wife died of yellow fever in 1804, he married one of their own, a Creole woman named Suzette Bosque. Opening Louisiana to refugees after the collapse of French rule in Santo Domingo, and suppression of the 1811 slave revolt on the river plantations between Baton Rouge and New Orleans, cemented his popularity with the province.

William C, Claiborne

Claiborne died only ten months after being elected U.S. Senator, at the age of forty-two. He had done much to win over the Creole population, even beating out a Creole candidate, Jacques Villere, for governorship. Claiborne's efforts, and the considerations given to the Creole population, began to sway their opinion. They know felt more inclined to consider themselves Americans, despite their dislike for their Anglo-Saxon neighbors. New Orleans legend, Jean Lafitte, who was popular among the Creoles, threw his support behind America, which also went a long way toward mending the feelings of the French descendants. The Creoles stood by America during the War of 1812, and were instrumental in Andrew Jackson's victory in 1815, over the British at the Battle of New Orleans.

The Lafitte Brothers: Pirates and Heroes

The legend of the famous Lafitte brothers is an interesting tale, shrouded in mystery and delicious speculation. The facts are, however, as follows.

Jean Lafitte (1776-1823) was a French pirate and privateer in the waters off the Gulf of Mexico, in the early 19th century. Pierre, his older brother, was also in the family business of smuggling, and other nefarious means of making ends meet. Jean operated a warehouse in New Orleans in 1805, to help disperse the goods smuggled by his brother Pierre. Things were going great, as they had a nice little export business going through the port of New Orleans. In January of 1808, the climate changed, and the governor bore down on the Embargo Act of 1807, which barred American ships from docking at foreign ports. The ever-resourceful Lafitte brothers packed up their business and moved it to Bartaria Bay near Grand Isle, at the bottom of the state. Here they were virtually unseen by U.S. naval ships, and they could smuggle in goods aboard *pirogues*, or barges, through the Louisiana bayous and into New Orleans.

Jean and Pierre Lafitte

Pierre set up shop in New Orleans, and looked after that end of the business. Jean Lafitte managed the daily routine of outfitting privateers and arranging the smuggling of goods they had stolen from unsuspecting vessels, from his headquarters in Bartaria. Bartaria Island began to boom by 1810, and seamen flocked to the island to work on the docks, in the warehouses, or join the crews of privateer ships.

It was at this time, that the ingenious Lafitte brothers ramped up their game. They purchased a schooner in 1812, and hired Captain Trey Cook to sail it, as a privateer. In January of 1813, they netted their first large fish, a Spanish hermaphrodite brig loaded with 77 slaves. They sold the slaves, and additional cargo, for a hefty $18,000 in profit. They turned that ship into another privateer, named *Doruda,* and within weeks, *Doruda* captured another schooner loaded with $9,000 in goods. This captured ship was not a good fit for privateering, so after unloading its cargo, the Lafitte's thanked the

Captain and crew, and returned it to them! The brothers began earning a reputation for treating the captured crew members well, often giving the ships back after they had looted them.

SMUGGLED GOODS
LAFITTE'S BARATARIA PIRATES

Next came the take-over of a third ship, the *La Diligent*. The ship boasted 12 fourteen-pounder cannons. Meanwhile, the *Doruda* captured their fourth ship, the *Petit Milan*. The Lafitte's stripped down their original ship and used its guns to outfit the new ship. They were now a fleet of three ships, which Jefferson
Davis described as "one of the largest privately-owned corsair fleets operating on the coast, and the most versatile."

The clever brothers had a system that went undetected for several months. They would send the ships to New Orleans with a legal cargo, and take on outgoing provisions from the city. A phony ship's manifest was then created listing *not the provisions* that had actually been purchased, but instead smuggled items waiting back in Lafitte's warehouse in Bartaria. Custom agents rarely noted what items *left* New Orleans, and manifests went largely unchecked. The ships would then sail to the mouth of Bayou Lafourche, load the contraband goods, and then sail legally back to New Orleans, as those goods were already listed on their manifest!

The bottom soon fell out of the illegal shipping expeditions. Thomas B. Robertson, acting governor during Claiborne's leave of absence, in September 1810, was furious over the Lafitte operation. He called the men "brigands who infest our coast and overrun our country." The citizens of New Orleans were not as offended. Lafitte's merchandise, that constantly made its way into their city, was cheaper than local merchants' goods and offered some luxuries not seen in the Louisiana territory. Upon Claiborne's return, the matter was left on the back burner, as there were bigger fish to fry.

On June 18, 1812, the United States declared war on Britain. Only seven weeks prior, Louisiana had been admitted to the Union, on April 30, 1812, and was now an official state. This included the Florida Parishes and the Territory of Orleans. New Orleans was crowned the capital and Claiborne as acting governor. The problem was, Britain's naval ships far outnumbered the naval power of the newly created U.S. The United States was forced to offer a letter of marque* to private armed vessels, which just happened to include the smugglers working for Jean Lafitte at Bartaria. These smugglers often held letters of marque from different countries, giving them permission to capture goods from differing nations. It was the equivalent of a Pirate Gold Card that you didn't leave Bartaria Bay without!

> *In the days of fighting between ships, a Letter of Marque and Reprisal, was a government license authorizing a person (known as a privateer) to attack and capture enemy vessels and bring them before admiralty courts for condemnation and sale. Cruising for prizes with a Letter of Marque was considered an honorable calling, combining patriotism and profit, in contrast to unlicensed piracy.

Lafitte dutifully handed over to America any booty he captured from the British ships, but somehow the goods from other ships found their way into Lafitte's warehouse in Bartaria. This greatly affected the amount of revenue the custom offices were collecting, and American authorities went after the Bartaria operation. On November 10, 1812, U.S. District Attorney John R. Grymes, charged Lafitte with "violation of the revenue law." 40 soldiers marched on Barataria Island, capturing Jean and Pierre Lafitte, 25 unarmed smugglers, and several thousand dollars of contraband. Bond was posted and the smugglers were released and disappeared, refusing to return for trial.

The arrests did little to detour Jean Lafitte, who, on March, 1813, registered himself as captain of *Le Brig Goelette la Diligente* for a journey to New York, supposedly to obtain a letter of marque from Cartagena, and to establish himself as a privateering captain. Lafitte got his letter, but never sent any booty there as promised. Instead all the captured booty went...you guessed it...to his warehouses in Bartaria Bay. All this was done, while he was still under indictment by the United States.

Governor Claiborne had enough. He issued a proclamation on March 15, against the Bartarian "banditti...who act in contradiction of the laws of the United States...to the evident prejudice of the revenue of the federal government."

In October, after Lafitte's smugglers wounded one of the authorities ambushing them, the governor offered a $500 reward for Lafitte's capture. Within two days of the offer, handbills were posted all over New Orleans, offering a similar reward for the arrest of the governor! Although the handbills were in Lafitte's name, rumor had it that they were created by the fine citizens of New Orleans, who were still opposed to losing the goods Lafitte supplied. In a final thumbing of the nose at the local authority, Jean Lafitte hosted an auction of smuggled goods right outside New Orleans! A gunfight ensued between Lafitte's men and the authorities. Two revenue officers were wounded and one was killed.

Claiborne appealed to the new state legislature, requesting approval to raise a militia to "disperse those desperate men on Lake Barataria whose piracies have rendered our shores a terror to neutral flags." The legislature set up a committee to study the matter, but there was a small glitch...most of the committee constituents benefited from Lafitte's smuggled goods, so no militia was raised. A Grand Jury did indict Pierre Lafitte, after one of New Orleans' leading merchants testified against him. Pierre was now behind bars accused of "having knowingly and wittingly aided and assisted, procured, commanded, counseled, and advised" persons to commit acts of piracy.

War of 1812: All Pirates Welcome!

While his brother Pierre languished in jail, Jean continued to operate the smuggling business. Over the next few months, the British Navy increased her patrols of the Gulf of Mexico. By August, they had set up a base at Pensacola. On September 3, 1812, the British ship HMS *Sophie* fired on one of Lafitte's smuggling ships returning to Barataria. Lafitte's smaller privateer sailed into shallow water that the larger British ship was unable to traverse. The British raised a white flag and sent a small dinghy with several officers. Lafitte and several of his men rowed out to meet them. Lafitte was about to be offered a bargaining chip that would turn his reputation from pirate to American War Hero.

The commander of the *Sophie* had come bearing a package for Lafitte. Inside were two letters. The first bore the seal of King George III, and offered the Baratarian's British citizenship and landholdings in the British colonies in the Americas, if they would promise to fight with the British against America, and return any stolen goods taken from Spanish ships. Lafitte saw the letters as a way back into American graces. He asked for 15 days to consider the offer and sent copies of the letters to Jean Blanque, a member of the state legislature, and someone sympathetic to the Barataria operations. Lafitte reminded Blanque that Pierre was still in jail, and "deserved an early release." Lafitte then sent a note to Claiborne, reassuring him of his loyalty to America and that he would volunteer himself and his men to help in the defense of New Orleans from British invasion. Within two days of Lafitte's notes, his brother Pierre "escaped" from jail.

Andrew Jackson arrived in New Orleans on December 1, 1814, and found the city wide open to the promise of attack. No defensive measures had been taken. Basically, all New Orleans had to offer was two ships and about 1,000 unseasoned troops. Jackson agreed to meet with Lafitte in mid-December. Lafitte said he would be willing to serve the United States and fight for New Orleans' safety if he and his men were pardoned. The pardon was granted, and the Baratarian's signed on to join the New Orleans militia; and just in time.

December 23, the first advance units of the British fleet arrived at the mouth of the Mississippi River. Lafitte alerted Jackson that he felt the American line of defense was too short, and advised expanding it to a nearby swamp; Jackson gave the order to expand. The British began their attack on December 28, but were surprised to see the volley heading back at them coming from two of Lafitte's former lieutenants, Renato Beluche and Dominique Youx. The Barataria men, who had agreed to defend New Orleans, had skill with artillery that far surpassed that of the British. The victory at the Battle of New Orleans was a glorious win for Andrew Jackson, and brought unity, respect, and political clout to the new state of Louisiana.

Jackson issued a statement praising the troops that fought so gallantly to protect the port of New Orleans, especially the cannoneers who were Lafitte's men. Jackson also singled out Jean and Pierre Lafitte for having "exhibited the same courage and fidelity." The Major General then went on to pardon the Lafitte brothers, and all of their men, on February 6, 1816. The
Battle of New Orleans helped cement Jackson's election to the Presidency.

Pierre continued to reside in New Orleans while his brother continued his nefarious dealings at sea. The brothers even became spies for Spain for a time. It was during this time, that Jean moved his base of operations from Barataria Island to Galveston Island, and built a huge community which he named *Campeche,* after the Mexican outpost down the coast. Lafitte created Letters of Marquee from a nation that didn't exist and went on a pirating spree. The letter, in essence, gave him permission from *all* nations to attack. He amassed a fortune, and built a headquarters called Maison Rouge, due to its red color. It was a two-story structure facing the harbor of Galveston. In

1818, an Indian tribe, by the name of Karankawa, attacked the colony, killing five members of Lafitte's crew. After that, a hurricane swelled over most of the island, killing several people and destroying fours ships, and most of the colony's buildings, leaving only six habitable homes.

Around 1820, Lafitte married Madeline Regaud, and finally left the colony he had created on Galveston, burning his fortress and settlements and taking immense amounts of treasure with him. All that remains of Maison Rouge is the foundation, located at 1417 Harborside Drive near Galveston wharf. Pirate Lafitte continued to take Spanish ships in the Gulf of Mexico, often taking the treasure to Galveston, or the barrier islands near New Orleans, to unload cargo or pick up supplies his brother Pierre had waiting for him. He then turned his attention to the waters of Cuba and continued his rampage there.

In February 1823, Lafitte was cruising near the town of Omoa, Honduras, on his 43-ton armed Columbia schooner, the *General Santander*. Omoa was home to the largest Spanish forts in Central America, and it guarded silver shipments from the mines of Tegucigalpa to overseas ports. On February 4, Lafitte moved in on two Spanish merchant vessels. It was a cloudy night and the visibility was poor. The Spanish ships were actually heavily armed Spanish privateers, or warships. They outmaneuvered Lafitte in the fog and came back around in a frontal attack. During the heavy gunfire, Lafitte was mortally wounded, and died just after dawn, on February 5. He was buried at sea in the Gulf of the Honduras. No American newspaper ever carried an obituary about him.

And poor Pierre, Jean's brother? He ran a respectable blacksmith operation in New Orleans, using it as a front for the brother's smuggling trade. He was the public face of the Lafitte operation, and was well known for his charm and wit, in addition to his adept trading skills of smuggled pirate booty. Pierre also commanded artillery units during the Battle of Orleans and was instrumental in the victory. He died near Dzilam de Bravo, in 1821.

Today you can still see Jean Lafitte's base of operation in New

Orleans. It is now called "Pirate Alley."

Pierre Lafitte's Blacksmith Shop still standing today on Bourbon Street in New Orleans, Louisiana.

Pirate Treasure in Louisiana

Jean Lafitte is rumored to have buried treasure all along the Galveston and Louisiana coastline, namely Contraband Bayou in Lake Charles, Louisiana, and Clear Creek near Nassau Bay, Texas. Grande Isle has been dug up by gold enthusiasts for centuries, as has most areas frequented by Lafitte and his men.

In W. C. Jameson's wonderful book, *Lost Treasures of American History,* he tells of the ongoing search for Lafitte's buried treasures. In his report, is a hapless man named Crazy Ben, who told all who would listen during his drunken recitations that he had been a cabin boy aboard Lafitte's last ship, *the Pride*, and watched as treasure-laden rowboats with Lafitte's men rowed up Clear Creek from Galveston to bury their loot in at least a dozen locations. Many would have scoffed at the old man's story if it weren't for one small thing…he paid for his drinks with Spanish gold coins! Crazy Ben was murdered by a group of men who followed him one evening from the bar, as he made his way, in a drunken stupor, to his poor living quarters. When Ben refused to divulge the location of his treasure, the men slit his throat and threw him in the bay.

Since 1950, rumors of a gold coin or two have surfaced near Clear Creek. Others have reported silver and jewelry washing ashore along the Louisiana shoreline. Perhaps the old wooden casks and chests, leather pouches, and buried jars have deteriorated over time, finally yielding up Lafitte's precious cache to the unrelenting intrusion of water. Experts today guess that the value of Lafitte's treasure is worth several hundred million dollars.

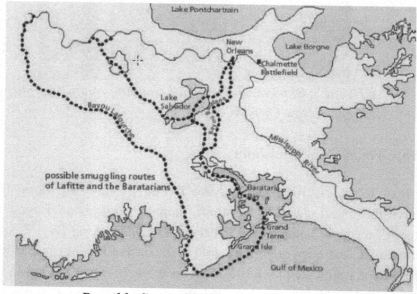

Possible Smuggling Route of Lafitte

Chapter Eighteen

Closer to Home:
Bayou Sara and St. Francisville, Louisiana

Only minutes down the Old Woodville Road (now Highway 61), from where the beginnings of the Myrtles Plantation rose from the ground in 1794, sits the picturesque town of St. Francisville. As one drives along its quaint streets, lined with historic buildings, potted flowers, more antique stores than any collecting enthusiastic could hope for, Mom and Pop eateries, and mansions dating back to the 1700's, it is hard to believe this small town was once the capitol of the Republic of West Florida, during the time just prior to the Civil War.

History rolled through the winding avenues here. Cannonballs bombarded the quiet, as the homes and once-thriving businesses were shelled by gunboats on the Mississippi River, that sent Union soldiers onto the shores of the small river port of Bayou Sara, and ultimately into the private grounds of the wealthy plantations dotting the nearby countryside.

Antique shopping in St. Francisville, Louisiana

Saint Francisville and Bayou Sara are located within the West Feliciana Parish of Louisiana. Following the founding of Bayou Sara, by Franciscan/Capuchin monks in the late 17th century, the area was explored further by France, Spain, and England. Originally part of the Florida colony, West Feliciana was conjoined with the other Florida Parishes during the Louisiana Purchase. The parish existed for a time as the independent Republic of Feliciana, but eventually joined the United States in

1810, as Feliciana Parish. In 1824, it was divided into East Feliciana and West Feliciana parishes. As mentioned earlier, Louisiana is divided into parishes, not the more commonly known counties.

St. Francisville is the second-oldest incorporated municipality in Louisiana, and the oldest in the Florida Parishes. In 1729, when the French established a small fort called Ste. Reyne aux Tunicas, it was the first attempt at European settlement in the area. It was later abandoned. Spanish Monks of the Capuchin order established a church and monastery on the west bank of the Mississippi River in Pointe Coupee Parish, after Louisiana was ceded to Spain, in 1762. The constant flooding of the Mississippi made internment of their dead impossible so they began looking across the vast river toward a bluff on higher ground. In the 1770's, the monks began transporting the sacred bodies of their dead to the east bank, even though it was not Spanish territory. They named the area Saint Francisville, in honor of their patron, Saint Francis. The new settlement grew up around the new burial ground.

History marched on, and Spain took over the east bank and the new area, in 1779, during the Revolutionary War, ousting the British. It was at this time, that land grants began being offered to Americans.

Americans had already lived in West Florida for decades. They had left behind British colonies and come to Louisiana to build plantations. Now they were in a confusing environment. Their neighbors had become American citizens, but with Spain still claiming this segment of territory, they found themselves still under Spanish rule. The Louisiana Purchase did not clear things up. On September 16, 1810, the disgruntled denizens declared the area the independent Republic of West Florida, with Saint Francisville as its seat of government, and marched on Fort San Carlos in Baton Rouge. Using a dairy cow path, the rebels slipped into the Spanish Fort with scatterguns and side arms, and raised their flag of a single white star on a blue field. Their independent rein as West Florida lasted a little over two months. Shortly after that, President James Madison declared West Florida part of the Louisiana Purchase, and in

December, West Florida was annexed. Finally, on April 30, 1812, the Territory of Orleans, including the Florida Parishes, was admitted to the Union as the state of Louisiana.

While all the skirmishes were going on, a Scotsman named John H. Johnson, platted the town site for St. Francisville and began selling the first lots in 1807. Not long after, the settlement received its municipal charter.

Just below the bluff, where the newly burgeoning town was evolving, another small entity was beginning to grow. Bayou Sara was sticking its toe into the Mighty Mississippi to test it position as a possible river port town. The area had long been used by flatboat men as a safe place to anchor. John H. Johnson joined his friend, and fellow Scotsman, John Mills, in establishing a trading post and cotton port. A primitive shantytown known as Bayou Sara Landing was born. Once again, the Mississippi River exerted her legalese and the small river port exploded. Bayou Sara Landing became one of the largest shipping ports between New Orleans and Natchez, before 1860.

As with all growth, things changed. The small town became known for its saloons, gambling dens, and bawdy houses. Riverboats were stopping at her port for more than just the importing and exporting of goods—primarily cotton. While warehouses dotted the river bank, the night was filled with the laughter and drunken howling of the visiting merchants.

Bayou Sara, Louisiana

J.W. Dorr, a newspaperman from New Orleans, visited Bayou Sara during 1860, and on May 9th of that year, wrote the following:

"If St. Francisville is stronger on the ornamental, Bayou Sara is out of sight ahead of her on the practical, for she does all the business and a great deal of business is done, too. It is a thriving and bustling place, and contains some of the most extensive and heavily stocked stores in Louisiana, outside of New Orleans, and there are few in New Orleans even which can surpass in value of stock, the concern of Meyers, Hoffman and Co., dry goods dealers and direct importers."

Mr. Dorr went on to list a number of established stores, including groceries and western produce, books, stationary and periodicals, a prominent bank called Robinson Mumford's Bank of Exchange and Deposit, the China Grove Hotel, saloons, bars and a Methodist Church, "where Rev. Thomas Donner can listen to your confessions of your trysts from the night before." Bayou Sara was also known as the great horse market for the surrounding country, and a good deal of horse trading went on. Large droves of horses from Kentucky were brought there for sale. The introduction of the West Feliciana Railroad, one of the country's first standard-gauge railroads, in 1831, did much to enhance the river port's commerce. The depot stood upon the levee in the lower part of town, having been moved from the upper part above Bayou Sara. A steam ferryboat also carried passengers back and forth across the Mississippi to Pointe Coupee at the charge of fifty cents each, and two dollars if they traveled with a horse and buggy. The town boasted one post office and a newspaper, *The Bayou Sara Ledger*, "edited and conducted by Jas. R. Marks, who is mayor of the town of Bayou

Sara."

Mrs. Beula Watts Smith was six years old when she began going to Bayou Sara from their plantation, Solitude. She recorded her memories, which were published in 1976, called

"Then and Now." The latter days of Bayou Sara have been taken from her booklet:

"I was told that before my recollection, Bayou Sara was, in its earliest days, a notorious river town. Ladies did not dare go on the street in daytime unescorted and never after dark. Barrooms were plentiful. Max Mann and Ben Mann each had a barroom. Henry Martin, George and Ellis Massey, Henry Kaufman, John Levy and John Irvin all had barrooms. Most of them had gambling tables. No wonder there were so many drunken brawls and killings. Five men were killed one evening, three white men and two negroes, including Willie and George Rucker, Bob Brannon and Clint Briggs. Two were killed in a freak shooting.

Everyone carried pistols, as men today carry wallets or cigarettes. But as I remembered Bayou Sara, it had quieted down to a very nice and pretty town.

"There was a lovely hotel managed by Mrs. Burton right near the river front... Joe Mayer also had a hotel.... There were no schools in

Bayou Sara. John F. Irvine had a big saw mill…there were two saw mills…one was called 'The Black Cat'…. there was a fish market owned by Jack Fields and his wife Elsie. There was a restaurant in connection where excellent fish dinners were served.

1910 Ringling Brothers Circus ad.

"About once a year a giant show boat, *Bryant's Floating Palace*, docked at Bayou Sara and presented nightly shows with its orchestra. A calliope announced its arrival. You could hear its organ-like whistle for miles around. Bayou Sara held a parish fair once a year. There was always a display in booths of jams, jellies, preserves, pickles, cakes, pies and canned vegetables. Prizes were given for the most excellent pieced quilts, and embroidered linen was also on display. There was a big pavilion on the fairgrounds where there was dancing all day and early evenings. Once a year, Ringling Brothers Circus came to Bayou Sara. We went from school to watch them unload. Of course, school closed for the day of the circus!

Bayou Sara

"Bayou Sara at that time was a bustling business center sprawling along the bluff below St. Francisville. The business life "is in Bayou Sara, the social life in St. Francisville." The riverboats brought merchandise from St. Louis upriver, and New

Orleans downriver, to Irvin & Son's large warehouse. Merchants came by horse and buggy with large wagons drawn by yokes of oxen, four to five to a wagon, to pick up goods for resale in their communities."

St. Francisville and Bayou Sara were thriving! The area surrounding the two towns was blessed with rich, fertile soil, long growing seasons, obliging climate, a proximity to the Mississippi River, and all its business wealth that was coveted. And so, they came....in droves! This was English Louisiana; settled by Anglo-Saxon aristocrats journeying down from the East Coast right after the Revolutionary War. They came with their trunks filled with finery,

409

herds of livestock, and the money to begin their lives as wealthy plantation owners. This part of Louisiana was different in its topography. Here were gently rolling hills, verdant woodlands teeming with flora and fauna, seen nowhere else in the Pelican State. The roads, instead of running for miles on one level, rose and fell, clearing softly flowing streams only to rise steeply, offering a view of cultivated fields where cotton, corn, indigo and sugar cane were flourishing.

The land also offered up rich clay that came in handy during construction of homes, brick walls, and roadways. Picturesque towns, large plantations and graceful homes, claimed their spots amidst this verdant landscape. St. Francisville rose to a pinnacle of prosperity. With plantations unrivaled in any part of America, and an enormous cotton crop yearly, the Feliciana parishes were assessed for more than thirty million dollars!

Mr. J.W. Dorr, journalist for a New Orleans newspaper, wrote:

"West Feliciana is one of the wealthiest parishes in the state, being considered the second rating in wealth and population next to New Orleans. The total assessed value of property is about $8,200,000 on which it pays a state tax of over $26,000, of which over $8,000 goes to the public school fund. There are thirteen public school districts in the parish and about 500 educable children. The total population of the parish is 12,000 in round numbers, of which, about 2,000 are white and about ten thousand slaves, the free negroes being few. Cotton is the principal product. Of the 227,367 acres forming the entire area, about 35,000 are in cotton, 5,000 in cane, and 19,000 in corn, leaving 165,000 or 170,000 uncultivated.

"St. Francisville, at that day, was very beautiful, with splendid homes, well laid out gardens and thriving stores. These two places (including Bayou Sara), were settled for the most part by families that came from Virginia, the Carolinas, and other Northern places, not as hardy pioneers to carve out their fortunes out of the wilderness, hewing the logs for their cabins with their own strength; but by a class for the most part that stemmed back to the aristocracy of England and Ireland

and Southland, who brought with them great chests of gold and silver coins, hundreds of slaves, wagon loads of fine furniture and paintings, who built palatial mansions, still standing, bearing witness of the above statements. These aristocratic families established a culture unsurpassed in America, the center of which revolved around beautiful St. Francisville." By 1785, the population had grown to the point to warrant creation of the District of Neuva Feliciana, from which the two parishes derive their names.

This euphoric time of prosperity and peace was not to last.

The Civil War

Shortly after 1860, when the towns of St. Francisville and Bayou Sara were at their "hay day," a fire raged through the river port of Bayou Sara, destroying nearly all the buildings in the main part of town. Flames leapt into the sky and licked at the nearby timbers as the residents of St. Francisville watched in horror from their position on the bluff above the port. The two towns were still reeling from the loss, when another enemy, more deadly than the inferno that had gutted the river port town, came calling. It came with gunfire, cannon explosions, and shells, that ripped apart the two once-prosperous towns.

The Southern states had not been happy all-in-all with the way the Union was handling things. Since the late 1820s, when the "tariff of abominations" threatened their overseas trades, there had been murmurings of discontent. Things really began to heat up in the 1850s. Initially, Louisiana was opposed to secession, and the planter class was particularly nervous about it. The planters were more conservative and realistic, and understood that while the abolitionists might keep slavery from expanding into new states and territories, it would, in all probability, continue to be legal where it already existed. The South just had to be quiet about it. If the slave trade was abolished, the plantations would fail. The field hands were the only thing bringing in the crop that consequently brought in the money!

The election of Abraham Lincoln, along with his views on slavery, put the final wrench in things. On January 26, 1861, Louisiana became the sixth state to leave the Union. Only nine days later, several Southern states formed the Confederate States of America. On April 12, the inevitable war broke out.

The Union understood Louisiana's importance in terms of location for strategic military command. Their first move was to gain control of New Orleans and its port, and block the lower Mississippi River, which they did. Next came the control of the railroad that served the heart of the area. Once the Union defeated Vicksburg, they controlled the river and divided the South in half.

The Anaconda Plan, named for the large constrictor snake, was a military squeeze tactic. The Confederate heartland was surrounded by water. The Mississippi-Tennessee-Cumberland river system encircled the west. The Gulf of Mexico hemmed in the south, and the east was cut off by the Atlantic Ocean and Chesapeake Bay. He who controlled the waters would win the war. If the Northern troops managed to take over the water egresses, the South would be cut off from the world. The Anaconda raised its head first at the mouth of the Mississippi, effectively setting up a blockade. The Confederates rallied and won a few small victories, but it was not enough. By autumn, they were running out of food in New Orleans and lower Louisiana. Though the northern section of Louisiana had an overabundance of food, thanks primarily to the plantations, they could not move it or sell it.

When the Union attacked New Orleans from the sea, a move the Confederates had not foreseen, it was a crippling blow. They had put all their fortifications at Vicksburg and Port Hudson, and left the Gulf of Mexico wide open. The North took over New Orleans, on April 26. When Port Hudson, a mere ten miles from the Myrtles Plantation, fell in July of the following year, the Union took control of the Mississippi River, splitting the Confederate Army in half, and cutting off its supplies from the West. Confederate General Richard Taylor wrote in 1863: "Louisiana, from Natchitoches to the Gulf, is a howling wilderness and her people are starving!"

Those awful days of 1863, followed the fall of New Orleans. The army of Butler terrified the people of New Orleans, bullying and robbing, while the Fleet of Federal gunboats kept continually going up and down the river, bombarding recalcitrant Confederates. In this fleet, was *U.S.S. Albatross*, with Captain John E. Hart of Schenectady, New York, as Lieutenant Commander.

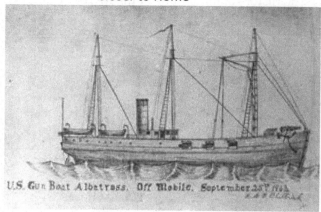

U.S. Gun Boat Albatross. Off Mobile. September 20th 1861.

Albatross

The *Albatross* prowled the waters of the great Mississippi and finally set her eye on the port of Bayou Sara, not far from the defeated Port Hudson. They came ashore here, looking for provisions, horses and mules, and information of where they could find wealth of any kind at the local plantations. The Myrtles was literally right next door! The Union troops found men in Bayou Sara who were from St. Louis firms, dealing in horses in the river port town. They helped the troops, putting a wedge between Bayou Sara and St. Francisville. In fact, it was to become St. Francisville's demise.

The official reports of the incident can be found in the National Archives in Washington D.C. It is written by Lieutenant Commander P. Foster, U.S. Navy to Rear Admiral David D. Porter, under the date of January 29, 1864, almost seven months after the destruction of St. Francisville by their military. During the discourse, he informs Porter, that Bayou Sara has been kind to them and in no way harboring Confederates or blocking their cause. He goes on to say that St. Francisville, however "has been a hotbed of secession ever since I have been in command of this place, and has been the constant resort of Confederates, where they are continually entertained and urged on acts of plunder and abuse upon the people of the lower town. Moreover, there is not one inhabitant of the place of St. Francisville who has ever shown himself favorable to the Union, while a majority of those in the lower town of Bayou Sara have ever proved themselves good and loyal citizens."

An order was sent to St. Francisville by the Union officers, allowing the women and children 24 hours to leave the place. "This order was subsequently prolonged," wrote Foster, "and ample time given. When the allotted time had elapsed, the shelling commenced, at noon on the 16th, continuing about four hours. In all, 108 shells were fired slowly, and with very great accuracy, each one telling."

Mrs. Wm. Walter Leak, who is a daughter of Captain Robinson Mumford, the leading banker of Bayou Sara, had a quite different telling of the shelling, and the advance warning "supposedly" given the women and children of St. Francisville. She and her three children were in their home located on the bluff overlooking the river, awaiting the arrival of her husband, Captain William Walter Leak, C.S.A., who was coming home on a brief furlong—as well as innumerable others who had been off fighting the war. Only a small handful of men remained in St. Francisville, and they were either elderly, or physically unable to fight. The rest were women and small children.

The shelling began without preamble, and the returning Confederates heading home to their families were caught in the havoc wrought by exploding shells. Mrs. William W. Leak and her children fled to a place of safety beneath a stair leading to the cellar of their large brick mansion, which threatened to collapse every moment during the bombing, while the town was being demolished. There was not one piece of artillery in the town with which to answer the onslaught. It seemed as if the end of the world had come to those who stood helplessly by as the court house, Grace Church, and mansion after mansion and place of business were attacked. The handful of old men, hysterical women and children, and one or two Confederate soldiers on leave, could do nothing but watch the scene of destruction. It is here, that the story takes a very thought-provoking twist. It is in times of war, that the good in man often shows its true face. For the people of St. Francisville, it became known as the *Day the War Stopped.*

While the shelling of St. Francisville continued its relentless attack, a single gunshot was heard coming from the Captain's Quarters aboard the *Albatross*. An officer ran in to find Lt.

Commander John E. Hart shot through the head by his own pistol. There were many theories as to the reason the young Commander, whose bravery had been heralded during his naval career, had taken his own life. Some attributed it to delirium from yellow fever. Others had another belief. Many believed Captain Hart had killed himself due to remorse. He had friends in St. Francisville, and had been entertained there. There were even rumors he was in love with a young woman living in the town. Whatever the reason, there was a lull in the shelling, and the handful of war-ravaged citizens of St. Francisville, their town lying around them in rubble, watched as a lifeboat, fully manned and waving a white flag, left the *Albatross* and crossed to Bayou Sara's soil.

The men got out of the lifeboat and asked if there were any Masons in the town, and learned there were two brothers who owned the ferry and the steaming. These Masons told the officer that in St. Francisville, the place they had just shelled, was a Masonic Lodge, and informed him that S.J. Powell, who was away with the Confederates, was its Master, but that Captain W.W. Leak of the Confederate Army (whose wife and children had just hidden beneath their staircase during the attack) "is home on furlough and can convoke the Lodge."

The officer sent word to Captain Leak that the commanding officer of the *Albatross* was dead, and requested that he be given a Mason's funeral, and be interred in the earth instead of being sunk into the Mississippi River. "We have Masons on board who can vouch for him and his standing. We will await your answer." Captain Leak, while looking about him at the desolation of the once beautiful town of St. Francisville, replied, "As a Mason, it is my duty to accord a Masonic burial to a brother Mason, without taking into account the nature of our relation in the world outside Masonry. Go tell that Union officer to bring the Captain's body ashore. There are a few Masons left in the town; most of us are at the front. I shall assemble all I can."

The body of Captain J.E. Hart, in uniform, was brought ashore, and four members of Feliciana Lodge No. 31, still wearing their Confederate uniforms, with their Masonic regalia worn above, received him. Together, with the Union Masons, they bore his body to the little Mason's Lodge, still standing— now the town library— and when the full Mason's funeral rites were completed, carried his body to the newly dug grave at Grace Episcopal Church—whose bell tower had been such a tempting target for their shells—and placed him among the others whose headstones were now torn and broken. Here, they, with "masonic ritual consigned all that was mortal of Lieutenant Commandant John E. Hart, Unites States Naval Officer of U.S.S. *Albatross* gunboat, to sleep his eternal sleep."

As the last clod of dirt fell on the new grave, the officers of the *Albatross* saluted and departed, and reaching their ship, sailed down the river.

Grace Episcopal Church and cemetery.

And then, the war resumed on different ground. Lee's northern invasion turned back at Gettysburg July 3, Vicksburg fell on July 4, and Port Hudson, only minutes down river from Bayou Sara, surrendered July 9, all in one catastrophic week. But for one brief touching moment of brotherhood, the war had stopped in St. Francisville, and this moment is re-enacted one weekend each June there. As a touching note, you will see fresh flowers placed on the Union's soldier's grave on each Memorial Day and All Saints Day, as they have been since the *Day the War Stopped*. It was Captain Leak who first started putting flowers on the Union officer's grave, a practice that has been honored ever since.

The Remains of War

Records have been kept, detailing the cost of the wars that ravaged Louisiana, from her conception to her statehood, and beyond. One particular report was very telling. It is a running account of the sessions held before Congress in Washington City, Dec. 7, 1831. The various sections are replete with land owners, business owners, and private citizens, petitioning for compensation for their grievous losses during the wars that marched across their properties. Reports of soldiers helping themselves to their food and water supplies, chopping down trees to use in the building of temporary houses and defense perimeters, completely taking over the homes and outbuildings to use as they pleased, were replete; page after page of destruction.

Here is an excerpt from that large report, that brings home the devastation felt by the people, who watched in horror as war overtook their hard work and lifestyles:

The House of Representatives, at the First Session of the Twenty-Second Congress, Begun and Held at the City of Washington, Dec. 7, 1831. Rep. No. 386.

"Does the conclusion follow that the Government is in no way bound to afford indemnification to the sufferers? Let the facts be examined.

"The declaration of war found in the settlements..., which had recently emerged..., progressing rapidly to a condition of prosperity and improvement. Their enterprising inhabitants, after having, by painful labor, converted forests into fruitful fields, were solacing the recollection of their hardships with the prospect of speedily attaining to those social comforts and blessings, which a deprivation, incident to their condition, rendered even more dear to them. The annunciation of this event (war), produced a complete revolution of their affairs. Pursuits of business were suspended; habits of social intercourse interrupted; and the relationship of neighborly kindness and friendship changed to feelings of deadly hostility and strife.

"Their houses, by the exigencies of the occasion, are converted into hospitals and barracks; their other buildings into magazines of arms and ammunition, or into storehouses for clothing and provisions; and their peaceful fields are made a bloody arena, on which are exhibited, years together, successive scenes of alarms, skirmishes, battles and massacres".

Many lives never recovered after the Civil War. Fortunes were lost, homes destroyed, and loved ones gone forever. The Myrtles Plantation was not immune to the onslaught. Due primarily to her proximity to Bayou Sara and St. Francisville, let alone Port Hudson right down the road, the Union soldiers found their way to her doors handily. There are rumors that she was overtaken, and a temporary headquarters for the Union army set up within her graceful walls. There is still visible damage to the fireplace in the Gentleman's Parlor from a sword smashing into its marble. In the ledgers reporting the good men of the St. Francisville area that joined in the fight to protect Louisiana from the Union, Clark Woodruff and David Bradford, Jr. of the Myrtles Plantation are listed as riflemen, who fought bravely for their territory and loved ones. It was a common practice for the military to simply take over a plantation and pitch their tents on her property, using the privy, helping themselves to the gardens and pantries, and giving a different twist to the meaning of "the spoils of war."

The Passing of an Era

Of Bayou Sara, nothing today remains. The terrible bombardment of St. Francisville also spelled its doom. Shortly after the destruction of that beautiful place, great fissures appeared in the sandy soil of the lower town. These fissures gradually grew larger, forming rivulet-like places that were filled with the debris taken from the ruined buildings which the people of St. Francisville knew would never be rebuilt. Left like a wrecked barge to rot on shore, Bayou Sara was practically abandoned for years. Boll weevils had taken a toll on the cotton plantations, and with the war and the unpredictable flooding of the Mississippi, the river port town met its end. It was the flooding of 1912, that finally left Bayou Sara a ghost town. Mrs. Beula Watts vividly recalls the flood that finished the once burgeoning river port:

"The rainy season began in early spring of 1912. The melting snow and ice from the north began to swell the river. The Mississippi River began to rise and flood the low land. The levee which protected the town became threatened. Rains and winds caused alarm. The citizens of Bayou Sara worked day and night in the rain, filling sand bags to bank the levee in weakening places. School boys worked with them. Sand boils began to appear. Citizens of Bayou Sara were ordered to move livestock and possessions to higher lands. The rains had stopped but the winds were high. The school was in St. Francisville and on May 2, 1912, before classes had started, whistles began blowing and bells began tolling.

"We knew what had happened! School was dismissed and we pupils ran to Catholic Hill to see the water rushing in, swallowing the town of Bayou Sara. The roar of onrushing water could be heard for miles. The crevasse was 187 feet wide! The next day, nothing but the tops of houses were visible. Most of the houses were swept away by the strong current of rushing water, and debris floated in the river.

"The once-rich merchants moved away and were rolled up the hill to St. Francisville. Other homes and stores were deserted and rapidly fell into decay. Only a couple of brick buildings and the railroad station remained."

The Flooding of Bayou Sara.

In 1926, the State Legislature removed the Charter of Incorporation from Bayou Sara, and in a short while the little ghost town became a wilderness of willows.

Mrs. Stephen Dart has a wonderful description of the history of Bayou Sara when she says:

"In two hundred years, Bayou Sara has come full circle. Once again as we view it today, the river bank looks very much as it did long ago when LaSalle passed by with his group of Indians and French explorers, and the once important port is now just a memory."

St. Francisville has rebuilt her beautiful streets, and the stately mansions can still be seen on the bluff overlooking the Mississippi. Here, were the haunts of John James Audubon, when after a day's tramp through the forest and glen in search of a new subject for his brush, he rested and refreshed himself before returning to the plantation mansions where he and his wife lived. Not far away stands Oakley Plantation, where Audubon taught painting to the children of the family. He remained here during the summer months of 1821, from June to October, and wintered in New Orleans. The paintings of the area birds are found in his immortal *Birds of America*. Each year a celebration is held in his honor. The Audubon Pilgrimage rolls back time in St. Francisville and the surrounding plantations, as doors are flung open to visitors who are encouraged to join in the celebration of the famous painter that made his home here. Louisiana's gorgeous blooms burst forth during this March celebration and remind the lucky guest that you are still standing in English Plantation Country.

In 2012, Louisiana celebrated their 200th anniversary of statehood. The area has also been blessed by a far-sighted historic preservation movement which has spearheaded the rejuvenation of historic downtown St. Francisville, as a National Register Historic District, encouraging vast renovations of many of the surrounding plantations.

During a recent visit to the Myrtles Plantation, to research this book, Teeta Moss, the Myrtles Plantation's owner, was kind enough to drive me through the streets of St. Francisville and down the gentle slope to the banks of the Mississippi where Bayou Sara once stood. There is nothing left of the town, even the ferry that was still giving tourists rides across the "Father of the Waters" is gone, as a new bridge replaced its need. There is a bayou to your right, its ghostly cypress trees tenaciously holding on through their broad green roots. You can see the water level markings along their tall trunks, proof that the river will not be tamed. It is quiet here, and you can't help but feel sadness and a deep wish to see the bustling river port town, as it was in its glory days. Time is no respecter of memories.

Chapter Nineteen

Indian Treasure and Burial Grounds Near the Myrtles Plantation

INDIANS OF LOUISIANA :
Their Contemporary Locations and Linguistic Retention

Before many of the wars had found their way into the lush area of West Florida, Indian tribes lived here, enjoying the vast woodlands, rivers and fertile soil. The Tunica Indians were especially prevalent in the St. Francisville area. Here, buffalo roamed freely across the expanse where swampland was not as ubiquitous as it was in other parts of the region. The soil yielded up clay that came in handy for the creation of pottery, weaponry, and modest dwellings.

One of the many legends regarding the Myrtles Plantation, is that she was built by David Bradford on sacred Indian burial grounds. Though it is almost a certainty the Tunica tribe wandered through her perimeters in search of food, timber, and buffalo, their burial site was actually farther to the northwest in West Feliciana Parish. The Tunica Hills Preservation Area is located 20 miles north of the town of St. Francisville, which would make it a good 15 miles north of the Myrtles Plantation location. The Mississippi frontage is framed by a high bluff, approximately 200 feet above the river. Old Tunica Road is an unimproved historical road with steep lichen-covered inclines and winding turns. One of the greatest cultural assets within the property is the location of a large Indian burial ground. It contained one of the most extensive collections of artifacts of both Indian and French origin. The artifacts are known as the Tunica Treasure and the burial ground is known as the Trudeau site, as it is found on the Old Trudeau Plantation property. It was not David Bradford, but a man by the name of Leonard Charrier, who discovered the site, and made headlines. It became known as *The Curse of the Tunica Treasure*.

Tunica Indians in West Feliciana Parish

In the blistering summer heat of 1968, an untrained pothunter, named Leonard Charrier, unearthed what became known as "the greatest archeological find in the lower Mississippi valley," and "one of the greatest archeological finds of the 20ᵗʰ century." What Charrier found, was a sacred mausoleum that held over 100 Tunica Indian graves. It was the chosen location for the tribe's revered dead to rest in peace and to remain undisturbed. Through extensive study of 18ᵗʰ century maps (which would be for the years of the 1700s), and early colonial period documents, Charrier figured out the exact location of something that had been jealously guarded by history for 240 years; something archeologists had been actively searching for since the 1930s. With all this research and hunting, it is certain the Myrtles Plantation area was looked at as well, and passed over, as the sacred burial ground of the Tunica, which controlled that area. Armed with a metal detector, and the casual permission of the

Trudeau Plantation's caretaker to poke around on the property, Charrier went in search of the long-hidden grave site of the Tunica Indians and the wealthy 18ᵗʰ century chief, Cahura-Joligo. Legend had it, that the great Tunica chief was buried with a cache of gold and silver coins given to him by French monarch, Louis XV, in gratitude for his tribe's military assistance to French settlers in colonial Louisiana.

When Charrier first stood on the land where his research had guided him, it didn't take long for his metal detector to start reacting…and strongly! Beneath the soil was metal, and lots of it!   The long undisturbed ground now began yielding up her treasures, as Charrier returned every weekend to dig up huge sections of the sacred soil. European glazed earthenware pieces, Rhine valley stoneware, blue and white Dutch delftware, brass and iron pots, pans and kettles, musket parts, ceremonial pipes, iron tools, pewter bowls, shell ear pins, jugs, bowls and jars, brass bells, glass beads, cooking utensils, iron knives, and brass buttons all testified to the unique relationship the Tunica Indians shared with the French and Spanish settlers, during the early colonization of Louisiana.

Bowls from the Tunica Treasure

This impressive tribe lived at, what is now known as, Angola, Louisiana, and just a few miles north of their chosen burial site at the Old Trudeau Plantation site. During this time, members of the Natchez were exacting their revenge on the Tunica for their military assistance to the French, killing Cahura-Joligo during a surprise early morning raid. Immediately after the death of the great Tunica chief, the tribe relocated to the Trudeau site where they lived and prospered for the next sixty years. The tribe eventually joined with the Biloxi

Indian tribe, forming the Tunica-Biloxi Tribe, and now lives in Marksville, Louisiana, where they have been for the past 200 years.

Without the Old Trudeau Plantation owner's knowledge or permission, and without any archeological training, Charrier began his search for treasure, unearthing the contents of more than 100 Indian graves, between 1968 and 1970. The artifacts he found were removed surreptitiously from the site, and carried away in his car across the Mississippi River on the Saint Francisville ferry, then piled and stuffed into every nook and cranny of his small residence in Bunkie, Louisiana.

In late 1969, Charrier was in the market to sell the artifacts he had unearthed to date. He brought into his confidence, Louisiana archeologist Stu Neitzel who, after his initial shock at seeing such marvelous artifacts piled up in the closets of Charrier's house, immediately contacted archeologist Dr. Jeffery Brain, of the Peabody Museum in Essex, Massachusetts, the leading authority on Tunica Indian history. When Dr. Brain finally arrived in Bunkie with Neitzel to see the items for himself, he offered Charrier $4,000 for the entire collection. Charrier countered and demanded $40,000, even though he could not provide proof of ownership. Brain then offered $8,000, but Charrier turned it down. He eventually sold the collection to the Peabody Museum where it would be restored, studied and displayed.

However, four years later, the legal rollercoaster began, as Charrier, the widow Louise Bell (who owned the Trudeau
Plantation), and the Tunica-Biloxi Indian tribe, all asserted rights to the treasure. Court cases ensued, with the Tunica Indians demanding the remains and artifacts of their ancestors be returned to them. The Tunica's were not recognized as a tribe at that time and so no rights were afforded them.

The battle raged on for years, until finally on July 27, 1981, an announcement appeared in the Federal Register, putting an end to the Tunica tribe's 60-year quest for official recognition:

"Notice is hereby given that the Assistant Secretary acknowledges that the Tunica-Biloxi Tribe exists as an Indian

Tribe."

March 18, 1985, what had begun nine years ago, in the crowded second-story courtroom of the West Feliciana Parish Court House in St. Francisville, had now arrived at its remarkable conclusion—the bones and grave goods remain the property of the descendants, who in this case are the Tunica-Buloxi Indians.

Charrier continued to appeal all the way to the Louisiana Supreme Court, but Judge Sartain's common sense ruling stuck. The message to all pothunters was clear: those who hope to be rewarded for plundering Indian graves for profit in Louisiana, are in for a big disappointment.

The Tunica Treasure has now been returned to the Tunica-Biloxi tribe from the Cabildo Museum in New Orleans, where it was housed for a time. As of August, 2003, the Tunica-Biloxi Tribe have restored 78-percent of the fragile goods that were unearthed 44 years ago, a stunning 255,000 artifacts. In 2004, the collection found its new home in the Cultural Resource Center on the Tunica reservation in Marksville, Louisiana, where the display is on exhibit.

The property the Myrtles Plantation stands upon, was inhabited by buffalo, as is made clear by the pond only a few feet from her doors. The pond began as a buffalo wallow, exposing the clay contents of the earth which was used by the Bradford's for creating brick for their new home. Indian tribes always followed the buffalo and made camp wherever they were found. The buffalo was to the Indian tribes a "traveling department store of the early days" or what I call "one-stop shopping." Indians used the buffalo for every part of its body. Without him the Natives would not have survived. Buffalo was used for meat, roasted and boiled for food; hides were used for clothing and teepees; muscles were used for thread and bowstrings; bones became weapons and tools; horns were used for utensils and toys; buffalo hair was made into rope; beard was used for decoration; tail for whips; brain to soften the skin; hoofs were boiled to make glue; the fat was turned into soap and candles; dung was used as fuel; teeth were made into necklaces; the stomach and bladders created containers; and the skull was used as ceremonial masks.

Buffalo Wallow

The evidence that buffalo did indeed graze in the pastures of what was to become the Myrtles Plantation is plain. The supposition that the Tunica Indians also prowled these grounds is warranted. But Indian tribes were not in the habit of burying their sacred ancestors all over the countryside. One area was blessed and sanctified, and guarded! Sacred rites were held there to send the loved ones on after they died. That burial ground was 15 miles to the northwest, on the Old Trudeau Plantation.

Appendix I:

The Myrtles Dance with Fame

The Myrtles Plantation has been featured in numerous newspaper, magazine and online articles. Production crews from the realm of television and movies have set up their cameras in her doorways and grounds, for both historical and paranormal projects. Here is but a sampling of her continued dance with fame:

Television:

A&E
Oprah National Geographic Explorer
Fox TV Scary Stories
MSNBC True Believers
Fox TV Haunted History
Hauntings Across America
True Tales of Haunted Houses

Unsolved Mysteries
Mysterious Journeys
ABC Discovery Channel
Indigo Films-Secrets
TV Asani of Japan
Film Garden Entertainment
WJTV Jackson Mississippi
Café Productions of London
Ghost Adventures
Ghost Hunters
History Channel
Learning Channel
WWL TV New Orleans
Louisiana PM Magazine
WBRZ Baton Rouge
Taste of Louisiana

Books:

Coast to Coast Ghosts
Dixie Spirits
Ghost Research Society
Ghost Trackers
Ghosts Along the Bayou
Ghostly Encounters
Guide to New Orleans
Haunted Bayou
Haunted Hotels
Haunted Houses
Haunted Houses & Chilling Tales
Haunted Houses USA
Haunted Inns
Haunted Louisiana
Hauntings Across America

Here a Ghost, There a Ghost
Historic Haunted America
House of Horror
Louisiana-A Treasure of Plantations
Les Plantations Du Vieux Sue
Marvelous Old Mansions
National Discovery of Haunted Places
New Orleans Ghosts
Southern Fried Ghosts
The Best Haunted Inns
The Haunting of Louisiana
The History and Haunting of the Myrtles Plantation
Ghosts Along the Mississippi

Magazine Features:

55 & Fine
AAA Southern Traveler
Acadian Times
ALlt Om Resor Swedish Travel American Spirit Magazine
Arrington's Bed & Breakfast Journal
Atlanta Homes
Baton Rouge Business Report
CNN/Money Magazine
City Social Magazine
Colonial Homes
Commercial Appeal
Country Inns
Country Roads Magazine
Courier Magazine
D—The Magazine of Dallas Dallas Morning News
Delta's Sky Magazine
Discovery Magazine

Fate Magazine Forbes

Gothic Journal

Gourmet Magazine

Home Magazine

Homestyle Magazine

Inn Register Magazine

Life Magazine

Louisiana Country

Louisiana Life Magazine

Meetings & Tourism

Moonlight Road

National Enquirer

New Choices

New Orleans Magazine

Newsweek

Oxford America

Reader's Digest

SA Pharmaceutical Journal

Southern Living '96, '98, '2000, '01,'02, '03

Southern Living Vacations

Touring Club Magazine

Travel & Leisure

Travel South

Veranda Magazine

Wanderlust Travel Magazine

Woman's Day

Woman's World

Zink Magazine

Newspaper Features:

Advocate Fun Section

Advocate Magazine Section

Advocate People Section
Biloxi Sun Herald
Boulder Colorado News
Boston Globe
Dallas Morning News
FLT Swedish News Agency
Ft. Worth Star
Good News Antiques
Hallandsposten/Sweden
Houston Chronicle
Kalamazoo Gazette

Kiplinger's Report
Knoxville Sentinel
Montreal Gazette
Morning Advocate, Louisiana
New York Post
New York Times Daily Newspaper
New York Times Travel Section
Old News is Good News Gazette
San Diego Union Tribune
St. Francisville Democrat
St. Louis Post Dispatch
Sunday Oklahoma Newspaper
The Observer Pennsylvania
The Times of Acadiana/Lafayette
The Times Picayune/New Orleans
The Times Travel/New Orleans
Toronto Sun
USA Today Weekend Edition
Wall Street Journal

Movies:

The Long Hot Summer (TV mini-series)

Appendix II:

Louisiana Recipes

Beignets

Trying to choose recipes indicative of Louisiana is like to trying to select a flower that represents a garden. It can't be done. There are the stand-outs, and food that decidedly originated from this diverse region of the United States, but for each chef, the ingredients will vary, that extra touch of spice will make it his own, and the way the dish is prepared will become his signature. Here are just a few recipes that, to me, scream "Louisiana Flavor Explosion!"

Beignets

The word beignet (pronounced ben-yai) comes from the early Celtic word 'bigne' meaning to raise. It is also French for 'fritter'. Beignets, a New Orleans specialty, are fried, raised pieces of yeast dough. They are dusted with sugar or topped with icing. They are like a sweet doughnut. They were brought to New Orleans by French colonists in the 18th Century.

Ingredients:

1 envelope active dry yeast
1 ½ cups warm water
½ cup sugar
1 tsp. salt
2 eggs, beaten
1 cup evaporated milk
6 ½ - 7 cups all-purpose flour
¼ cup shortening softened
Oil for deep frying
Powdered sugar

In a large bowl, sprinkle yeast over the warm water; stir to dissolve and let stand 5-10 minutes. Add the sugar, salt, beaten eggs and milk. Mix well, add 4 cups flour and beat until smooth. Add shortening and blend in remaining flour. Cover and chill 4 hours or overnight. Roll out on floured surface to ¼ to ½ inch thickness. Cut in to 3 inch squares. Heat oil to 360 degrees. Deep fry a few at a time until lightly browned on both sides. Drain on paper towels and sprinkle with powdered sugar. Serve immediately. Makes 24-36 beignets.

Crawfish Etouffee

Ingredients:
1 # crawfish tails (fat pack if available)
1/4 # butter
2 tbsp. all-purpose flour
1 medium onion - diced
1/2 bell pepper- diced
3 stalks celery- diced
2 pods garlic or 1 tsp- minced
1 tsp sweet basil
1 tsp leaf thyme
1/4 c. diced parsley
1/4 c. diced onion tops
1/2 c. shrimp or seafood stock, water if unavailable
Red, white, black pepper, and salt to taste

Sauté flour and butter together to form a blonde roux. Add celery, onion, bell pepper and garlic, sauté until the onions clear. Add shrimp stock and fat if available. Add basil and thyme, some pepper. Simmer 20 minutes minimum. Ten minutes before serving, add crawfish tails and bring back to a light simmer. Adjust salt and peppers to taste. Immediately before serving, stir in onion tops and parsley. Serve on hot Louisiana rice. Serves up to 4 people.

You may also use this recipe to fill a Crawfish Pie:

Let cool and add to puff pastry or other pastry squares, about 5" square, fold over as an apple turnover, crimp two edges and egg wash. Bake at 375 for 15 minutes. Serve with extra Etouffee over or under pies.

Uncle Dewey's Bar-B-Q Ribs

Ingredients:
4 racks of Baby Back Pork ribs (1 rack per person)
1-liter Coke
1-liter Pineapple juice
1 cup brown sugar

Bar-B-Q Sauce
2 large onions, chopped
2 cloves of garlic, chopped
1 bell pepper, chopped
1 small can tomato paste
2 tablespoons canola or corn oil
2 tablespoons Worcestershire sauce
1 large tablespoon Dijon mustard
1 cup Balsamic vinegar
1/2 teaspoon cayenne pepper
1/2 teaspoon black pepper
1/2 teaspoon white pepper
1/2 cup lemon juice

1. Boil ribs in mixture of Coke, pineapple juice, brown sugar. If ribs are not submerged in liquid, add water. Boil 1 hour. (Don't throw out the liquid!)
2. Grill ribs on Bar-B-Q for 5-10 minutes on each side.
3. To make sauce...sauté onions, garlic, bell pepper in oil for about 5 minutes. Then add tomato paste and about 3 cups of the liquid remaining from boiling. Now add Worcestershire sauce, mustard, vinegar and spices. Let boil down until thick like Bar-B-Q sauce. Add lemon juice at the end. (Here's a little trick...if you like your B-B-Q sauce a little sweeter, add more brown sugar here!)
4. Dip ribs in sauce, then put back on Bar-B-Q pit on LOW HEAT for another 10-15 minutes. Don't let the sauce burn...

5. Now it's time to get dirty...the meat will fall off da bones and into yo mouth. Enjoy!!!

Mardi Gras Scampi

Ingredients:
60 peeled and de-veined 21-25 count shrimp, tail on
4 oz. butter
10 mushrooms sliced
2 bunches green onions sliced
5 tbsp. garlic
5 tomatoes wedged
3 Golden bell peppers, julienne
3 red bell peppers, julienne
1/2 c. lemon pepper seasoning
5 c. white wine salt, red
pepper, dill 10 tbsp.
butter, frozen
5 tbsp. grated Parmesan cheese
30 oz. cooked pasta- angel hair, capellini, fettuccini

This is a fast sauté item. Put the first 4 oz. butter in a heated sauté pan or rondo. Add shrimp, mushrooms, green onions, and garlic, then sauté. When the shrimp begin to turn pink, add the tomatoes, both peppers, lemon seasoning, other seasoning, and sauté for 1 minute on high. Add white wine and blend together. When the wine has heated, lower the fire, add frozen butter, Parmesan cheese and shake/stir. Fold in the pasta. Serves 10, serve immediately.

Oysters Bienville

Ingredients:
1/8 # bacon
4 oz. sliced mushrooms
4 cloves garlic-minced
1/4 bunch green onions-chopped
1/2 stick butter (1/8 #)
2 c. flour
1 1/2 qt. milk
1/4 tsp. egg shade food color
1/2 # boiled shrimp diced
1/2 pt. oyster juice
1/2 c. lemon juice
1/2 c. sherry
1/4 c. chopped parsley
6 doz. oysters with shells

Cut bacon into small pieces and fry until brown. Sauté mushrooms, garlic and green onions. Add butter and when it has melted, blend in flour. Cook slowly 5 minutes, and then gradually stir in milk. After sauce thickens, add egg coloring, shrimp, oyster juice, lemon juice, sherry, and parsley. Simmer slowly 15 minutes.

Have 12 pie pans half filled with rock salt. Arrange 6 oyster shells in each pie pan. Put a raw oyster (at room temperature) on each shell and top with sauce. Place under broiler (6 inches from heat) until heated thoroughly and browned on top. Serves 12.

Soft Shell Crabs Juliette

Ingredients:
12 medium soft shell crabs
3 c. light oil
2 cups milk and 2 eggs or just 2 cups buttermilk
4 cups fish fry or seasoned corn flour
2 cups seasoned flour salt, granulated garlic, red-white-black pepper
   to taste, thyme and basil.
3 large tomatoes
2 eggplant
Béarnaise Sauce

Wash crabs thoroughly under cold water. Lift the end points on the crabs and remove the gills (dead man). Wash again. flip crab over and remove the back flap. Wash again. Cut off the mouth and cut out the eyes and eye stems. Wash again. Let crabs drain in colander about 30 minutes to drain. Season them with salt, peppers, basil, thyme and garlic.

Peel and slice eggplant, soak eggplant in salted water about 30 minutes. If you have a grill, thickly slice tomato and grill the slices, keep warm. If you have no grill, just lightly warm them in a buttered sauté pan. Fry the eggplant by dipping in egg wash or buttermilk and seasoned flour. Dip crabs in egg wash then corn flour, shake off, repeat then pan fry in
375-degree oil. Place two eggplant slices on the plate, top with grilled tomato, then the crab, top with béarnaise sauce.

Okra, Shrimp and Andouille Gumbo

Ingredients:
1/3 c. light oil
2# cut okra
2 c. chopped onions
1 c. celery
1 c. bell pepper
2 c. chopped tomatoes
1 # smoked or Andouille sausage
5 # peeled head on shrimp (make a stock with the shells)
1/2 c. chopped green onions
2 tbsp. minced garlic
10 c. seafood or shrimp stock
Salt, white pepper, leaf thyme, cayenne pepper, black pepper

Sauté half the okra in hot oil, season with white, red, and black pepper and cook until browned. Stir in the onions, celery, bell pepper, and garlic. Cook about five minutes. Add 1 c. of the stock and simmer another five minutes. Stir in the tomatoes and two more cups of stock. Simmer; add the remaining okra, leaf thyme, season with red, white and red pepper, and then the last of the stock. Bring to a boil, reduce and add sausage. Simmer 45 minutes, add shrimp and green onions. Skim the surface for excess oil, serve over rice. Serves about eight.

Louisiana Pralines

Ingredients:
2 cups light brown sugar
1 cup white sugar
1 cup water
1 c heavy cream

1 tbsp. vanilla
1-1/2 cups chopped pecans
1/2 cup pecan halves

In a heavy bottomed pan, combine sugars, water and cream. Cook and stir until soft ball stage. (238 degrees) Remove from heat, whip with a heavy whip for ten to fifteen minutes, add nuts and vanilla, drop by spoonsful onto buttered pan or parchment. Cool, wrap in film.

Bananas Foster

Ingredients:
1 c. brown sugar (light or dark)
1/4 # butter
2 bananas
2 oz. banana liquor
1 oz. rum
1/2 tsp vanilla extract
1/2 tsp cinnamon or 1 cinnamon stick
1 oz. Rum (if it is to be flambéed)
Vanilla ice cream

Cook the sugar and butter for about 5 minutes. Add bananas, simmer another 2 minutes, add cinnamon, vanilla flavoring, banana liquor and 1 oz. rum, simmer another 2 minutes. If flambéing, pull the sauté pan back and super heat the front edge of the pan, add another 1 oz. rum with a jigger, (do not pour out of the bottle!!) and light with a long match, or roll the flame over the
edge of the pan if using gas, jiggling the sauté pan will increase the flame. Serve over vanilla ice cream.

Bananas Foster. Photo courtesy of foodnetwork.com.

Louisiana Festivals, Pageants and Parties

"Laissez les bons temps rouler!" Let the Good Times Roll!

No one loves a party like Louisianans! And if there was ever a doubt about how much they adore food…the list of festivals dedicated to eating is three times as long as any other category! Enjoy!

Arts and crafts festivals

* Angola Prison Rodeo & Arts and Crafts Festival — Angola
* Antique Festival — Denham Springs
* Cultural Crossroads — Minden
* Dirty Linen Night — New Orleans

* Fall Festival in Antique Village — Denham Springs <u>Hot Air</u>
  <u>Balloon Festival</u> Championship — Baton Rouge
- Louisiana Book Festival — Baton Rouge
- Louisiana Tournoi — Ville Platte
- Melrose Arts & Crafts Festival — Natchitoches
- NCLAC Holiday Arts Tour — Ruston
- Nicholls State University Jubilee — Thibodaux
- Red River Revel — Shreveport
- Shakespeare Festival — New Orleans
- Sippin' in Seer Sucker — New Orleans
- Spring Arts Festival — Minden
- Tennessee Williams/New Orleans Literary Festival — New Orleans
- Three Rivers Art Festival — Covington
- White Linen Night — New Orleans
- Gumbo Gala: Food, Art & Music — Shreveport, Louisiana

Community festivals and celebrations

- Baker Buffalo Festival — Baker, Louisiana
- Baton Rouge Fest For All Festival — Baton Rouge
- Christ Fest Community Festival — Deville, Louisiana

Food, harvest and wild game festivals

- Alligator Festival — Luling, Louisiana
- Andouille Festival — Laplace
- Bayou Lacombe Crab Festival—Lacombe
- Blues and BBQ Challenge Festival—Hammond

- Boudin Cook-Off—Lafayette
- Bucktown Seafood Festival — Bucktown, Louisiana [2]
- Cajun Hot Sauce Festival — New Iberia
- Catfish Festival — Des Allemands, Louisiana
- Catfish Festival
- Cattle Festival (Abbeville)
- Chef Soiree — Covington[3]
- Cochon de Lait Festival — Mansura
- Cracklin Festival — Port Barre
- Crawfish Festival — Breaux Bridge
- Crawfish Étouffée Cook-off Festival — Eunice
- Teacher Festival — Gueydan
- Etouffee Festival — Arnaudville [4]
- Franklin Parish Catfish Festival — Winnsboro
- French Food Festival — Larose, Louisiana
- Frog Festival — Rayne
- Fur and Wildlife Festival — Cameron
- Great Gator Race — New Iberia LA
- International Rice Festival — Crowley, Louisiana
- Jambalaya Festival — Gonzales
- Lecompte Pie Festival — Lecompte
- Louisiana Cattle Festival — Abbeville
- Louisiana Cotton Festival — Ville Platte
- Louisiana Gumbo Festival — Thibodaux
- The Louisiana Swamp Stomp Festival — Thibodaux, Nicholls
  State University, Louisiana
- Louisiana Pecan Festival — Colfax
- Louisiana Pepper Festival — St. Martinville
- Louisiana Watermelon Festival — Farmerville
- Mirliton Festival—New Orleans

- Mudbug Madness Festival—Shreveport
- Natchitoches Meat Pie Festival—Natchitoches
- New Orleans Food & Wine Experience—New Orleans
- New Orleans Seafood Festival—New Orleans
- Giant Omelette Celebration — Abbeville
- Amite Oyster Festival — Amite, Louisiana
- Ponchatoula Strawberry Festival — Ponchatoula[6]
- Plaquemines Parish Fair & Orange Festival — Buras
- Rabbit Festival — Iowa
- Ruston Peach Festival — Ruston
- Seafood Festival — Mandeville
- Shrimp Festival — Delcambre
- Shrimp and Petroleum Festival — Morgan City
- Sorrento Boucherie Festival — Sorrento[7]
- Strawberry Festival — Ponchatoula
- Sugarcane Festival — New Iberia
- Swine Festival — Basile
- Tales of the Cocktail — New Orleans
- Tamale Fiesta — Zwolle
- Tomato Festival — Chalmette, Louisiana
- *Viande BoucAnne* (Smoked Meat Festival) — Ville Platte
- Yambilee Festival — Opelousas
- The Taste of Louisiana Festival — Lake Charles, Louisiana

Earth and nature festivals
- Bayou Teche Bear Festival — Franklin
- Earth Fest at Audubon Zoo — New Orleans
- Earth Day Festival — Baton Rouge
  Forest Festival — Winnfield

Louisiana Nursery Festival — Forest Hill
Southern Garden Symposium – St. Francisville

Film and media festivals

- Contraband Film Festival — Lake Charles
- New Orleans Media Experience Festival — New Orleans
- Outhouse Film Festival — Baton Rouge
- Ozone Film Festival — Covington
- Red Stick International Animation Festival — Baton Rouge
- Sawmill Festival -- Patterson

Heritage and folk festivals

- Annual Germantown Festival — Minden
- Black Heritage Festival — Lake Charles
- Balfa Cajun/Creole Heritage Week — Ville Platte
- Buggy Festival — Church Point
- Baton Rouge Cajun Day Festival — Port Allen
- Celtic Nations Heritage Festival — Lake Charles
- Festivals Acadiens — Lafayette
- French Settlement Creole Festival — Baton Rouge
- Greek Festival — New Orleans
- International Acadian Festival — Plaquemine
- International Heritage Celebration Festival — Baton Rouge
- Independence Italian Festival — Independence, Louisiana
- Italian Festival — Baton Rouge, Louisiana
- Los Islenos Festival — St. Bernard
- Louisiana Folklife Festival — Monroe
- Louisiana Renaissance Festival — Hammond
- Mardi Gras – New Orleans

- Mensaje Spanish Festival — New Orleans
- Northwestern State University Folk Festival —
- Natchitoches Oktoberfest Festival — Gonzales
- The Day the War Stopped – St. Francisville
- The Audubon Pilgrimage -- St. Francisville
- Wooden Boat Festival — Madisonville

Holiday festivals

- Baton Rouge Bonfire — Baton Rouge
- Baton Rouge Festival of Lights — Baton Rouge
- Christmas in the Country – St. Francisville
- Christmas Under the Oaks — Sulphur
- Courir de Mardi Gras — Acadiana
- Festival of the Bonfires on the Mississippi River — Gramercy, Lutcher and Paulina
- Go 4th On The River — New Orleans Baton Rouge
- Holiday Trail of Lights — North Louisiana
- La Grande Boucherie des Cajuns — St. Martinville
- Mardi Gras – New Orleans
- Myrtles Plantation Halloween Experience – St. Francisville
- Natchitoches Christmas Festival — Natchitoches
- NCLAC Holiday Arts Tour — Ruston
- New Orleans Mardi Gras — New Orleans
- Port Allen Bonfires on the Mississippi River — Port Allen
- Pow Wow and Trade Days Festival

Music festivals

* Ark-La-Tex Jazz & Gumbo Music Festival — Shreveport

* Bluegrass on the Bayou Festival — Baton Rouge
* Blues Week Festival — Baton Rouge
- Cajun French Music Association Festival — Lake Charles
- Cajun Music Festival — Mamou
- Cane River Zydeco Festival and Poker Run Natchitoches
- Creole Zydeco Festival — St. Martinville
- DeltaFest — Monroe, Louisiana
- Essence Music Festival — New Orleans
- Festival International — Lafayette
- French Quarter Festival — New Orleans
- Highland Jazz & Blues Festival — Shreveport
- Gas, Food and Lodging Music Festival — Baton Rouge
- Lagniappe Dulcimer Fete Festival — Port Allen
- Le Cajun Festival Music Awards — Lafayette
- New Orleans Jazz & Heritage Festival — New Orleans
- Satchmo Fest — New Orleans
- South Louisiana Blackpot Festival and Cook-off Lafayette
- Strawberry Jam'n Toast To the Arts Festival Ponchatoula
- Swamp Pop Festival — Gonzales
- Tomato Festival — Chalmette, Louisiana
- Voice of the Wetlands Festival — Houma, Louisiana
- Voodoo Experience — New Orleans
- Zydeco Festival — Opelousas

Louisiana Definitions

Louisiana has a diverse background of ethnicities, which greatly influences its perspective and languages. To define Louisiana through terms in a glossary, would be an injustice. Here are a few terms, however, that may aid the reader in understanding the terminology used throughout this book.

According to Charles M. Robinson III in his wonderful book, *Roadside History of Louisiana*, he explains the references to this area as follows:

Acadian (Cajun) and Creole: Both Acadian and Creole are considered distinct cultures. The two terms are sometimes confused, but they are not the same. *Acadians* (or Cajuns) are descended from the French Canadians of Acadia (Nova Scotia). Acadian is the dominant ethnic group in southwestern Louisiana, a region officially designated as "Acadiana." Most Cajun terms are simply French words, though often pronounced somewhat differently than in France or French Canada. Many oft-used terms have to do with parties: a *cochon de lait* (coo SHON de LAY) is a pig roast; a *fais-do-do* is a dance; and *"Lassez les bon temp rouler"* means "Let the good times roll!"

Creoles are people of French or Spanish descent born in the New World. Their ancestors were immigrants who came either directly from France, from France by way of Santo Domingo (now Haiti and the Dominican Republic), or, late in the colonial period, from Spain. The Creoles are now spread throughout the state, but they were traditionally centered in New Orleans and along the Mississippi.

Bayou (BY-you):   Strictly speaking, the plural is "bayoux", but common usage dictates the Anglicized "boyous." Bayous are streams that flow every slowly along flat, low-lying terrain. The lack of slope creates almost no current from source to mouth, and the surrounding soil consists of soft alluvial deposits. With few natural obstructions such as rocks, bayous often flow for miles in straightaways. Their natural banks may look man-made.

Centuries, even millennia, ago, many of Louisiana's bayous were channels of the Mississippi River, and as such they were navigable. Until the arrival of the railroad, these waterways supported a thriving steamboat trade, and even today, many provide access from interior ports to the Gulf of Mexico.

Plantation: Today the word *plantation* is used to describe any large Southern estate. Originally, however, it meant a landholding on which both crops and livestock were raised, though a plantation often specialized in one particular crop. Below Baton Rouge, cotton was king. Properties used almost exclusively for crops were called *farms*, while those focusing on livestock were called *places* (known in the West as *ranches*). A place on which cattle were raised was called a *vacherie.*

ARCHITECTURAL TERMS:

Allée: French for "alley", a clearly defined pathway, usually leading from the river to the house; often bordered by oak trees.

Balcony: An overhang supported by the internal structure of the house. In New Orleans, it is also known as a *banquette.*

Doric columns: Heavy columns with simple crowns; a common feature of Greek Revival-style plantation homes.

Gallery: A second-floor outdoor walkway supported from the ground by columns or other braces, found on plantation houses and New Orleans townhouses.

Garçonnéirre: Separate quarters on a plantation for older boys, allowing them to come and go at their own convenience.

Jalousie: A window or door covering arranged in slats, similar to a Venetian blind.

Pigeonnier: Dovecotes, where pigeons are raised for food and their droppings collected for fertilizer.

Verandah (also spelled veranda): A large, columned porch without a gallery.

LOUISIANA SLANG

"Where Y'at?" In New Orleans, this is the same as asking "How are you doing?" or "What are you up to?"-- *not* your location. Due to this frequently used sentence, along with "Who Dat?", Louisianans are sometimes affectionately nicknamed "Y'ats."

Crawfish...not "crayfish".

Beignets: Donuts with corners, not hole. They were made famous by Café du Monde in the French Quarter.

Cher: French word traditionally used by both Cajuns and French speaking Creoles as a term of endearment. Pronounced "shaw" or "share."

Dressed: Sandwiches in Louisiana either come dressed—with lettuce, tomato and mayonnaise—or they come undressed.

Etouffee: French for smothered. It's a Creole and Cajun cooking technique often used with shellfish, like shrimp or crawfish, or even duck. The main ingredient is cooked in a brown sauce with tomatoes, onions and seasonings. Pronounced eh-TO-fay.

Faubourg. French for neighborhood.

Gris Gris. Something magic or a good luck charm. Gris gris bags and little totems are often the symbols of cast voodoo spells. Pronounced gree-gree.

Making Groceries: Y'at speech for shopping for food.
Parish: Louisiana has parishes instead of counties. New Orleans is in Orleans Parish.

Po' Boy: A sandwich of anything from roast beef, sausage, shrimp, oysters, to alligator…served on French bread. If you add tomato, lettuce and mayonnaise, it is "dressed."

Praline: A super sweet cookie made from melted sugar.
Originally a French recipe with almonds, the locals have generally preferred the more readily available pecan.

Roux: Roux is the basis for many Cajun and Creole recipes, including Gumbos, soups, sauces and other dishes. A roux is simply flour and oil cooked in a pan until brown.

Second Line: As a noun or verb, the second line is the funky walking/dancing part of a parade just behind the main band, which is the first line. Second lines always include marching brass bands. The tradition comes from jazz funerals.

Shotgun: This is the term for the New Orleans' style of long thin houses, the reference being that if you stood at the front door, you could fire a shotgun straight out the back one! Usually they stretch for four or five rooms in a row with the doors lined up. A house adjoining two such homes is a "shotgun double." And a shotgun double with a second floor added in the back is a "Camelback shotgun." Camelbacks came about when the city- based taxes on how many floors a building had on the street.

Streetcars are the correct term, not trolley.

Vieux Carré: French for 'Old Square'. This is the old term for the French Quarter—still used today by many who live there.

Zydeco: The accordion and rub-board led sound of South Louisiana's Creoles. A sort of twin to Cajun music but with a rhythm and blues sound.

Appendix V:

Bibliography

Louisiana History

1. *Africans in Colonial Louisiana: The Development of Afro-Creole Culture in the 18ᵗʰ Century.* Louisiana State University Press. Hall, Gwendolyn Midlo (1995)
2. *Louisiana Voodoo and Superstitions related to Health.* Associations of Schools of Public Health.
3. *Voodoo in New Orleans.* Nickell, Joe (2006) 4. *Voodoo & the Life of Spirits in New Orleans.* Fodor's New Orleans (2005).
5. *Wedding Customs in Antebellum America.* Cooper, Meagan. Online article.
6. *Women's Life and Work in the Southern Colonies.* (New York: W.W. Norton & Co. Inc. 1972)
7. *Civil War Etiquette: Martine's Handbook & Vulgarisms in Conversation.* (Mendocino, California: R.L. Shep, 1988)
8. *Background: The Plantation Way of Life.* Louisiana Studies in Historic Preservation.
9. *The Plantation Mistress: Woman's World in the Old South.* Clinton, Catherine.
10. *Antebellum Homes of Louisiana: A Tour Through History.* Deborah Anderson. Online.
11. *The Cabildo: Antebellum Louisiana: Urban Life.* Louisiana State Museum.
12. *Manners and Etiquette in the Antebellum South.* Southern Banner, March 16, 1833.

13. *Everyday Life in the United States before the Civil War 1830-1860*. Robert Lacour-Gayet. (Librairie Hachette: Paris, 1969) **14.** *Jean Lafitte*. Wikipedia.

15. *"Arrrrr!"* Hayes, Greg (May 2, 2007) Online article.

16. *Remains of the War*. (Congressional Edition, Volume 226)

17. *The Smithsonian Guide to Historic America*. Logan, William B. & Muse, Vance.

18. *A Cultural Gumbo*. Fodor's New Orleans 2005.

19. *Roadside History of Louisiana*. Robinson III, Charles M.

20. *Off the Beaten Path, Louisiana*. Martin, Gay N.

21. *Lost Treasures of American History*. Jameson, W. C.

St. Francisville & Bayou Sara

1. *The Day the War Stopped*. Grace Church of West Feliciana Parish—St. Francisville.

2. *The St. Francisville Area, West Feliciana Parish, Louisiana*. McCoy, Jan & Johnson Donald W.

3. *Bayou Sara*. Dorr, J.W.

4. *The Legend of the Tunica Treasure*. Hennessy, Jefferson.

5. *St. Francisville History*. St. Francisville Historical Society.

6. *West Feliciana Parish, Louisiana*. Wikipedia.

7. West Feliciana Historical Society, St. Francisville, Louisiana. Helen Williams, Historian.

The Myrtles Plantation

1. *Famous Haunted Houses and Places.*
   Encyclopedia of the Unusual & Unexplained.

2. *Plantation Poltergeists.* Opdyke, Jeff D. (D Magazine, June 1993)

3. *The Myrtles Plantation: "Where the Past Lives On".* Courtesy of the Louisiana State Library.

4. *Stephen Saunders: Research of the Myrtles Plantation for Consideration for the National Historic Register.* Donated by Arlin Dease, June 13, 2001.

5. *Myrtles' New Look May Yet Prove Discouraging to Lonely Old Ghosts.* Champagne, Mary, Women's Editor, Sunday Advocate, Baton Rouge, Louisiana, March 21, 1976.

6. *LSU Digital Library.*

7. *Bradford House Organization.* Washington, Pennsylvania. Tom and Myrna Hart.

8. *National Register of Historic Places, Louisiana.*

9. *Census Records, Death Indices and Property Records of Louisiana World Family Tree.*

10. *Ancestry.com*

11. *Family History Book of Alexander Stirling and Ann Alston.* Weller, Ann.

12. West Feliciana Historical Society, St. Francisville, Louisiana.

13. West Feliciana Court House, St. Francisville, Louisiana.

14. Grace Episcopal Church, St. Francisville, Louisiana.

15. *The Wall Street Journal, October 31, 1984.*

16. *Louisiana Life, Feb. 1990.*

17. *Personal Interviews with Past Owners, Curators, Library Archivists, Newspaper Archivists, Museum Overseers, Historical Societies and Research Experts.*

18. *Fright Night.* (*The Times-Picayne*, New Orleans, Louisiana, October 28, 2007)

19. *The Rich Era of the Myrtles.* (*Southern Living Magazine*)

20. *Report and Analysis of Mysterious Photo of "The Myrtles Plantation".* Bourgeois, Norman.

21. *Myrtles Historical Tour.* The Myrtles Plantation.

22. *Myrtles Plantation. Explore the History and Culture of Southeastern Louisiana, A National Register of Historic Places Travel Itinerary.* National Park Service, U.S. Department of the Interior.

23. West Baton Rouge Museum, Baton Rouge, Louisiana. Lauren Davis, Curator.

24. West Feliciana Parish, St. Francisville, Louisiana.

25. West Feliciana Historical Society, St. Francisville, Louisiana. Helen Williams, Historian.

26. *St. Francisville Democrat Newspaper.* St. Francisville, Louisiana.

27. *Bayou State Periodical Index.* Baton Rouge, Louisiana.

28. East Baton Rouge Parish Library, Baton Rouge, Louisiana.

29. State Library of Louisiana, Baton Rouge, Louisiana. Charlene Bonnette, Head, Louisiana Collection, State Library of Louisiana.

30. LSU Hill Memorial Library, Baton Rouge, Louisiana. Barry Cowan and Judy Bolton, Head of Public Services, Special Collections, LSU Library.

31. West Feliciana Parish Library. St. Francisville, Louisiana.

32. Arlin Dease, former owner and recognized restorer of the Myrtles Plantation. Current owner of Hemingbough Plantation, St. Francisville, Louisiana.

33. Teeta Moss, current owner of the Myrtles Plantation. Extensive restoration and expansions of property.

34. The Louisiana Digital Library.

35. *Furnishings of the 17th Century.* Online article on Louis XIV and XV antiques.

36. Clerk of Court, West Feliciana Parish Court House.

37. Ann Weller, author, historian and descendant of the Ruffin Gray Stirling Family. Owner of Wakefield, Plantation, St. Francisville, Louisiana.

38. Shirley Lang, Louisiana Government Record Archives.

39. William Drew Winter, *World Family Tree* Vol. 4, Ed. 1, Tree #2356 and the 1850 United States Federal Census.

40. Tulane University Jones Hall Louisiana Collection.

41. *The Murder of William Winter. Point Coupee Democrat Newspaper,* January 1871.

42. *The Murder of William Winter. Feliciana Republican,* January 27, 1871.

43. *LDS Church, Family History Center, Computer Records.*

44. Application for Spanish Land Grant, Madrid, 1792, in David Bradford's name.

45. Certificate granting land, Bradford Collection, LSU Archives.

46. David Bradford's will, dated 1803, West Feliciana Courthouse.

47. Title Search—West Feliciana Courthouse.

48. Clark Woodruff Letter, Mss. 4021, Louisiana and Lower Mississippi Valley Collections, LSU Libraries, Baton Rouge, Louisiana.

49. Slave Census for Clark Woodruff, 1820-1850. Alice L. Luckhardt, researcher and writer for FamilyTree.com.

50. *Ghosts Along the Mississippi.* Laughlin, John.

51. *Within the Plantation Household: Black & White Women of the Old South.* Fox-Genovese,
Elizabeth. (1988 University of North Carolina Press)

52. *The Haunting of Louisiana.* Sillery, Barbara.

53. *Louisiana's Haunted Plantations.* Pascoe, Jill.

54. *Sarah Morgan: The Civil War Diary of a Southern Woman.* Edited by Charles East.

55. *Feliciana Republic Newspaper,* clippings courtesy of LSU Special Collections.

56. Louisiana Division of Historic Preservation and
Office of Cultural Development, Department of Culture, Recreation and Tourism. Nicole Hobson-Morris, Executive Director.

Appendix VI:

Recommended Reading

1. *Sarah Morgan: The Civil War Diary of a Southern Woman.* Edited by Charles East. (A Touchstone Book, 1991)
2. *Lost Treasures of American History.* Jameson, W.C. (MJF Books, NY, 2006)
3. *Roadside History of Louisiana.* Robinson III, Charles M. (Mountain Press Publishing Company, 2007)
4. *Louisiana's Haunted Plantations.* Pascoe, Jill. (Irongate Press, 2004)
5. *The Haunting of Louisiana.* Sillery, Barbara. (Pelican Publishing Company, Inc., 2001, 2003, 2006, 2010)
6. *Within the Plantation Household: Black & White Women of the Old South.* Fox-Genovese, Elizabeth. (University of North Carolina Press, 1988)
7. *Family History Book of Alexander Stirling and Ann Alston.* Weller, Ann.
8. *Off the Beaten Path Louisiana.* Martin, Gay N. Revised and updated by Jackie Sheckler Finch. 2009. (Morrison Book Publishing)
9. *Family History Book of Alexander Stirling and Ann Alston.* Weller, Ann.
10. *Off the Beaten Path Louisiana.* Martin, Gay N. Revised and updated by Jackie Sheckler Finch. 2009. (Morrison Book Publishing)

Appendix VII:

Photo Courtesy and Information

Photography for this book was offered by the following sources:

Rebecca F. Pittman

Jim Zaccone Photography www.JimZaccone.com

Jason Phillip Reeser:
Jason Phillip Reeser, editor of Saint James Infirmary Books, lives and writes in southwest Louisiana. His ghost story anthology, The Cities of the Dead, which Louisiana Poet Laureate Julie Kane called "a twist of Louisiana Gothic," is set in the cemeteries of New Orleans. This year he published Kiss of the Lazaretto, the third book in his Lazaretto trilogy, which mixes science fiction and hard-boiled detective thrillers. His blog, *Room With No View,* has featured interviews with poets as well as fiction author David Morrell, the creator of Rambo. He lives in Louisiana with his wife, the poet Jennifer Reeser.

Amanda Folce DeVille with the Myrtles Plantation.

Various websites, artists, and bloggers, as noted.

You can access the Myrtles Plantation's official website by going to: www.myrtlesplantation.com.

Their address and phone are:
The Myrtles Plantation
7747 US Highway 61
St. Francisville, Louisiana 70775
(225) 635-6277

Reservations are recommended for overnight stays, and encouraged for tours.

Original photograph of the Myrtles Plantation, circa late 1790s. You can see the water piping leading from the roof gutters to the cistern for the collection of rain water. This cistern is still there today, at the south end of the house. The building that housed the Bradfords, while the main house was being constructed, is seen at the left. The tree stump in the foreground may be a hitching post.

Appendix VIII:

Myrtles Plantation Timeline

1792: David Bradford (1760-1808) buys 500 acres @ $1.40/ac

1794: Construction on kitchen pre-building begins. Property is called Richland.

1796-1797: Laurel Grove Plantation is completed and renamed Laurel Grove. David, along with wife Elizabeth (m. 1785) live at Plantation with 8 children: Sarah Matilda (later marries Clark Woodruff), David (later marries Amanda Jane Davis), Eliza, Octavia, Abelard, Jane, Sophia and Edmund.

1808: David Bradford dies.

1816: Elizabeth Bradford buys Laurel Grove for $8,000 on Dec. 3.

1817: Clark Woodruff marries Sarah Matilda Bradford. They manage Laurel Grove for Elizabeth Bradford. They have 3 children: Mary Octavia (Oct. 3, 1818 – Jan. 21, 1889), James and Cornelia (twins). They died two months apart in 1824 from yellow fever.
 Sarah Matilda and Clark Woodruff buy Laurel Grove from Elizabeth Bradford for $2.50/ac. Woodruff plants cotton and indigo on 5,000 acres with 450 field hands and 50 house slaves.

1820? Possible house fire resulting in death of a mother and two children at the plantation when both Bradford's and Woodruffs were living there.

1823: Sarah Matilda Woodruff dies of scarlet fever on July 21, 1823. Woodruff remains with mother-in-law.

1824: James and Cornelia die of yellow fever, two months apart— James in July and Cornelia in September.

1825: Woodruff purchases another 650 acres of land, expanding Laurel Oaks property.

1830: Elizabeth Bradford dies. Woodruff and daughter, Octavia move to Covington, LA, leaving a caretaker to manage the plantation.

1834: Ruffin G. Stirling (Apr. 5, 1795 - July 17, 1854), married to Mary Cobb on Feb. 14, 1813, buys Laurel Grove for $46,853 along with slaves on Jan. 1, 1834. Woodruff and Octavia move to New Orleans. Ruffin G. Stirling renames Laurel Grove, The Myrtles. He builds a new wing, almost doubling the size of the house. Ruffin and Mary have 8 children:

Stephen, Clarence, Lewis, William, Ruffin, Henry, Sarah, Mary Ann. Only four lived at the plantation after Ruffin died in 1854, leaving Mary a widow at 41.

1850's: The Stirlings do extensive remodeling, friezework, etc. Mary buys a 300 lb. chandelier in Baccarat crystal from France. Stirling buys more land extending the property to Bayou Sara.

1851: Clark Woodruff dies in New Orleans. No one claims his grave years later during re-interment.

1852: Sarah marries William Drew Winter at the Myrtles in the wedding of the decade.

1854: Ruffing Sterling dies of consumption.

1861: The War Between the States begins. Louisiana secedes from the Union.

1863: The Siege at Port Hudson. Union soldiers shell Bayou Sara and St. Francisville.
1867: William Winter is declared bankrupt due to devastation of crops from the war.

1871: William Winter is shot on the verandah and dies on Jan. 26.

1878: Sarah Winter dies at the age of 44 after becoming a recluse in the house following William's death.

1880: Mary Cobb Sterling dies. Buried next to Ruffin.

1881: Stephen Stirling (son of Ruffin and Mary) buys Myrtles for $3,000 on Feb. 5.

1886: Oran D. Brooks buys the Myrtles for $10,000 in March.

1889: Property is split between Harrison Milton Williams, Aaron Schlessinger.

1891: Harrison Williams buys the Myrtles and moves in along with 2nd wife Fannie Lintot and young son. Six more children are born at the Myrtles. The oldest boy, Harry drowns in Mississippi while trying to save cattle being swept away in flood waters.   Fannie's spinster sister and maiden Aunt Katie (the Colonel) live with them. More cotton is planted.

1909: Fannie Williams (now widowed) buys the Myrtles for $7,313 from M & E Wolf on June 6.

1927: Reported stabbing of caretaker at caretaker's cabin.

1930: The Great Depression begins.

1942: Fannie Williams' younger brother, Edmund Haralson, is living in small house on plantation and is killed during a robbery at his house.

1948: Fannie Williams turns over management of the Myrtles to son Surget Minor Williams who marries Jessie Folkes. He provides a home at the plantation for Fannie's spinster sister and Maiden Aunt Katie.

1950's: Property surrounding the house is divided among William's heirs and the main house is sold to Marjorie Munson of Oklahoma, a widow in Dec. of 1953. She marries Dolor   Michaud. The Gentleman's Parlor is turned into a Music Room.

1975: Arlin Dease and Mr. and Mrs. Robert F. Ward take over. Only 10 acres remain. Stephen M. Saunders begins extensive research to nominate the Myrtles Plantation as a Historic   Places.

1977: John L. Pearce buys the Myrtles.

1978: September 6, 1978, The Myrtles Plantation is officially entered into the National Register of Historic Places.

1980: Frances Kermeen and Jim Meyers buy the plantation. They do remodeling and turn it into a B & B with 11 Guest Suites.

1990: The Myrtles is sold to Mark Sowers

1991: Arlin Dease reclaims the Myrtles.

1992: Teeta and John Moss buy the Myrtles and continue its career as a B&B. They do extensive improvements and add a barn and four cottages, as well as a bricked courtyard, fencing, landscaping and renovations. The Carriage House is a full-service restaurant.

Appendix IV:

Myrtles Plantation Map and Legend

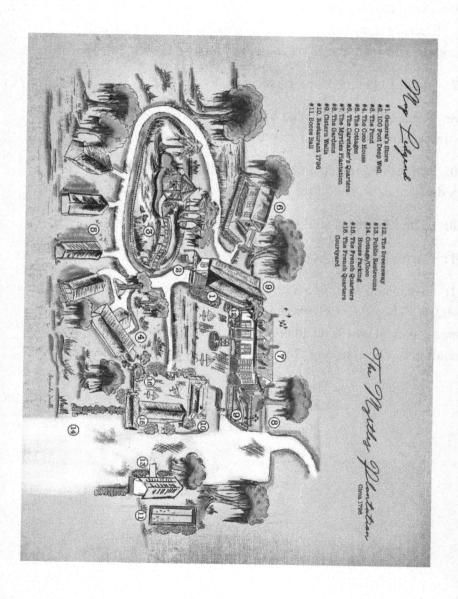

Map Legend

#1. General's Store
#2. 100 Foot Deep Well
#3. The Pond
#4. The Coco House
#5. The Cottages
#6. The Caretaker's Quarters
#7. The Myrtles Plantation
#8. The Gardens
#9. Cistern Wells
#10. Restaurant 1796
#11. Bocce Ball

#12. The Breezeway
#13. Public Restrooms
#14. Cottage/Coco
    House Parking
#15. The French Quarters
#16. The French Quarters
    Courtyard

The Myrtles Plantation
Circa 1796

ABOUT THE AUTHOR

Rebecca F. Pittman is a paranormal historian with a passion for mysteries. Her series of books under *The History and Haunting* titles have garnered her a faithful following. They include *The History and Haunting of the Stanley Hotel, The History and Haunting of the Myrtles Plantation, The History and Haunting of Lemp Mansion*, and *The History and Haunting of Lizzie Borden*. Ms. Pittman's works of fiction also center around "things that go bump in the night." *T.J. Finnel and the Well of Ghosts* is Book One of a 5-book series. *Don't Look Now!, The Diamond Peacock Club,* and *Hourglass* are due out in 2018/2019.

Other books, on how to create businesses in the creative arts, and a dating and marriage relationship guide for women, called *Troubleshooting Men, What in the WORLD do they want?* are also in demand.

You can find out more about Rebecca at her website, www.rebeccafpittmanbooks.com, and sign up for her free monthly newsletter *Ghost Writings.* It covers all things paranormal, upcoming books, and signings. It also keeps you apprised of your favorite haunt's on-going events. She just released the first of her paranormal card game series. *The Lizzie Borden Paranormal Card Game* is now on sale and can be found at her website. Other games, including *A Dark and Stormy Night* are scheduled to be released soon.

Rebecca makes her home in the foothills of the Colorado Rockies where she pursues her love of golf and boating. She is the proud mother of four sons and has been blessed with their families who (to date) have given her 9 grandchildren.

Other Books by Rebecca F. Pittman

Paranormal Non-Fiction:

The History and Haunting of the Stanley Hotel,
1st & 2nd Editions

The History and Haunting of the Myrtles Plantation,
1st & 2nd Editions

The History and Haunting of Lemp Mansion

The History and Haunting of Lizzie Borden (November, 2016)

The History and Haunting of the Crescent Hotel
(Spring, 2020)

The History and Haunting of Salem (Summer/2019)

Self-Help Books:

How To Start a Faux Painting or Mural Business,
1st and 2nd Editions

Scrapbooking for Profit,
1st and 2nd Editions

Troubleshooting Men, What in the WORLD do they want?
(A Dating & Marriage Advice Book of Secrets for Women)

Supernatural Thrillers:

T.J. Finnel and the Well of Ghosts (Book 1 of a
5-Book Series)

Coming Soon:

Don't Look Now!
The Diamond Peacock Club

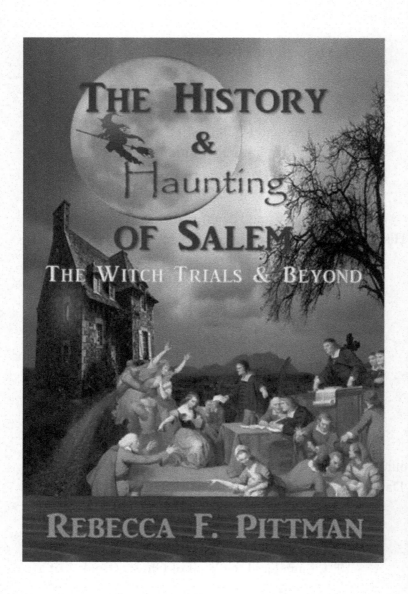

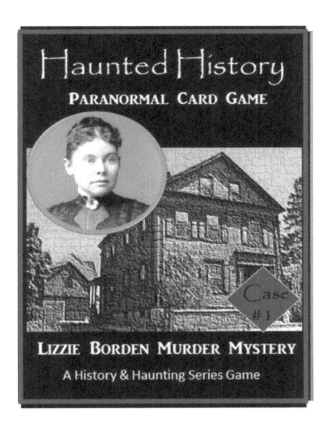

Coming Summer 2019